A RINGSIDE SEAT

A Ringside Seat

THE AUTOBIOGRAPHY

Michael Brunson

Hodder & Stoughton

First published in Great Britain in 2000
by Hodder and Stoughton
A division of Hodder Headline

10 9 8 7 6 5 4 3 2 1

British Library Cataloguing in Publication Data
A CIP catalogue record is
available from the British Library.

ISBN 0 340 728361

Typeset by Hewer Text Ltd, Edinburgh
Printed and bound in Great Britain
by Clays Ltd, St Ives plc

Hodder and Stoughton
A division of Hodder Headline
338 Euston Road
London NW1 3BH

For Sue,
Jonathan and Robin

CONTENTS

LIST OF ILLUSTRATIONS

Unless indicated, photographs belong to Michael Brunson.

PREFACE

Good dictionaries are a delight, as well as being very useful. The best not only tell you how to spell, but offer telling insights into where words come from and how they have been used and developed, and they frequently do so with great precision and clarity of thought. It was not, however, the vast multi-volume *Oxford English Dictionary* that was most helpful as I mulled over the title of this book. Greater assistance came from its slimmer, though still voluminous, and more up-to-date relation, the *Shorter Oxford*. For the figurative use of the words 'ringside seat', it offers the following definition: 'a place affording a clear view; an advantageous or privileged position from which to observe or monitor something'.

That is it precisely. The 'something', in my case, has been the course of events, at various points across the world, over some thirty-five years. My employment and credentials as a radio and television journalist during that time have indeed allowed me 'an advantageous or privileged position' from which to tell other people what has been going on, or what is likely to happen, and, on occasion, what it might all mean.

During that time, my words, and the pictures to which they were attached, have often survived in some shape or form, sometimes in scripts that I have kept myself, but most often in the archives at ITN, my employer for most of my working life. I have not kept a diary, though I have maintained a sort of working logbook, so it is to the staff of ITN's film and video library and news information department that I owe a special word of thanks, for the help they have provided not just during my working years, but during the preparation of this book.

Similar thanks must go to Denis Chadwick, known to everyone as Chad, who edited most of my reports during fourteen years at Westminster and also maintained a special video archive of ITN's political output. Chad is a meticulous operator, who does not compromise on standards. Many is the time that I have urged him to push the red button on the editing console, which actually performs the sound and vision cut required, rather than other buttons that allow you to see in advance what will happen if you go ahead. Many is the time that he has refused to do so until he is certain that the operation will meet his high standards, and he has brought the same care and attention to the maintenance of a unique videotape library, which he has helped me to raid.

Many other friends and colleagues have been of great assistance in jogging my memory, and in helping me to sort out the true sequence of events, to which memory is often a very uncertain guide. David Lomax, John Mahoney, Marshall Stewart and Anthony Teasdale have been especially helpful. Michael Alcock, Roland Philipps and Roseanne Boyle gave help and encouragement in advance of and during the writing of this book. At ITN, Judy Toohey conjured up still photographs from film and video clips. Anne Lingley, who runs ITN's nerve centre in the House of Commons Press Gallery with such great skill, has so organised my professional working life that more spare-time authorship has been possible. As with every reporter, however, it is my name that's on the page. The end result is down to me and to me alone.

Introduction: The Glamorous Life?

'What,' asked the Director-General of the BBC, 'makes a good broadcaster?'

The imposing figure of Sir Hugh Carleton Greene, a former journalist and distinguished war correspondent, did not, in truth, expect an answer. This was the man who, throughout the 1960s, ran an organisation that was regarded throughout the world as the epitome of broadcasting excellence, especially in the field of radio and television news. He knew, better than most people, the answer to the question he had just posed to an audience of young hopefuls gathered in Bush House, the headquarters of the BBC World Service. Many of them were from overseas, especially the countries of the Commonwealth, who had come to London for training. This was 1964, and I was a trainee too, having just started at the BBC. The Director-General's question was merely rhetorical, but his answer was both surprising and, to myself at least, immensely reassuring.

'I think', said Sir Hugh, 'that a good broadcaster is probably someone who likes the sound of his own voice!'

I heaved a private sigh of relief. I had never, ever, been shy on that score. From my first appearance on a public stage during my early years at primary school as Mr Grumpy, through school debating societies and church choirs, to a

1

succession of later stage appearances, both at school and at Oxford, I had never been reluctant to perform in public. Yes, I had to admit I *did* rather like the sound of my own voice, but I also had the sense that for a potential broadcaster to admit it was rather like someone saying he wants to be a clergyman because he likes dressing up.

I also knew, however, that enjoying public performance was, in part, what had led me to the BBC after taking my degree. I had no clear idea of precisely what kind of broadcaster I wanted to be, but I did have the certainty that I wanted to be one. Once I had decided, during the course of my brief stay at Bush House, that I wanted to be a broadcast *journalist*, rather than just a broadcaster, I began to understand that becoming one would involve very much more than the simple ability to perform. I had never suffered from stage fright, and it may have been a great help from the start that I never had any real problems about the broadcasting side of broadcast journalism. Almost the only thing that might have given me pause about such a career was the fact that, since the age of seven, I had been stone deaf in my left ear, the result of a severe attack of measles. The real challenge, though, as it must be for any journalist, was exactly what facts to discover, and how to discover them.

Now, almost forty years on, the challenge is not the lack of information but the sheer extent of it. A fable for our own age is that striking opening to Dickens' *Hard Times* in which Mr Gradgrind famously declares to the cowering schoolmaster, 'Now, what I want is, Facts. Teach these boys and girls nothing but Facts . . . In this life, we want nothing but Facts, Sir; nothing but Facts!'

Today, even Mr Gradgrind might feel moved to complain of information overload. We are deluged with facts. Facts come at us from every source imaginable. Facts pour out, for example, from every government department, including

Number Ten itself, from the official Opposition, and from every other political party, whether represented at Westminster or not. Beyond politics, no organisation, be it official or voluntary, no pressure group, no group of any kind, nor, indeed, any individual with a case to put, is slow in putting it forward. By every possible means, on television, whether delivered by aerial or satellite or cable, on radio, in newspapers, magazines and topical books, and on the Internet, facts are beamed at us twenty-four hours a day, seven days a week, 365 days a year.

Sorting out the facts, and making some sense of what they mean, is the journalist's job, and especially the job of a television journalist, since television is, by a very large margin, most people's primary source of news. Yet nowadays the television news industry is often 90 per cent logistics and 10 per cent journalism. Of course there are news editors, and resource managers, and producers and technical directors whose job it is to look after the logistical side of things. The great risk, though, is that television journalists themselves increasingly get sucked into the whole non-stop, whirling merry-go-round that is the apparatus of the modern information circus. As a result, we can often fail to stop and ask ourselves that basic question which all journalists must ask: 'What the hell is *really* going on?'

There is another problem. Television journalists live in a goldfish bowl. You cannot walk down any street without being recognised. Such encounters range from cheery over-familiarity ('Allo, Michael me old son, how are yer?'), to wonderful cases of mistaken identity, like the gentleman who rushed up to me in Norfolk with the words, 'Yes, yes, I know you. You're a solicitor in Great Yarmouth!' You cannot make the smallest mistake, or commit the tiniest misdemeanour, without a gossip columnist writing about it. You are not just a

journalist, but a television personality too. You are supposed
to be living rather a glamorous life.

In Stephen Sondheim's musical *A Little Night Music*,
there's a bittersweet song about the relationship between a
famous actress and her daughter. The refrain throughout is
'Heigh-ho, the glamorous life!' The song itself, however, is all
about how distinctly unglamorous it all is – the actress's
packing and unpacking, the boring official events she must
attend, the grim hotels she must stay in, and how she and her
daughter have an impossibly strained relationship. The par-
allels with late-twentieth-century television journalism are
close.

To many people outside the world of television news, a TV
correspondent's job really does represent a very exciting life.
Jetting off at a moment's notice to the world's hot-spots,
hobnobbing with kings and queens, presidents and prime
ministers, always there, ahead of the queue, to claim that
ringside seat to watch history being made. The bittersweet
reality is rather different. It's a life entirely governed by events,
in which no plan for the days, weeks or months ahead can
ever be guaranteed. It's a life of living out of a suitcase during
frequent absences from home, of impossible working hours
once you have returned, of horrors as well as triumphs to
report. That is not to complain. It is just the other side of the
coin.

Of course, there is the glamorous side of it all, especially the
travelling. My reporting has taken me to the High Arctic,
where the insides of your nostrils freeze, and to the scorching
deserts of Saudi Arabia, where a cold beer tastes more
wonderful than the finest champagne. I have walked along
the Great Wall of China with a British Prime Minister, and
visited the pyramids of Egypt with a British Foreign Secretary.
I have been twice to the North-West Frontier and the Khyber
Pass, in the mountains between Pakistan and Afghanistan –

with a British Prime Minister on one occasion, and with a British Foreign Secretary on another. International conferences have taken me to all the world's major capitals. Royal tours have taken me to the ancient Mayan cities in Mexico, the temples of Bangkok and Chiang Mai in Thailand and the beaches of the Indian Ocean islands – the Maldives, the Seychelles and Mauritius. Covering every kind of official visit has taken me from Ayers Rock in Australia to Zambia and Zanzibar.

There have been plenty of glittering banquets, including the most spectacular of all for a thousand guests in the Great Hall of the People in Beijing in 1984, after Britain agreed to hand back Hong Kong to China. The menu, full of local delicacies, was magnificent, and two full orchestras serenaded the guests, one to play British music, the other Chinese. There has, remarkably, been other music to enjoy while still on official duty, a particular treat for someone for whom music, especially classical music, is a great passion. I think still of a special performance of Baroque Concerti Grossi which, with immense style, the Italian authorities laid on especially for the press, in the church of San Giorgio in Venice, during a European summit. I think back, with equal pleasure, to a particularly lively performance, by the civic organist, on the magnificent instrument which dominates Leeds Town Hall. That is not the sort of prelude you expect to the opening session of a Labour local government conference, but he gave it his all, and the pleasurable surprise was all the greater. Every year, one of the best Government receptions is that given by the Scottish Secretary, the balcony of whose office overlooks Horse Guards Parade, from where his guests can enjoy the summer performance of Beating Retreat. There was even, once, a performance to watch at the Folies Bergère in Paris, strictly in the line of business of course, as a group of journalists helped to inaugurate a new air service from London.

Yet, for every moment of glamour or unexpected pleasure, there have been the grim moments of life to be witnessed and reported on. It was in Belfast, and not in some far-flung country in the grip of civil war, that I once found myself lying, face-down, in a gutter, to avoid the danger of a sniper's rifle. It was in Belfast, too, standing on the roof of Ulster Television, that I saw the horizon ablaze, marked out by the fires from burning barricades and hijacked vehicles when internment of IRA suspects was introduced in August 1971.

Over the years, I have done my fair share of reporting disasters, both natural and man-made. In Iran, Nicaragua and the Soviet Union, I saw for myself the incredible devastation and loss of life caused by major earthquakes. In Nigeria and Zaire, I reported on the killing and starvation that civil war can bring. One of my earliest assignments after joining ITN was to report on the crash of a British plane in Belgium, and to see and to film, with due care, the bodies being removed from the wreckage. A little later I was to learn, with incredulity, the simple cause that had resulted in the loss of so many lives: a leaking toilet had created such serious corrosion in the airframe that the whole tail assembly of the aircraft had broken off.

Far less obvious to the cameras, but just as devastating to the individuals concerned, have been the careers lost and reputations ruined in and around Westminster. It is hard to convey what hurt those families and friends go through when the great fall from grace occurs, even if, on occasion, their political careers are later rehabilitated. Yet, as journalists, we are often directly, and properly, involved in the exposure of exactly that failure of duty, or misbehaviour, which brings people down.

So a life in broadcasting has brought every kind of contrast. As a correspondent in America, I had access to the White House, and there were visits to New York or Chicago or Los

Angeles with three Presidents, Reagan, Ford and Carter. Yet there was the collapse and the disgrace of the Nixon Presidency to report on during the scandal of Watergate. There were the journeys, too, to report on the dark side of the American Dream – the soaring murder rates in Detroit and Atlanta, and the grinding poverty of the West Virginian coalfields.

In the Far East, I saw for myself the magnificence of the Sultan of Brunei's palace, and the more formal splendour of the Emperor's residence in Tokyo. Those images only served to heighten the sense of absurdity as I watched the ridiculous military posturing at Panmunjom on the border between North and South Korea, and saw the desperation of the Vietnamese boat people as they waited in the detention camps of Hong Kong. In Africa and India too, the dignity and authority of Nelson Mandela and Indira Gandhi, and the quiet, cool atmosphere surrounding their official residences, reinforced the impact of the squalor and the noise which I saw and heard in the shanty towns around Cape Town and Johannesburg, or in the slums of Calcutta.

In Europe, I was constantly struck by the exuberance of the various national election campaigns, involving huge tented rallies in the cities of France or vast gatherings in Bavaria, enlivened with beer and oompah bands. There were, equally, many moments of quiet dignity and pauses for reflection across Europe – especially the ceremonies in Germany to mark events like the ending of British Military Government in Berlin, or the anniversary of the Allied airlift into that city. There were, too, the constant reminders of Europe's cultural heritage – the funeral of the composer Igor Stravinsky in Venice, for example, in 1971, on which I reported, when his coffin was carried along the canals to one of the city's magnificent churches in a flower-filled gondola.

Funerals, by the way, have always moved me greatly, which

is just as well, since journalists tend to go to rather more of them than the average human being. At many of the official ones, there is not only the sense of occasion and ceremony to savour, but the rare chance to stop and look back, and to reflect a little on the past, as represented by one person's life.

Can anyone who was involved, as I was, in reporting any part of the funeral of Princess Diana ever forget it? I doubt it, but other, less grand occasions, from the respectful but warm formality of the funeral held in Edinburgh for the Labour Leader John Smith to the stern dignity, matching the man, of the service in St Margaret's, Westminster, for Enoch Powell, made an equal impact. So, too, did events like the funeral of President Nasser, which I witnessed in Cairo in 1970. A million people crowded the city, and the coffin had, at one stage, to be galloped through the crowd to prevent it being torn from the gun carriage by over-zealous mourners. Among those mourners, I came face to face with Leila Khaled, one of the Arab terrorists who had hijacked and blown up three Western airliners at Dawson's Field in Jordan the previous month. She told me she had no regrets for what she had done.

At Harold Macmillan's funeral, held early in 1987 in a country church near his Sussex home, Birch Grove, I saw just what old-fashioned journalism could sometimes produce. It was meant to be a simple family occasion – the great memorial service in London would follow later. We were gathered in the churchyard just after the service, where his grandson, the Earl of Stockton, had agreed to talk to us. One local journalist, drawing on years of experience of attending such events, politely enquired, 'Were there any last words, my Lord?' 'Yes,' the Earl replied. 'My grandfather simply said, "I think I'll go to sleep now." ' It was the headline in many of the national newspapers the next morning.

Reporting on the living, there is no stranger kaleidoscope than life in and around the Houses of Parliament. There is the graceful behaviour of the House of Lords, where there is no exact equivalent of the Speaker of the House of Commons. Nevertheless, their Lordships and Ladyships, by using their own, discreet pecking order or by relying on instinct, seem able to find a quiet consensus in deciding who shall rise to make a speech. In stark contrast, there is the rowdy behaviour of the House of Commons, where Madam Speaker often has to shout like a fishwife to try to restore order. Yet how much more immediate and relevant can the Commons seem, compared to the discussions of legal, technical or political niceties in which the Upper House immerses itself.

As Political Editor of ITN, I reported on three very different Prime Ministers. Margaret Thatcher, determined to shake Britain out of what she saw as the wicked grip of socialism and the resulting lack of individual responsibility by its people, and, in the end, losing touch with both the people and her Parliamentary party over the poll tax and Europe. John Major, pinioned from the start by the Tory split over Europe, always searching for a consensus within that party, which the problems of a tiny, and diminishing, Parliamentary majority made ever more difficult to achieve. Latterly, Tony Blair, pursuing his 'Third Way' embracing the economic efficiency of a market-driven economy and the social justice of high-quality public services and welfare support. All three, in addition, were responsible for leading Britain in time of war, in major campaigns in the Falklands, the Gulf and the Balkans.

A life in broadcasting has also, for the most part, meant actually getting to the places and events about which I am reporting. Even in the House of Commons, I much prefer to be in my seat in the Press Gallery above the Speaker's chair, though I could rely on the television or radio feed from the chamber. Since the microphones are deliberately controlled to eliminate extraneous noise, so many of the nuances of what is actually going on – the cheeky aside, the *sotto voce* insult – can be picked up only if you are there in person. They can, though, make all the difference to the 'feel' of a report.

Every autumn, there are the party conferences to get to in person, in the British political world's annual pilgrimage to the seaside. There are, too, the overseas trips with various members of the Government, aboard the official planes, with their first-class service. There could be no greater contrast to that than my flight aboard an ancient ex-RAF freighter I once hitched a ride on, while reporting the civil war in Zaire. On that occasion, the in-flight catering was a Spanish omelette made with dried vegetables and egg powder, cooked up by the pilot as he crouched over an open-flame, butane gas stove, which he had set up on the cargo deck.

One of my most extraordinary journeys by train took place in 1976. The previous year, the former Prime Minister Edward Heath had become a bestselling author with a book called *Sailing: A Course of My Life* about his principal hobby – ocean racing. Now there followed a second book about his other great interest – music. His publishers, Sidgwick and Jackson, decided a hefty promotional tour was in order, and hired a special train, normally used for travelling exhibitions, which made its way from London to Bristol, with stops along the way. At each of these, the public were invited aboard, first to purchase one or two of the books, and then to discover the author in an adjacent, and suitably decorated, baggage car, seated behind an ornate eighteenth-century desk, ready to sign their purchases. The general bonhomie of the occasion was greatly enlivened, between stops, by the liberal supplies of the author's favourite malt whisky which were also on board. I had enormous fun with the script, describing that day, which I wrote in the form of a station announcement. 'The train now leaving Paddington Station,' it began, 'is for making Edward Heath a great deal of money.'

Journeys by road have ranged from travelling in the sleek limousines of official motorcades to bouncing across Nigeria or the India–Pakistan border in army Land Rovers. Sometimes it's been quicker to cross New Delhi or Bangkok, in the rush to the TV station, by motorised rickshaw rather than by standard taxi. I have chartered aircraft and rented sea-going yachts, including a Trinity House cutter to meet round-the-world yachtsman Chay Blyth on his way home. When the European Parliament hired a hot-air balloon to publicise the 1999 European elections, I made good use, during our filming, of another balloon, normally used to show tourists the sights of London, which happened to be operating beside it. That night I was able to sign off, 'Michael Brunson, ITN, *above* Westminster.'

On many occasions, though, getting the story has meant going absolutely nowhere, and for long periods of time. I cannot count the thousands of hours I have spent waiting in Downing Street, a thoroughfare down which the wind always seems to whistle, and on which the sun never seems to shine. Thousands more hours have been spent on various doorsteps, official and private, in Britain and abroad, waiting for information, and often not getting it. Sometimes, though, while the hanging around was immensely long and tedious, the end result was a great story. Waiting outside Stormont Castle in Belfast for the Good Friday agreement on the future of Northern Ireland was one of the longest and coldest of those vigils. To be present, however, when that agreement was hammered out and announced, and to sense the exhilaration of those who had done the deal, was to witness something quite unique, even though the hopes of an early settlement raised by that agreement were premature.

Relieving the tedium of the wait on most doorsteps is one other factor. In journalism you are rarely alone. Unless you are pursuing a genuinely exclusive story, other journalists will be waiting, and working, alongside you. As a television journalist, I am almost never alone in any case, since my cameraman and my producer are usually with me too. It all makes for a great deal of friendship within the profession.

Of course, there are the loners, journalists who instinctively prefer to work on their own. There is the real danger, too, of 'pack journalism', of going along with an easy, and too readily agreed, version of events. Equally, when someone is pursuing a well-founded independent line or an exclusive story, and you get to hear about it, there is the conflict of reconciling your efforts in trying to match or beat his or her report with respect for that colleague's professionalism or enterprise.

Most journalists are, by nature, convivial souls, ready at the drop of a hat to come to the aid of a colleague who, through no fault of his or her own, may be in trouble. Sometimes, however, they can be as wicked or devious as any other members of the human race, even when dealing with each other. *En masse*, journalists can also behave quite badly, especially if faced with 'jobsworth' press officers, officials or other government employees, at home and abroad, who see it as their main role in life to hinder rather than to help us. Never will I forget the terrible abuse we hurled at a certain government bus driver at the end of an official visit by Mrs Thatcher to Switzerland. He insisted on driving us through the middle of the Geneva rush hour, rather than taking any alternative route, as we tried to rejoin the Prime Minister's plane for the journey home. Perhaps we should have forced the miserable man, who eventually got us to the airport some two hours late, to undergo a dressing-down from the Iron Lady herself. There she stood, her face a picture of barely concealed rage over the long delay in taking off for London, as she watched the cause of that delay, the errant press corps, climb sheepishly aboard.

It is not only Prime Ministers who can reduce swollen journalistic heads. Members of the public are perfectly capable of doing it too, as I was forcefully reminded during another visit Mrs Thatcher made, this time during the 1983 general election campaign. Four years of the Thatcher Government had begun to produce some very vocal opposition on the streets during that campaign, with groups of demonstrators, usually formed by a hard core from the Socialist Workers Party, waiting for her at many of the places she visited. They were usually in fine voice, too, maintaining a constant chant of 'Maggie, Maggie, Maggie! Out! Out! Out!'

On this occasion, I had arrived well ahead of the official motorcade outside a brewery in Stockport in Greater Manchester, and the chanters were in full cry. One of the Socialist Workers spotted me, and, presumably because he had got bored with his usual refrain, decided to change his slogan. Gradually, I realised that all the demonstrators had taken it up, as I heard them shouting, 'Michael Brunson, *News at Ten*, Out! Out! Out!' I went over to them to suggest that they were out of order and should stop. Whereupon the man who was leading the shouting stopped, put his face very close to mine and bellowed, 'Why don't yer get yerself a proper job, yer great pillock!'

CHAPTER ONE

Making a Start: Oxford, Africa and the BBC

S o what does a young Oxford graduate, with a not very good degree in Theology, who has spent a lot of time mucking about in student theatre, do for the rest of his life? That was the question facing me in 1962 as I set about the business of trying to find a job.

I was coming to the end of seventeen years of full-time education. I had started that education in the state sector, at an infants' school in London and a primary school in Bedford. I had won a scholarship in 1951 to an independent school, which only the English could refer to as a 'public school'. I had spent eight years at Bedford School, including two terms as an assistant master in the preparatory department there. That was after I had gained entry to Oxford, and was waiting to take up my place, the nearest I ever came to the traditional 'gap year' between school and university.

I had spent four years reading Theology at Oxford. My choice of degree had been heavily influenced by the fact that I had been brought up in a very religious family. My stepfather, who had adopted me at the age of four, after my natural father had been killed in the war in 1942, had himself begun to train for the priesthood before he had married my mother.

They had met largely as a result of their connection with the Church Army, the Church of England's version of the Salvation Army.

During the 1950s, I had regularly been going to church three times on a Sunday. I attended twice as a choirboy at Morning Prayer and at Evensong – these were the days before the Parish Communion had taken hold as the main C of E service. There was a third visit to church for a modern version of Sunday School called Junior Church, which my stepfather ran on Sunday afternoons. It was therefore hardly surprising that I believed that I had a calling to the Anglican priesthood. Indeed, shortly before going to Oxford, I had been formally taken under the wing of the Church's training body, the grandly named Central Advisory Council for the Training for the Ministry. After attending a selection board, I was put in touch with the Director of Ordinands for my home diocese, St Albans. He turned out to be a rather elderly clergyman, with a wonderfully old-fashioned turn of phrase. In his first letter to me, he enquired about my plans for further education. I wrote back, reminding him of my place at Oxford. 'I am so sorry,' came the reply. 'I had no idea you were such a swell!'

I had applied to The Queen's College, Oxford, as a result of a meeting, through the Student Christian Movement, with that college's chaplain, David Jenkins, who later was much in the news during his time as the controversial Bishop of Durham. I have always suspected that I was accepted, after a reasonable but not spectacular set of A-level results, for two reasons: because there was not exactly a rush of young people wanting to read Theology, and because I had agreed to take part in a new, four-year course intended to match Oxford's famous four-year degree course in Classics, commonly called 'Greats'.

'Theology Greats' was an equally demanding course. I had

already learnt Greek at school, but for those who had not it involved learning Greek from scratch. It also required all of us to learn Classical Hebrew. This is an even more difficult language than Greek. It reads from right to left, not left to right, and employs a whole new set of characters. Those characters are only the consonants, and the vowels, at least when you first begin to learn it, are added in the form of tiny dots and dashes underneath. The whole thing was not made any easier by the fact that we were taught it by a very stern non-conformist minister, who was working on a new translation of the Old Testament. He insisted on holding his demanding thrice-weekly classes at nine in the morning, a terrible time for most people, let alone young undergraduates.

But learn Hebrew I did, and sufficiently well to be able to read at least some of the Old Testament in its original language. At that stage I was diligent enough to get a second in the halfway examinations, taken after five terms. But, after that, things rather began to fall apart.

For a start, I had lost my vocation. This came as no surprise, incidentally, to my mother, who told me later that she had constantly told my stepfather, 'I do hope Michael will change his mind. He'll make a rotten priest!' I tried to switch courses, but was firmly told by David Jenkins that this was out of the question, and that if I wanted a degree I would simply have to soldier on. So I did, spending less and less time at my work, and more and more time on student drama.

That might not have done much for my formal education, but it was good fun. My contemporaries on the student theatrical scene included people like Esther Rantzen and the man who later became the Hollywood star Michael York, but who was then still called Michael Johnson. Sheridan Morley was there too, though he was frankly valued more for his ability to deliver his famous father, the actor Robert Morley, to our various productions than for any great acting skill of his own. Another contemporary was Peter Snow, who was later to become an extremely well-known television journalist. Even at Oxford, however, his exuberant style of performance tended to dominate any play in which he took part, including a production of George Bernard Shaw's *The Devil's Disciple*, in which I was supposed to have a starring role.

I spent more time, in fact, directing plays than acting in them. Whether acting or directing, however, the play was certainly the thing. I got involved in any dramatic production I could, especially those in the Oxford Playhouse, which was about to become, disastrously, the University theatre. There were plays in almost any other location, inside or outside, to which we could gain access. One of the most spectacular was in my own college, Queen's. Every summer we were allowed to stage a production on the terrace of Hawksmoor's magnificent library, which looked out across the Provost's garden and which, for a couple of weeks every year, he gamely surrendered to the College dramatic society. One year I decided that the production of Jean Anouilh's *Time Remembered*, which I was directing, needed a particularly large addition to the set – a pre-war Austin Seven car. We found one at a car dump just outside the city, and had it delivered to the front of the college, the entrance to which consisted of a very elegant but somewhat steep set of stone steps. Fortunately, the vehicle's engine had been removed, which made its transfer by half a dozen of us up the steps, past the porter's lodge, across the quadrangle and into the Provost's garden slightly easier. Whether the Provost relished the sight of an ancient automobile occupying his elegant terrace for a fortnight, I rather doubt.

The result of giving more attention to my life as a 'luvvie' than to my academic studies was a pretty poor third-class degree. Fortunately, it seemed to matter very little to my future employers at the BBC what kind of degree I got, and, indeed, whether I got a degree at all. Astonishingly, they never asked. I had applied to them before my results were known and had been accepted by them, and that, apparently, was that.

Their selection procedure for one of their greatly prized General Traineeships was, on the face of it, rigorous enough. I gather that in the year I applied there were, as usual, over a thousand applicants, and I believe that, in the end, they took less than half a dozen. But, looking back on it all, the way in which I was chosen as a trainee was extraordinary. It simply consisted of completing a long questionnaire, and of appearing twice before a selection board.

I am convinced to this day that I would not have made it but for the fact that one of the board members was the BBC's Head of Religious Broadcasting. At the time, this was a man called Kenneth Lamb, known throughout the Corporation as 'The Lamb of God'. Without knowing that he would be a board member, I had made a strong pitch in my application about my interest in becoming a religious broadcaster. My actual devotion to such a calling was less than skin-deep. I had arrived at it only because I could not immediately think of any other occupation that would naturally call for a combination of a Theology degree and an ability to perform in public.

It seemed to work, though the questioning at both boards was geared to establishing that I was some kind of young 'Renaissance man' who would benefit from the essentially broad-brush approach of BBC training. So, in addition to their interest in the fact that I had apparently mastered three ancient languages – Latin, Greek and Hebrew – the board members also wanted to know, in some detail, why I had once played the double bass in my school orchestra. There were some additional exchanges, which, even at the time, seemed less than relevant to the task in hand. At one stage, someone suddenly asked me, 'So what lost causes are the dreaming spires of Oxford espousing now, then?' I cannot begin to imagine how I answered that one, but, however inadequate the reply, it did not prevent me from being offered a job.

Nonetheless, it was soon clear that, however rounded a person the BBC had now decided to include among its employees, in their view still more rounding was in order. It was suggested to me that, as part of my training, a year abroad as a VSO volunteer might be an excellent thing. In 1963, Voluntary Service Overseas was still something of a fledgeling organisation, and it seems that someone may have suggested that a bit of high-profile support from an organisation like the BBC would be immensely helpful. So, after an introductory six weeks with the BBC African Service at Bush House, and a brief VSO induction course, I was put on a plane to Sierra Leone.

I had never flown before. I had only seldom been out of England before. That may seem astonishing, but it was not that uncommon for a twenty-something in the early 1960s. Suddenly, here I was, experiencing my first-ever take-off, leaving Gatwick at around midnight with a ten-hour flight by turbo-prop aircraft to tropical Africa ahead of me.

I have immensely mixed feelings about my time as a VSO volunteer. Uppermost is a sense of failure, because I had to come home before the end of my appointed year. My step-father had suddenly died, and my mother simply could not handle the prospect of her only child, even one aged twenty-two, remaining in Africa and leaving her to cope on her own. As a result, those whom I had been teaching in Sierra Leone suddenly found that, two-thirds of the way through their year-long courses, their teacher had disappeared. I was also a very bad teacher. I had been assigned to the Prince of Wales School in Freetown, the capital of Sierra Leone. I was asked to teach some A-level English and some lower-level French, and I am now frankly ashamed of how poorly I did it, even before my sudden departure made things worse.

However, like most people who have been a VSO volunteer, I can attest that it was a valuable, character-building experience. Tropical West Africa was not then, and is not even now, the easiest place in which to live. Sierra Leone, after all, is the original 'White Man's Grave', as the Victorian tombstones in Freetown's oldest cemetery showed. In row upon row, the crumbling headstones recorded the deaths of those who had left the United Kingdom for service in the former British colony, and who had died from various tropical fevers and other such diseases, often within weeks or months of their arrival. For most of the year, the temperature in Freetown is extremely high, and the atmosphere humid. The rainy season provides some relief, though the thunder and lightning is violent and the downpours are long and severe.

There were, nonetheless, many compensations. The school day ended at around two in the afternoon, so it was possible to be on a wonderful tropical beach an hour later. Astonishingly, I had arrived in Sierra Leone without being able to swim, so now I taught myself how to do so.

I was also conducting a courtship by airmail letter. I had met Sue on my very first day at the BBC. Indeed, it was she who was sent to greet me at the Bush House reception desk on the morning of my arrival. Subsequently, we had been out together during my brief spell in London before I left for Africa, including a visit to the Proms, where we had sat in the steep upper reaches of the Albert Hall. There, she told me later, I had deeply shocked her by deciding to occupy not one, but two seats, by putting my legs over the back of the unoccupied one in front of me. I thought it was a rather sensible solution to the cramped conditions. She thought it was an extremely odd way to behave.

The relationship, however, survived this early hiccup, and throughout my time in Sierra Leone we kept up a regular correspondence. Saturdays became a particularly important day, since I discovered that it was far more reliable for her to send letters, *poste restante*, to the Central Post Office in Freetown, to which I dashed early every Saturday morning. It all ended, incidentally, in the best possible manner. We were married about a year after my return to England.

On my return, I resumed my traineeship in the BBC African Service, where I came into contact with the man who played an important part in my becoming a journalist. Frank Barber had worked in Fleet Street on the old *News Chronicle*, and, even though he worked from Monday to Friday as the BBC's West African Programme Organiser, he still did a regular Saturday shift, editing the front page of the *Sunday Times*.

My work for Frank did not directly involve me in hard news, but, with understandable logic after my recent spell in Sierra Leone, I was put in charge of a programme called *Calling Sierra Leone and the Gambia*. Even by the standards of the early 1960s, it was a curiously old-fashioned programme. One regular item was a sort of radio gossip column, written and presented by a clergyman from Sierra Leone who was working in North London. He was called the Rev. M.G.M. Cole (I never did find out what the initials stood for), and he always began his broadcast with the words, 'Well, well, well, here we are again!' The rest of the programme seemed to consist almost entirely of a long list of the people who had arrived and departed by the ships of the Elder Dempster line which, in those days, still regularly sailed between Liverpool and Freetown.

I decided to sack the Rev. Cole, and told him that I intended to do so. He was far from pleased, and he raised merry hell. He appealed to my boss, Frank Barber, and I was overruled –

an early encounter with the office politics of broadcasting. But in this, as in many other things, Frank's guidance was sound, and invaluable. He would offer his advice in his bluff Yorkshire way, his words always reinforced by the printed sign which hung above his desk, declaring 'Do It Now!' He taught me how to write for radio, and how to focus on the main points of what I was trying to say. Throughout, he kept up a steady stream of anecdotes and examples of good, and bad, journalism from his Fleet Street days, just as my thoughts were turning ever more frequently towards the BBC's news programmes.

It was becoming increasingly clear that I would determine my own BBC future, since I quickly discovered that the Corporation's much vaunted training programme on which I was enrolled was haphazard in the extreme. In charge of it was a man called Hallam Tennyson, a distant relative of the great poet, but with whom I had very little contact.

Training, as such, was minimal. I was sent on just one formal course, which lasted a fortnight. It dealt with every subject under the sun, and drew together a disparate group of people. During a discussion on the future of television, an austere lady, who worked for BBC Radio in the wonderfully named Gramophone Department, declared, 'Television is something about which I know little, and care less!' One unfortunate instructor, demonstrating the use of what was laughably called a midget recorder – a vast green box containing a reel-to-reel tape recorder – decided to play a number of recordings made in and around his house, to demonstrate the machine's capabilities. Unfortunately, he prefaced the last of these with the words: 'Here is a recording which I made in my back passage.'

The course was valuable, however, for one opportunity which it gave me. Each of us had to compile a radio programme, to be played to and judged by the course directors.

Given the lack of any clear sense of direction from on high about my future career, I had spotted local radio as an area into which I might move. I decided, therefore, to make what turned out to be a pretty dreadful tape of what I imagined local radio might sound like in the town where I'd been brought up. 'Radio Bedford' was extremely boring, but it did mean that I was able to demonstrate my growing interest in moving into journalism. Hallam Tennyson duly took note, and I was transferred, not to one of the fledgeling BBC local radio stations, but to Broadcasting House, to work in the South East Regional News Unit.

South East News was run by a veteran journalist called Maurice Ennals, a kindly man, who offered encouragement and gentle criticism to the young journalists who worked for him. He had, however, two particular eccentricities which could make life difficult for his staff. First, he constantly appeared to be going for what used to be called a 'wash and brush up'. At almost any hour of the day, Maurice could be seen, towel, toothbrush and toothpaste tucked under his arm, either making for, or returning from, the gents' loo, or engaged in his ablutions inside it. Since his office was separate from the main *South East* newsroom, editorial decisions on the programme were often made as a result of a chance encounter in the corridor or the washroom.

Maurice Ennals also had a passion for tidiness and good order. Like all the young reporters on the programme, I edited my own sound tapes on a small bank of Ferrograph tape machines, installed behind a screen at one end of the newsroom. I admit that we were not the tidiest bunch of individuals, and the reels of tape, and tape boxes, left scattered around this area drove Maurice to distraction. Day after day, he tried to instil in us the need for good housekeeping, and, when all else failed, he would institute his own drastic spring-cleaning. Tapes carefully, if untidily, kept back for future reports would be swept up and sent off for recycling, and if we so much as hinted at a touch of annoyance, Maurice would sharply inform us that if things had been left in good order no problem would have arisen.

The same stern rules applied to the newsroom itself. Any papers left lying around, without any clear evidence of ownership attached to them, were in constant danger of being thrust into the nearest dustbin. I once, while making a brief visit to the studio some distance away, left some scripts for the day's programme lying in some spot which fell foul of Maurice's rules. When I returned, I found the scripts in the dustbin. Once again, I was lectured on the need for tidiness and order, though, as always, with such good humour that my frustration was short-lived. For the most part, however, Maurice left the day-to-day running of the programme to his deputy, Marshall Stewart, to whom I owe a very great deal. Marshall taught me how to be a journalist, and, above all, how to acquire and develop that most crucial of skills, news judgement.

Such judgement is a fine call when you are dealing with local news. Day after day, you must learn to assess the relative merits of very similar stories. Is the opening of a new concert hall in Brighton more important than the opening of a new police headquarters in Essex, and, if so, why? Of course, major stories broke in our area, but they would be reported on the national news, so what was our follow-up to be? What extra information could we add? Covering the whole of south-east England, why should anyone in one part of that vast area be remotely interested in anything we were reporting from another?

Marshall Stewart helped me to acquire the skill of how to judge the news and how to present it. It was the equivalent of serving time, and learning the trade, on a local newspaper, a world from which he himself had come. As a result, he retained a considerable affection for the West Midlands, where he had worked on the *Birmingham Mail*, coupled with an equal devotion to Coventry City Football Club. It was to him that I would return with my reels of tape, after a day dashing around London or the south-east in a red Mini, armed only with one of the sizeable machines which the BBC still insisted on calling a midget tape recorder.

I can claim no great scoop during my time on *South East News*. Later, Marshall Stewart, who went on to become Editor of the *Today* programme, and the BBC's Head of Publicity, would joke with me about my excitement at having interviewed Marianne Faithfull's mother, or even, on one occasion, the singer Frankie Vaughan.

A series of reports on famous people who had begun their careers in our region was a particular delight. The inventor of the Dambusters' bouncing bomb, Sir Barnes Wallis, took me back to his old school and his old science laboratory at Christ's Hospital near Horsham. Sir Freddie Laker told me, at Southend airport, how he had set up his first airline, using aircraft which were going cheap after the end of the Berlin airlift, and which he had converted to ship people, or cattle, across the English Channel. If there were too few passengers, the passenger flight would be cancelled, and would instantly become a cargo flight instead. A small herd of cattle was apparently kept corralled close to the airport for just such an eventuality. All went well, Sir Freddie explained, until, on one flight, a cow broke loose on take-off and smashed its head through the plane's window. The pilot was forced into the ultimate indignity – circling his home airfield to jettison fuel before his emergency landing, with a cow, mooing loudly, stuck out of the side of his aircraft.

Much that I did during my spell on *South East News* was great fun, but above all it was a time for acquiring new skills. There was no sterner test than the routine of the early-morning news broadcast. At that time, there was a five-minute slot allocated to regional news bulletins, immediately after the 7 and 8 a.m. national bulletins on what was still called the Home Service – Radio Four did not arrive until September 1967. These regional bulletins were written and read by one of the *South East News* staff, which frequently meant me. It also meant either getting in to work very early, or booking a bed in the dreary accommodation just across the road from Broadcasting House, in the old Langham Hotel, since restored to its former glory but used then as an extra set of offices by the BBC.

The greatest ordeal, however, involved not just the writing of the short bulletin but the submission of it, for approval, to one of the duty sub-editors in the main BBC radio newsroom. It was difficult enough having to decide the relevant merits of a fire in Basildon or a car crash in Billericay, but having one's efforts torn apart at the last moment by a vastly more experienced senior journalist was traumatic, though doubtless good for one's professional soul. Mostly, however, the sub-editors were kind, and checked it all through only to guard the BBC against libel or other legal problems.

That was all followed by a quick dash to one of the studios to read the thing. Here again you had to be careful. It may only have been a regional bulletin, but, because it was being broadcast in London as well as the rest of south-east England, an awful lot of senior BBC people might well be listening to it. Every one of them was ready to complain to one's own immediate superiors if anything went wrong. Fortunately, not very much did, and I was soon certain that this was the sort of job I wanted to do on a permanent basis. I therefore asked to end my status as a trainee so that I could apply for a staff job on the programme, which I duly got. My professional career as a journalist was under way.

However, I soon had ambitions to work in national news. It was always possible to apply for an attachment to other programmes, and the fact that I was working in Broadcasting House alongside the people who ran some of them was a great advantage, since they had a vague idea of who I was. After a while, I managed to get myself assigned on a temporary basis to what was then a rather new radio programme called *The World at One*. It is easy to forget, more than thirty years on, that *The World at One* was regarded at the time as quite an experiment, bordering indeed on the revolutionary.

Until then, news magazines were typified by time-honoured programmes like *Radio Newsreel*, still being transmitted at seven o'clock every evening, and so called because, when it was first thought up, it was meant to be the radio equivalent of the old cinema newsreels. It certainly reeked of that era, especially since it was introduced by stirring martial music. It consisted of the cream of the old-style BBC newsreaders introducing a succession of reports from famous BBC correspondents like Erik de Maunay in Paris and F. D. Walker in Bonn. As with the Rev. M. G. M. Cole earlier, most people never discovered what the F. D. stood for. He was always simply introduced as 'F. D. Walker'. So, and for many years later, was a famous BBC Belfast correspondent known to everyone in the profession and to most of the people of Northern Ireland as Billy Flackes, but always referred to, on air, as 'W. D. Flackes'.

The World at One brushed that entire tradition aside. A famous figure from Fleet Street, William Hardcastle, the former editor of the *Daily Mail*, was brought in as presenter, something that was completely unheard of. He conducted live interviews, as well as introducing other reports, which often consisted of packages put together by the programme's team of journalists, instead of dispatches by BBC correspondents. They also contained 'actuality', brief excerpts from interviews, or other natural sound recorded outside the studio, which proves that the 'soundbite' has a rather longer history than most people imagine.

That was all meat and drink to me as I began my short attachment. It was what I had been doing on *South East News* for months. Not surprisingly, as my temporary posting drew to an end, I pleaded with my superiors to let me stay with *The World at One* on a permanent basis. But here I ran into the roadblock of BBC bureaucracy. That was not the way things happened, I was told. I would have to wait my turn.

Frustrated, I applied for a vacancy as a national BBC reporter, based in Birmingham. In charge of all such posts was a fearsome character called Tom Maltby, a journalist of the old school, who had arrived from the tougher end of Fleet Street to become the BBC's grandly named Head of Home Correspondents. During my interview for the post, I became very pompous, and referred to a report I had seen on an ITN bulletin the previous evening. It had shown the wife of a missing trawlerman shortly after receiving the news of her husband's death. I suggested that this was not at all the sort of thing that the BBC should broadcast. 'Finest bit of reporting I've seen in years,' growled Maltby. I did not get the job.

Ever more desperate to escape from regional radio, I finally applied for and was given an attachment to BBC Television, to work on the precursor of *Newsnight*, a nightly programme called *24 Hours*. Only then did the Editor of *The World at One* plead with me not to desert radio. Andrew Boyle, a friendly though tough man, who, in addition to his BBC career, wrote the book which was chiefly responsible for unmasking Anthony Blunt as a traitor, told me that I could, after all, have a job on his programme. Asking me to call on him at his home in Putney for a private discussion, he even hinted that, on occasion, I might be able to stand in for the great William Hardcastle himself as the presenter. But it was too late. My mind was made up. I wanted to be a television journalist.

CHAPTER TWO

Scissors and Cardboard: Early Days in Television

W orking in radio had provided its own satisfactions. It was, and still is, a very 'immediate' medium. Little stands between the reporter and getting his story on the air. It was often a matter of simply going out with a tape recorder and recording what needed to be recorded, coming back to base and editing it. Editing meant putting the tapes on to a reel-to-reel machine, physically cutting out the material you did not want with a razor blade, and sticking the bits you did want back together again with little bits of white sticky tape. After the programme editor had listened to what you had done, and any corrections were made, it was then simply a matter of delivering your tape to the studio, for playing out at the right point in the programme. So much was in your own hands. If the recording quality or the editing was poor, or the tape was late arriving in the studio, it was your fault and no one else's.

Now, having moved into television, I was no longer my own master. Indeed, I was no longer a reporter, since my job was to be a junior producer, working on the preparation of items to be broadcast by other people. In many cases that meant being a dogsbody for someone who *was* a reporter. It was not a situation that I particularly relished, but it was the price I was prepared to pay to get my foot on the bottom rung of the ladder of television.

I was soon to learn that television depends on teamwork. It is not a place for those who like to work on their own. From the start, I discovered that everything involved someone else, and that everything seemed to take a very long time to accomplish. This was 1966, and the technology of television was still in its infancy. Pictures were still being transmitted in black and white, and the equipment we were using was cumbersome, and frequently unreliable.

Nowhere was this more obvious than in the matter of editing television videotape. The television equivalent of radio tape editing, which I now encountered, was akin to a surgical operation in a hospital. It involved the use of a machine the size of a sideboard, which needed special air-conditioning equipment to stop it from overheating. On to this the editor loaded the huge, and extremely heavy, reels of two-inch-wide tape. Editing took place with the help of a microscope, through which the editor had to search for a break in the 'pulse' signal on the tape, for it was only between these that the tape could safely be cut. This was done with a pair of scissors, and, after the section that wasn't required had been removed, the whole thing was glued back together again. Multiple edits were, therefore, heavily discouraged.

I came to dread Mondays, because *24 Hours* that evening frequently made use of excerpts from the American political talk shows, which even then were a staple of US television on Sundays. Recordings of the programmes were shipped to us overnight, and once we had received the giant reels, the search for the required passages began. This was a nightmare, because the great machines had almost none of the facilities that nowadays we expect to find on even the cheapest of home video recorders. The only way to see any picture at all was to play the tape at 'real time' speed, that is, the speed at which the original broadcast had taken place. Fast picture search was not available and frequent spooling, stopping and playing was frowned on, because at any time the machine might chew up the tape. The editors would rail against us young producers for not reading the 'dope-sheets', the documents which purported to give some detail of what was on the tapes, with sufficient care, so that what was required could be instantly found.

The preparation of graphics, the means of displaying and revealing words and figures on the screen, was an equal nightmare. Graphics are now created electronically on a computer, and there is virtually no limit to the clever effects that can be achieved. Then it was all a matter of cardboard. To one side of the main *24 Hours* office was a room occupied by the graphic artists. It resembled a painter's studio, with coloured card, paint, glue, easels and much else besides scattered all around it. A simple graphic was printed out in white letters on black card by the sort of machine then used outside television to produce price tickets in department stores. Anything more complicated required the production of something that looked like a page from a child's pop-up picture book. Elaborate constructions, consisting of bits of card sliding this way and that, to be operated by hand in front of the cameras, would take hours to make. Once again, an eager young producer like myself was frequently told that what I wanted was out of the question, either because it was too complicated or because there was insufficient time in which to make it. It was clear, though, that the graphics team were proud of their work. Their most ingenious triumphs could be seen hanging on the walls all around their workroom.

Much of my work was to do the research for items that would be broadcast live, and directly from the studio, during

the course of the programme. That frequently involved producing a first draft of the questions that one or more of our
star presenters would be asking during one of the studio
interviews or discussions which made up a large part of the
programme. Then, as now, such items were frequently set up
with a high regard to the potential they had for generating a
good punch-up.

The presenters were a very distinguished bunch. Among
them were Cliff Michelmore, Kenneth Allsop, Michael Barratt and Professor Bob McKenzie, famous for his use of the
swingometer, another triumph of the graphics department, in
the earliest of the general election results programmes.
Michael Parkinson was briefly a member of the team as well.
24 Hours was broadcast every weekday evening at 10.30
p.m., and two of the presenters would usually arrive at the
studios by mid-afternoon. They would soon be asking to be
briefed about the evening's interviews. These sessions were
conducted rather like an Oxford tutorial, with Kenneth
Allsop, in particular, forever asking, 'Why this?' or 'Why
not that?' as he got to the bottom of the matter in hand. Often
they would simply fine-tune what we had prepared for them.
Sometimes they would ignore it or throw it all away. They
could all be exasperating, and, in the case of Bob McKenzie,
there was the additional hazard of the wreaths of cigar smoke
which enveloped both him and me during our discussions, but
I learnt a great deal from all of them.

There was soon the opportunity to work away from base,
both at home and overseas. One such trip was a particularly
hazardous assignment during the course of the Nigerian–
Biafran civil war.

The reporter David Lomax had been asked to cover the
Nigerian side of the conflict, and I was asked to go with him
as his producer. Fortunately, David and I got on well, and it
was from him I learnt the importance in television journalism

of 'writing to picture'. That is another way of saying that it is not usually a good idea to assault more than one of the viewers' senses at the same time. If you ask them to listen to one point, while the pictures are making another, they will either get confused or irritated, or both. Of course, the practice can be taken too far. It was once brilliantly lampooned by David Frost on that early example of late-night satirical television, *That Was the Week That Was*. His reference to the Lord Privy Seal was illustrated by Blake's picture of God, an outside toilet and a circus animal with a ball on the end of its nose.

In Lagos, I first encountered that staple of overseas war reporting, the 'up country trip', so brilliantly mocked by Evelyn Waugh in his classic and very funny novel about journalism, *Scoop*. Governments in time of war do not like to have a whole bunch of foreign correspondents hanging around their capitals and making trouble because they are bored. A trip to the front, or as close to the front as the Government deems fit, is often arranged as a result. It usually turns out to be a long way from any action. This applied to the visit we were invited to make to Port Harcourt, in what had been part of the breakaway Republic of Biafra in the east of the country. It had just been recaptured by Federal troops, and so, for obvious propaganda reasons, the Nigerians were keen to show it to us.

Getting there was the first hazard. After several false alarms, we were told to report to Lagos airport, where we located an ancient propeller-driven DC-4 from which all the seats had been stripped out. Already aboard it were about a hundred Nigerian soldiers, sitting on the cargo, which turned out to be oil drums full of petrol. The captain, an elderly American, was wearing a pair of spectacles with the thickest lenses in them that I had ever seen. As he finished his pre-flight checks, he warned us that the aircraft had what he called 'about a dozen major unserviceabilities', the most serious of which appeared to be the fact that one of his engines was refusing to start. Outside, the ground crew struggled in the ninety-degree heat to get it going, which they eventually did by squirting large quantities of something or other into the front of it. Inside, the plane had become a sauna, with a hundred Nigerian soldiers, not to mention a British television team, sweating buckets. Ignoring the rest of the 'unserviceabilities', the pilot eventually took off, and we lumbered towards Port Harcourt. From the moment of our arrival, we quickly realised that we were going to have to keep on the right side of one of the most eccentric soldiers I have ever met.

The man in charge of Port Harcourt was the new military governor, Colonel Benjamin Adekunle, otherwise known as the 'Black Scorpion'. Colonel Adekunle greeted us and then proceeded to inspect his troops, no doubt for the benefit of our cameras. He carried a riding crop, which he used frequently, and a pistol, which we assumed was loaded and which he often placed against either his own temple or that of one of his men, in a sort of theatrical version of Russian roulette.

The Colonel's orders were issued as either a shout or a scream, and our first port of call was his headquarters. Port Harcourt had been a large commercial centre, through which millions of barrels of oil were shipped, and which had attracted foreign businesses of all kinds. Those who had run them were anxious to find out what had happened to those businesses, and waiting to see the Colonel was one such businessman seeking permission to inspect his former premises. He needn't have bothered. All he got for his pains was a torrent of abuse before he was sent packing.

We filmed in and around the devastated port, where the docks were full of packing cases containing the personal effects of many of the expatriate oil-company workers who had been forced to leave. Many of the cases had been ripped open and their contents looted. I decided on a little looting of my own, when I discovered, and retrieved, a small carved wooden statue of what appeared to be a tribal chief in his elaborate headdress being kicked around on the very edge of the dock.

In the absence of any military action, it was clear that the bulk of our report was going to have to be about the extraordinary Colonel Adekunle, and so we asked for an interview with him. This he agreed to do at his house, on condition that we helped him with what he described as his newly acquired home-movie camera.

The interview completed, a houseboy was dispatched, and reappeared with a large and, to our crew, very familiar-looking steel box. The Colonel's 'home-movie camera' turned out to be a complete set of professional television gear, almost identical to that which our own team was using, and which the Colonel had ordered directly from the manufacturers in Switzerland. Of course, he hadn't the faintest idea how to use it, and as our crew tried to explain its mysteries to him, David Lomax and I took up our own equipment and began filming what was going on. We expected to be roundly abused by the Colonel for so doing, but, as his deeply furrowed brow made plain, his concentration was being taxed to the full. So great was his concentration that our sound recordist, Freddie Downton, was able to swap some of his own rather worn-out cables with the brand-new ones which, he had quickly spotted, formed part of the Colonel's kit. Eventually, the Black Scorpion tired of the whole thing, and ordered his new toy to be taken away. I doubt whether it ever left its box again.

Much more hazardous was a second trip to a town called Enugu. This was a far bigger place than Port Harcourt, and had been designated by the rebels as the capital of Biafra. As a result, the Federal army was even more proud of having reclaimed it. We joined a group of about forty correspondents who were taken there from Lagos in a specially chartered Nigeria Airways plane, for what we had been warned in advance would be a day trip.

Our host on this occasion could not have been a greater contrast to the Black Scorpion. This Colonel was a sophisticated, almost urbane man, and, of course, we pleaded with him to let us stay on in Enugu after the others were due to go back to Lagos. He eventually agreed, but, once again, there was a condition, and this time it was a much more serious one. He could give us some accommodation, and even an old Peugeot staff car, which, it turned out, used almost as much brake fluid as it did petrol. But, after that, we were on our own. He would not be responsible for getting us back to Lagos.

After nearly a week of filming in an area which was very close to the front line, we made our way back to an almost completely deserted Enugu airport, and settled down to wait for a plane – any plane – and a flight back to Lagos. We were sure there would be one, and we soon discovered that there was not. We returned, sheepishly, to the local commander. 'What did I tell you?' he said. 'It's up to you to get yourselves back.' Eventually, however, he relented. We gathered that his change of heart was something to do with the fact that his girlfriend needed to be taken back to her home town. A Land-Rover and driver would transport us to Makurdi, a journey of some 150 miles through the bush on rough laterite tracks, where there was another airport from which, he understood, a flight to Lagos was due to leave.

David Lomax and I, our cameraman and sound recordist, and the Colonel's girlfriend, together with all our gear, somehow managed to squeeze ourselves into the Land-Rover, and the journey started well enough. We made good time, and, after several hours, we got close to the clearly deserted airport at Makurdi. Our spirits rose considerably, since we could hear the sound of aircraft engines. We made the fastest possible progress, and, once we had arrived at the heavily damaged airport terminal, we dashed through, only to see a large transport aircraft just taking off. We ran to the control tower, to see if we could radio the pilot to turn back and pick us up, but it was no use. The controllers told us that it was simply impossible, and that our best bet was to press on to Kaduna, another 200 miles further on, from where scheduled flights to Lagos were operating.

Fortunately, Kaduna turned out to be the home town that the commander's girlfriend was headed for. We set off for it, but the journey became increasingly hazardous, especially as darkness had fallen. Without our drivers, we would have become completely and seriously lost. After two or three hours at the wheel, one of them would come to a totally unmarked junction or fork, and still, even in the darkness, know which direction to take. We suffered several punctures, and eventually used up the spare wheels that we were carrying with us. At one point, after yet another puncture, we had to find somebody in a small bush village into which we had limped in the middle of the night to help us. Incredibly, someone was found, even at that hour, to effect a makeshift repair on the tyres, and we were able to continue.

After a hair-raising night bouncing along for mile after mile, we eventually made it to Kaduna airport, early on a Sunday morning. To our great relief we were told that a flight to Lagos was due to leave later that morning. We received the even better news that there were seats available on it. In addition, Nigeria Airways would accept credit cards for the payment of our fares – a fact that, in the middle of a war-torn African country in the late 1960s, was pretty remarkable in itself. Payment to our drivers, upon whom we had been totally dependent, was more straightforward – our entire spare cash, and lots of cigarettes.

As my time with *24 Hours* continued, I was on very rare occasions able to do a little reporting of my own. I recall, for example, going to see the London dockers' leader Jack Dash, in his small house in the East End, and, to my shame, employing for the first time one of the most dreadful clichés of television reporting, as I filmed him inspecting his roses. I tried and failed to get into Czechoslovakia in the early part of 1968, at the start of the 'Prague Spring', simply because I was not diligent or determined enough. Nonetheless, I was still certain that I wanted to become an 'on-screen' reporter, and, later in 1968, my chance came.

It was a particularly interesting time in the development of television news in Britain. In July 1967, ITN had introduced *News at Ten*, the first half-hour news bulletin ever on British television, to be presented by two 'newscasters'. It was totally different in style and content to anything that had been attempted anywhere else on British television. When news of its imminent launch reached the BBC, the Head of BBC Television, Huw Wheldon, summoned those of us working on current affairs programmes at the Lime Grove studios to a staff meeting. 'Now,' said Wheldon. 'It would be the easiest thing in the world for us to kill off this new venture, if the BBC decided to schedule something like a light entertainment programme against it.' 'What a very good idea,' I recall whispering to someone at my side. 'However,' he continued, 'we do not behave that way at the BBC. We shall rise to the challenge, and simply defeat them by the excellence of our own continuing efforts.' I suspect that as *News at Ten* began to build a steady audience soon after its launch, and to receive critical acclaim, there were those in the BBC who felt that Sir Huw Wheldon had made a dreadful mistake.

For my own part, I had a growing feeling that I was making a mistake in struggling on at *24 Hours*. In its way, it was rewarding, but I still had ambitions to be a full-time television news reporter. Working alongside me on the programme, specialising in reports on science and the exploration of space, was Peter Ryan, whose brother, Nigel Ryan, was about to become the Editor of ITN. Peter Ryan had somehow sensed my growing frustration, and simply said to me one day, 'You're not very happy here, are you? I think you should go and see my brother.'

I did just that, and Nigel Ryan suggested, after an initial meeting, that I should return, with some examples of my work, for a second session with himself and the outgoing Editor of ITN, Sir Geoffrey Cox. I persuaded one of the BBC film editors to put together what turned out to be a very meagre 'clip-reel', a compilation of my efforts on television thus far, including the shots of Jack Dash inspecting his roses, and back I went to ITN's headquarters. At that time, ITN shared an office block with the old Rediffusion television company, which was responsible for ITV programmes in London. The block was located at the bottom of Kingsway, just across the road from Bush House, where my broadcasting career had begun with the BBC four years earlier.

My second meeting with my future employers took place in the rather strange surroundings of the ITN preview theatre. This was a small, darkened room like a miniature cinema where, I learnt later, incoming film reports were viewed by a sort of editorial vetting committee, who sat in a row of cinema-style tip-up seats to watch them and to make instant decisions on their fate. My fate was almost sealed just as speedily, as I sat alongside Sir Geoffrey Cox and Nigel Ryan in those same cinema seats. The ITN projectionist could not get his machine to show my BBC clip-reel – something to do with the different operating procedures of the two companies.

Eventually, a lever was pushed or some vital knob was twiddled, and there, on the screen before us, was my offering in all its inadequate glory. Sir Geoffrey did not think much of it, and gently said so. Between the two of them, however, they must have seen something they liked. I was offered a job – the start of over thirty years' service with ITN.

Any doubts I had about whether I was doing the right thing were removed by one final meeting at the BBC. I went to see the Editor of *24 Hours*, Tony Whitby, to tell him that I was intending to leave and to join ITN, hopefully as a reporter on *News at Ten*. 'I wish you well,' he said, 'but I am not surprised. What I need on my programme, you see, are not reporters like yourself, but thinkers.'

CHAPTER THREE

'Get Rid of That Coat':
A Reporter at ITN

I left the BBC and joined Independent Television News in September 1968. I hoped, indeed expected, that my reporting career would resume very soon. In this I was guilty of wild optimism, since the Editor of ITN, Nigel Ryan, had made it perfectly plain that, while he believed that I would eventually become an ITN reporter, I was to start as a scriptwriter.

Once again, I decided that a foot on the ladder was better than having no chance of climbing the ladder at all, and, on this occasion, my instincts were right. ITN, I quickly discovered, was a very different place indeed from the BBC. For a start, it was very much smaller. It may have been a national news organisation, but the whole feel of it was much more akin to working in a regional newsroom. Everyone was literally bumping into everyone else in the cramped conditions, but, as a result, decisions were taken speedily, often instantly. It was a very friendly place, perhaps because so many people had been recruited relatively recently for the launch of *News at Ten*, which had first gone on air just over a year before I arrived.

I was immediately set to work. The usual practice at ITN

now is to ease people in slowly, to help them find their feet. Not then. We were so short-staffed that an extra pair of hands was a godsend to the hard-pressed producers, and I was given the job of writing 'lead-ins' – the introductions to the film packages which were the hallmark of *News at Ten*.

What really helped my career forward at this stage was having a halfway decent address book. A former Editor of ITN, David Mannion, told me recently that one of the questions he always asked those who were applying to him for jobs was whether or not they had a contacts book, and that he was staggered at the number of them who replied 'No'. Like me, he found it inconceivable that anyone could either be a reporter or hope to be one without a little black book full of the sort of addresses and telephone numbers which are not generally available to the public.

By the time I joined ITN, I certainly had one, and it turned out to be very valuable. Within days of my arrival, a story broke in the middle of the evening involving the proposed, and highly controversial, England cricket tour to South Africa. I am not a cricket fan, but I did gather that the News Editor desperately wanted to get hold of someone very senior in the management of the game. I knew that in my little black book I had the name and, more to the point, the home telephone number of a man called Les Ames, who was the manager of the England touring side. He was also the Secretary of Kent County Cricket Club, and in my days as a BBC radio reporter I had once interviewed him, and had been diligent enough to make a note of his number. ITN's own contacts system having failed, I had come to the rescue, and I was duly rewarded.

After just a couple of weeks as a scriptwriter, Nigel Ryan called me in, and told me that I was to be made a reporter forthwith. I could scarcely believe either my own ears or my luck. This is what I had joined ITN to achieve.

Once again, I was put straight to work. My first assignment was to report on the latest developments in the controversy within the Roman Catholic Church over the use of the contraceptive pill. I decided that in order to do the story I needed to obtain a packet of them, and so went to an astonished newsdesk secretary and asked her, 'Are you on the pill, and have you got any with you?' Fortunately, she was a broadminded young lady, and the answer to both my questions turned out to be 'Yes'. Armed with the vital packet, I went with a camera crew to Westminster Cathedral, and stood outside it, waving the pills about, as I recorded my first ever 'piece to camera' for my new employers. Opinion was sharply divided about my efforts when I returned to base, but eventually I persuaded the relevant programme editor that, without the waving of the packet, the story was nothing.

My career as a television reporter quickly flourished, but not always in quite the direction which I anticipated. A great deal of my time was spent 'on the taxi rank', as we called it, waiting, along with one or two other reporters on duty on any particular day, for a story to drop and for the news editor to assign us to cover it. Most coveted were assignments to cover foreign stories, for which you had to be ready to leave at a moment's notice. Those assignments usually involved quite short trips abroad, but one of my first turned out to be not only of a far longer duration than was usual, but of an altogether different nature.

ITN had committed itself to an arrangement with a strange man called John Fairfax, who had decided that he wanted to row across the Atlantic from the Canary Islands to Florida. As he got closer to the Florida coast, I was sent out with one of ITN's most senior cameramen, Cyril Page, and a sound recordist, 'Nobby' Pullen, to rendezvous with him at sea, and to interview him. Cyril had a reputation at ITN for not doing things by halves, and for speaking his mind. My first encounter with him had been on a story in Kent about the continuing speculation over the building of the Channel Tunnel. I was wearing a long black overcoat, a leftover from my undergraduate days, and when the filming was complete, Cyril had drawn me to one side, and asked, 'Do you want to get on at ITN?' I replied that of course I did. 'Well, get rid of that bloody awful coat!' was his terse response.

On this latest assignment, the three of us checked into Miami's plushest hotel, the Fontainebleau, the same hotel at which, several years later, the former Labour Minister John Stonehouse staged his 'disappearance'. It was immediately clear that the Fontainebleau was very much to Cyril and Nobby's taste, and they were not to be prevented from enjoying its facilities, since we spent some three weeks staying there in all. An even higher standard of living, however, was yet to come.

We first needed to find John Fairfax. Cyril hired a small seaplane, and we headed for the spot which Fairfax had indicated by radio was his position. Eventually, we caught sight of him. Unfortunately, we also learnt that another seaplane, hired by our rivals from the BBC, was in the area too. Our plan had been that we should land beside the boat, interview Fairfax and take the film back to Miami, but our pilot decided that what looked to us like a very slight swell made such a landing impossible. Even the fact that we could hear over the radio that the rival plane from the BBC was prepared to brave the conditions and land could not persuade our pilot to do likewise. Fortunately, John Fairfax stuck to his contract with us, and refused to talk to the BBC. We dropped him a packet from our plane, which contained among other things the large box of cigars he had asked for and a note telling him to stay where he was, and that we would be back as soon as possible, by boat.

Once we had returned to Miami, Cyril Page set about

finding a suitable vessel. Miami, of course, is teeming with boats for hire, but he decided that the only one which would have the range and other conditions which we required was a 140-foot luxury yacht, complete with a crew of seven. As always with Cyril, a great deal of haggling went on, and what he described as a superb deal was struck. We set off, found John Fairfax and his boat once more, and invited him aboard our yacht to be interviewed. This was the nearest thing to normal conditions that John Fairfax had experienced for a considerable period of time. After tossing around in a twenty-foot rowing boat in the middle of the Atlantic for several weeks, he was now able to enjoy the relative stability of the after-deck of a luxury yacht. More to the point, he was able to have a drink.

As the interview continued, more drinks followed, thanks to the ministrations of an attentive steward. (When we looked at the interview later, John Fairfax's growing inebriation during the course of it was clear for all to see. It was the more readily apparent since ITN, seeking a decent return on its investment, decided to use a great deal of the interview, and to devote most of the second half of *News at Ten* to it.) Late into the evening, by which time darkness had fallen, we eventually lowered a somewhat worse-for-wear, and clearly reluctant, oarsman over the side of our yacht. Having put him back into his little boat, we told him we would meet him again in Miami. Whether the alcohol had anything to do with it or not I do not know, but he immediately got caught up in a number of strange currents, which for a time took him closer to Cuba than to Florida. As a result, he ended up not in Miami, but in Fort Lauderdale, some forty miles further up the coast, where we filmed his official landfall.

On my return to London, I was quickly informed by my clearly envious colleagues that I should not expect such plum trips to come my way with any frequency, and that I had better return to the 'taxi rank', and await my share of less glamorous assignments. However, journalism is often a matter of being in the right place at the right time, even if you are simply the next person in the queue. A little later, I was the duty reporter in London when news came through of a serious incident involving the Queen, who was in the middle of a tour of New Zealand. The royal yacht *Britannia* had been caught in a fierce storm in the Cook Strait between the North and South Islands, so fierce that a seaman aboard one of the ships of the New Zealand navy which was escorting *Britannia* had been washed overboard and drowned.

ITN did not routinely cover royal tours in those days, but I was quickly dispatched to New Zealand and told to stay with the tour until its completion in Australia. I did so, though not without some difficulties. The local New Zealand-based cameraman who had been hired for me turned out to be one of the thinnest and frailest-looking men on earth, and he was carrying one of the biggest and heaviest of the cameras then in current use. The '600' model he was using, with a huge 'double O' film magazine stuck on top of it, was only normally used, with a tripod, to film things like cricket matches. Somehow Don, the cameraman, staggered round New Zealand with this contraption on his shoulder, and, when a locally hired cameraman on the next leg of the tour turned out to be completely incompetent, Don staggered round Australia with it too.

ITN had no regular royal – or as the BBC, then and now, stuffily put it, 'Court' – correspondent. But, after my rapid introduction to the craft, the job of reporting royal tours regularly came my way. The most exotic was a tour that lasted some eight weeks in all. It began in Kuala Lumpur, turned eastwards towards Borneo and Brunei, and then began a leisurely progress across the Indian Ocean. The Queen was using the royal yacht, while the RAF was responsible for transporting the accompanying correspondents. This imposed upon us the barely endurable hardship of being dumped in the Maldive Islands, as well as in the Seychelles and Mauritius, up to a week before Her Majesty and the royal yacht got there.

It also meant a visit to a strange place called Gan, a small island roughly halfway across the Indian Ocean. This tiny atoll, rising no more than a few feet above the sea, was used at the time as a staging-post by the RAF, and had been all but covered by a mile-long runway and the various buildings associated with an RAF station. To illustrate the scale of the mighty runway, I got my cameraman, with the help of some of the ground crew, stationed on a hydraulic loading platform high above it, so that I could be filmed walking down the immense expanse of concrete. Unfortunately, I was wearing a pair of extremely ancient and baggy army-surplus khaki shorts, of the sort that were regularly seen on the television programme *It Ain't Half Hot, Mum*. I have no idea exactly how I acquired them in the first place, though I do recall that I had owned them for many years. I was told later that the resulting pictures, when shown on *News at Ten*, produced gales of uncontrollable laughter in the ITN newsroom. I also heard later that when RAF personnel received media training from ITN staff the film was regularly shown as an example of when it is kinder *not* to help reporters with their sillier filming ideas.

We flew on to the Seychelles, where I got an early taste of the power of the press. We had decided not to spend the days ahead of the royal party's arrival in complete idleness. In between satisfyingly long spells on the beautiful beaches, we had filmed a short report about the islands, and, in particular, about the new Seychelles airport, which the Queen was due to open. This, as with all such reports at that time, had to be shipped by plane, undeveloped and in sealed cans, back to

London, and the British Airways representative at the newly completed but as yet unopened airport promised that he would make immediate arrangements. His arrangements, however, for the shipment of our film turned out to be totally inadequate. In short, the film cans were still sitting in the airport when I checked back later, and I made a terrific fuss. His solution was to arrange for a scheduled flight from South Africa to London to take a diversion out across the Indian Ocean, and to make an unscheduled landing at the new airport, simply to pick up our film. I can only assume that British Airways had already realised the enormous tourist potential of flights to and from the Seychelles and were determined to do anything to avoid bad publicity. I was to discover throughout my career that big businesses, even more than governments, regard poor publicity as something to be avoided at any cost, and that businessmen will move heaven and earth before, during and after any hostile reporting to get things changed. Whether the passengers aboard the South Africa-to-London flight in question appreciated the detour, I rather doubt.

My early days at ITN were not, however, a constant round of highly enjoyable experiences like royal tours. When I joined in 1968, the Troubles in Northern Ireland were just beginning, and, along with most of my general reporting colleagues, I was expected to do my turns of duty in Belfast. Strangely, it was many years before ITN established its own correspondent there. We relied for the most part on our colleagues at Ulster Television (UTV), the ITV station in the province, and, when things hotted up, reporters were sent out from London. As we reported the growing activities and demands of the People's Democracy movement, led by the young student Bernadette Devlin, we constantly heard Loyalist voices warning that it was all nothing more than a front for the IRA. With no great understanding of the recent history of the province, but with the sense that the Catholic and Nationalist community had, over the years, been seriously discriminated against, I thought the 'it's all an IRA front' argument unfair.

What I failed to understand, though, was the potential for the actions of the civil rights movement, and the reactions to them by the RUC, to trigger, in time, a new IRA offensive. As television reporters, we were more than mere bystanders. What we said and did had a profound effect on the situation. Pictures, for example, of the brutal suppression of the civil rights march in Derry in October 1968 by the RUC and the police reservists, the B Specials, were shown extensively on both ITN and BBC news bulletins, and around the world, and were greeted with outrage. As sectarian rioting and violence increasingly became the norm, a set of ITN ground rules evolved – above all, that we should do nothing to promote or encourage violence.

I personally became aware of the dangers that can arise when an outside 'fireman' reporter is sent in to cover a situation to which he or she does not have the full background, or does not give both sides of the story. On one occasion, I reported that Loyalists were laying the blame for an outbreak of rioting on Nationalists who had been waving the Irish tricolour flag. I was specifically told that my report had been seen on the news, and had immediately been the cause of much more serious rioting. I came to rely heavily on the expertise of Robin Walsh, the Head of News at Ulster Television, whenever I was sent over for duty in Belfast. On each successive visit, the situation seemed to have deteriorated. I was in the city, for example, in August 1971 when the internment of Republican sympathisers began in the early morning. The areas from which they had been taken echoed to the constant banging of dustbin lids on the pavements as their wives and families protested about the arrests. Four days of serious rioting followed, in which twenty-two people were killed. As well as reporting trouble at ground level, we could see and film the Belfast skyline from the roof of the UTV building. It was a mosaic of smoke and flames, a sight that was to be repeated over and over again for many years.

My regular trips to Belfast, and my time as a general reporter, were, however, about to come to an end. In the autumn of 1972, our correspondent in Washington, Robert Hargreaves, became ill, and I was asked to take over there on a temporary basis. Eventually, Robert's condition became too serious for him to continue, and early in 1973 I was formally appointed as his replacement. After just over four years' service, I had been given one of ITN's top jobs, and with it the chance to report on one of the most important stories of the decade.

CHAPTER FOUR

'You Sure Picked Your Time': Washington and Watergate

L et no one tell you that top-level journalism isn't tough on relationships and on family life. It is. At the highest level, the only way to succeed in the trade is always to put the job first, and that can be very hard indeed on those closest to you. While I was standing in for our regular Washington correspondent at the end of 1972, I was asked if I would remain on duty over Christmas. I said I would, provided that my wife Sue and my two young sons, Jonathan and Robin, could join me in the United States. It was agreed that they would, and they arrived in Washington three days before Christmas.

For three months, I had been living in an apartment hotel in Georgetown, a fashionable area of Washington very similar to Chelsea in London. It was pleasant enough, but it was decidedly not home. Sue and the boys joined me there, and we spent our first full day for many weeks together on a grand sightseeing tour of the American capital.

On Christmas Eve, there was a massive earthquake in the Central American republic of Nicaragua, in which it was immediately clear that thousands of people had died. The final death toll was some 10,000. ITN covered Central

America from its Washington office, and the only way into Nicaragua was by chartering a small plane from Miami, since the airport at Managua, the Nicaraguan capital, had immediately been closed to civilian flights. It was clear that I would have to go, but leaving a wife and young family to spend Christmas on their own in a bleak apartment building in a city which they had never previously visited was very, very hard. There was, however, one compensation. ITN realised how difficult the whole thing had been, and, on my return to Washington, agreed to pay for a short holiday for us all at Disneyland in Florida. One of the boys' earliest memories is of suddenly exchanging the freezing temperatures of Washington for the sweltering heat of Florida, and of swimming at midnight in an outdoor pool at our hotel in the middle of winter.

Early in 1973, my permanent appointment to Washington was confirmed, and I was immediately involved in reporting an incredible story which has become a by-word for scandal in high places.

Watergate was the name of the apartment and office complex close to the Potomac river in Washington where the original break-in and burglary which formed the heart of the story took place. In 1972, President Nixon, a Republican, was seeking a second term of office, and was eventually re-elected. But in June of that year five men, part of a White House 'dirty tricks' squad known as the 'plumbers', were caught red-handed by a security guard as they broke into the offices of Nixon's political rivals, the Democrats. President Nixon did not directly authorise the break-in, but the whole affair rested on the allegation, subsequently proved to be true, that the President had learnt about it at an early stage and had tried to cover it up.

Within days of my arrival in Washington in the autumn of 1972, I was sending the first of many reports on Watergate back to London. Details were beginning to emerge very regularly, mostly as a result of the tenacity and professional skill of two *Washington Post* reporters, Bob Woodward and Carl Bernstein. They were the clear leaders in the field. At one stage, I used to go to the *Post* office in the centre of the city at around eleven o'clock every evening to pick up the first edition of the paper, to make sure that I was well ahead on the latest developments.

By May 1973, the Senate had voted by seventy votes to zero to hold hearings into the matter, and to hold them in public. That meant that the television cameras, and television correspondents like myself, were admitted to the great committee room under the dome of the Capitol where they took place. Another British correspondent, Fred Emery of *The Times*, regularly joined me there. Although the hearings were being transmitted live on television and radio, it always surprised me that more of my colleagues from the resident foreign press did not decide to show up in person, as we were all entitled to do, provided we could get one of the precious press seats. As I was to find in the House of Commons later, nothing actually beats being there.

In charge of the hearings was Sam Ervin, an elderly, white-haired Senator from North Carolina, who would repeatedly describe himself, in his Southern drawl, as 'just an old country lawyer who wants the truth'. As a result of the constant probing by Senator Ervin and his committee, astonishing bits of the truth began to emerge. With these I filled the daily reports which I was sending back to London, where every twist and turn of the Watergate hearings was being given maximum coverage.

I prefaced one of my messages back to London with my own expression of near total disbelief. 'I know you're going to find this a bit far-fetched,' I told the Foreign Editor, 'but we've just been told that Nixon bugged his own White House.' That was after a Presidential aide called Alexander Butterfield had told the Ervin Committee that Nixon had a secret taping system, activated by a switch concealed under his desk in the Oval Office. On the day in question, rumours of a sensational development had begun to circulate among the journalists covering the Ervin Committee shortly before the break for lunch – another example of the value of actually attending such events. Immediately after lunch, the existence of the secret tapes was confirmed by Butterfield's testimony. That week, *Newsweek* magazine produced a brilliant photomontage for its front cover. Using an aerial photograph, they converted the roof of the White House into a reel-to-reel tape deck. Much later, those same tapes were the main cause of the President's downfall, once the courts had ordered him to hand them over. On what became known as the 'smoking-gun tape', the man who had declared 'There will be no whitewash in the White House,' and who had publicly denied any cover-up, was heard telling his staff, 'I don't give a shit what happens. I want you to stonewall . . . plead the Fifth Amendment, cover up, or anything else.'

There was considerable suspicion that the President or his aides, or both, had tried to doctor the tapes to remove such incriminating evidence. Certainly, when the contents of the tapes were eventually made public, there were discrepancies between the transcripts that the White House had earlier released and what Congressional aides actually found when they listened to them. But those differences were often to remove Nixon's bad language from the transcripts, and did not seem to involve anything of great substance. That was why the matter of one very large discrepancy, a gap of eighteen and a half minutes on one of the tapes, became such a huge story.

In addition to attending the Ervin Committee hearings in person, I also tried, as often as possible, to attend the many court hearings that were a very important part of the Watergate story, as it became, not just a political enquiry, but a criminal investigation. As a result, I was one of the very few people actually to have heard the Nixon tapes before the President left office. The transcripts of them were gradually being released as part of the cat-and-mouse game between the White House, the Congress and the prosecutors, but the actual sound recordings were not made available until several years later. However, whenever a contentious issue about the tapes came up in court, headphones were handed out, and everyone in the courtroom could hear sections of them. The quality was very poor, but Nixon's swearing (signalled as 'expletive deleted' in the official transcripts) could be heard quite plainly.

But quite the most sensational moment in Judge John Sirica's courtroom came when it was revealed that there was an eighteen-and-a-half-minute gap in one of the recordings. Richard Nixon's personal secretary, Rose Mary Woods, a woman who was fiercely devoted to the President, claimed that it was all the result of a dreadful accident. The mishap had occurred, she said, while she had been transcribing the tapes, despite the fact that she had previously told the court how careful she had been in undertaking the task.

In court, I listened and watched as Miss Woods explained, and demonstrated in a series of extraordinary physical contortions, how she had been distracted by a telephone call and had reached out to answer it. She explained that she had somehow managed to keep her foot on a pedal, which had continued to activate the tape machine she was using. She had also managed at the same time to press the machine's 'record' button instead of the 'stop' button, thus accidentally erasing a section of the tape. Once again the headphones were handed around the courtroom, and we all sat listening to the gap, eighteen and a half minutes of a sort of up-and-down hum, for which Miss Woods was taking the blame. To back up her story, the White House issued a series of remarkable photographs of her, posing in the same contortions she had demonstrated in court. Neither the photographs nor Miss Woods' testimony did much to dispel the rampant suspicion in Washington that the damage to the tape was no accident.

At the height of the Watergate story, I would be responsible for pulling together a major package of all the day's developments and having them ready for transmission by satellite to London by early evening. The time difference between Washington and London meant that we were working to an early deadline of about 4.30 p.m. local time each evening – 9.30 p.m. in London – so that the report could be recorded and turned around in good time for *News at Ten*. In the early 1970s, transmission by satellite was still something of a novelty. We could certainly not go live from the White House lawn at the drop of a hat, as we do now. Almost all my regular work in Washington consisted of reports on film, which were shipped by plane to London overnight and, as a result, the television coverage of American events was often seen in London a day late. If a really urgent story broke, I would send a report to London by telephone, and they would stick up on the screen a still picture of me and a 'reporting from Washington' caption.

I was also working inside a television studio, almost like a newscaster, far more than I usually did. My links between the excerpts, taken, for example, from that day's session of the Senate Watergate Committee, were pre-recorded in the studio and then cut into the package. Life was not made any easier by the fact that the studios were four or five miles from the centre of Washington. Studio work requires a particular technique. You need, for example, to seem relaxed, even if you are not, and to avoid the appearance of staring at the viewer as you read your script from the autocue. All this was not something I was used to, or very comfortable with, and the Foreign Editor in London, John Mahoney, and I used to conduct daily and lengthy post-mortems on how I was doing.

Richard Nixon finally resigned on 8 August 1974, and it had become clear a few days earlier that a fair amount of live broadcasting would be required from me. Unfortunately, the pressure on the local television companies' resources in Washington was so great that I had to go to New York to get the facilities required. I did so under furious protest. Here was the story that had been the talk of almost every Washington meeting and press conference, as well as every newspaper edition and dinner party, for the previous two years. The American capital may have been appalled, but it had been totally gripped and absorbed by every last detail. Yet I was not to be in town for the extraordinary denouement, as the disgraced President addressed his country on television, and then delivered a rambling and maudlin farewell to his stunned White House staff before taking off in the Presidential helicopter from the South Lawn for the last time.

In my contacts by phone with London, and on my brief visits home on leave, people constantly asked me why it was taking the Americans so long 'to get rid of Nixon'. He had been known even before he became President as 'Tricky Dicky', and had even been forced to declare in the middle of his latest troubles, 'I am not a crook.' Why, my British friends asked, hadn't the Americans thrown him out of office far sooner?

The answer was bound up with the mystique of the American Presidency. The aura that surrounded the Oval Office in the White House, and its occupant, was a potent force in the America of the 1970s. It is still very much part of America's collective consciousness. The President is the head of state, as well as the head of the US Government. Despite his failings, Richard Nixon, like many a President before and after him, was regarded to the end as the embodiment of all those virtues that Americans hold so dear. The President of the United States is their First Citizen, who represents something of which Americans are very proud – nationhood, founded on each citizen's individual rights and self-reliance. The President also carries for them the authority of their country throughout the rest of the world.

That is why Americans are so reluctant to see their President fall. Seeking to impeach him and remove him from office is the equivalent of Britain getting rid of its king or queen. Americans knew that Nixon's disgrace would be America's disgrace, and no one wanted to deliver the final blow. Throughout, Nixon had his staunch defenders, but there was, as there always has been, the strong feeling among ordinary Americans that their President could do no wrong.

It is for that reason that, during the impeachment of both Nixon and Clinton, the issue of exactly what it was that the President had done wrong was so crucial. The constitution talks only of impeachment for 'high crimes and misdemeanours', and the final decision rests on a two-thirds vote in the Senate. In Richard Nixon's case, the matter never came to a Senate vote, because during the hearings in the House of Representatives the so-called 'smoking-gun tape' was revealed. That showed clear evidence of the President's attempt to cover up a criminal act and demonstrated that he himself was guilty of criminal wrongdoing. In President Clinton's case, the legal argument raged around the somewhat less precise question of what constituted, or did not constitute, a sexual relationship. In addition, though America remains a deeply conservative country, the more liberal attitudes of the 1990s compared with those of Nixon's time meant that more people were prepared to turn a blind eye to what their President had been up to. It was, therefore, far easier for the Democrats to argue in 1999 that the whole thing was a political witch-hunt, got up by the Republicans. It is true that during the Watergate scandal twenty-five years earlier, the situation was reversed with the Republicans making the same accusation against the Democrats, but there was one crucial difference. Republican support for Nixon was itself far from solid; many Republicans had always harboured grave doubts about him. When it came to investigating the cover-up, it was, after all, the Republican Senator, Howard Baker, who uttered the classic distillation of the case against Nixon when he asked, 'What did he know, and when did he know it?' So Bill Clinton survived; Richard Nixon did not.

Back in 1974, with Nixon gone, and with his deputy, Gerald Ford, sworn in to replace him, America set about trying to repair all the damage Watergate had caused. Many Americans regarded Ford as a nice enough man, but not quite Presidential material. I had interviewed him as Watergate unfolded and before Nixon's departure, though with the chances growing that he might well have to take over. I had asked him then, very bluntly, about the public's perception of him as a dull man who lacked charisma. 'I think America has had rather too many so-called charismatic Presidents in its recent past,' the Vice-President of the United States growled, as he drew the interview to an abrupt close.

Eventually, in 1976, President Ford had to go out and seek his own mandate to stay in office. Throughout the so-called primary elections, those early beauty contests of every race for the White House, he remained a courteous and pleasant man. I interviewed him again, as he took a swing, on an old-style campaign train, across his home state of Michigan. 'Mr President,' I began, just before the camera was switched on. 'Could you please avoid getting too technical? I'm not sure many people in Britain understand the system of American primary elections.' He grinned as he replied, 'I'm not sure many people in America understand them either!'

In the event, however, plain, honest Gerry Ford was not the person Americans believed would pull them out of their post-Watergate depression. Instead, they turned to a peanut farmer from Georgia, who had become the Governor of that state. Jimmy Carter's appeal was that he was Mr Clean, a Southerner entirely free of all that Washington sleaze. Such scandal as did surround him was of an entirely different kind.

Governor Carter had also taken to a campaign train, and I was aboard it when, as it rolled through Pennsylvania, news came of an extraordinary interview he had given to *Playboy*. Carter was a deeply religious man, who was regularly filmed teaching a Sunday-school class back in his home town, and whose wife Rosalynn, known to some as the 'Steel Magnolia', was never far from his side. Yet *Playboy* reported that he had said, 'I've looked on a lot of women with lust. I've committed adultery in my heart many times. This is something that God recognises I will do and God forgives me for it.'

On board the campaign train, the campaign team's photocopier almost blew up as it reproduced countless copies of the interview, which were quickly passed along the carriages. Why someone on Carter's staff hadn't simply pulled the plug out of the machine, I couldn't quite understand. Next along the carriages was the Governor himself, accompanied as usual by a press 'pool' – a small group of reporters who would stick close to him and who would then write up what they learnt for the benefit of the rest of us. The tedium of this chore, in which the tiniest detail must be faithfully recorded, often produced some jokey writing at the best of times, but this one, written up by the correspondent of the *Boston Globe*, was a classic of its kind. I have it still. It begins, 'Okay, gang. Let's put on that wink and leer, and take a stroll with Jimmy Carter through the train.' The report went on to relate how

Governor Carter had turned aside all questions by saying that he hadn't read *Playboy*, only the 'analysis' of it prepared by his staff, and that he was not concerned about it. Certainly, when he came to the part of the train in which my crew and I were located, he quickly turned aside my attempts at an interview.

The American primary season of 1976 was interrupted by a meeting of the leaders of the world's industrialised nations, known as the G7, which was held in Puerto Rico in June that year. The British Prime Minister, James Callaghan, created a terrific stir by flying in on Concorde, which had caused such huge controversy when the first attempts were made to fly it commercially to the United States. This was the first time it had ever been chartered commercially, and Callaghan told me on his arrival, and later confirmed in his memoirs, that he had enjoyed the experience a very great deal. It had, he said, almost completely freed him from jet-lag, something that was entirely beneficial for heads of state. 'It would probably be better for us all if they used Concorde whenever possible,' he added. Other leaders since have not been slow to follow his advice.

While in Puerto Rico, I slipped and fell, tearing a ligament in my right foot. It had to be set in plaster before I returned to Washington and reset once I was there. Unfortunately the replastering took place on the day I was due to drive the 300 miles to New York, for the Democratic National Convention in Madison Square Garden. This was the great gathering that would finally choose the Democrats' candidate for the Presidency. I had to take with me from Washington an extremely bulky video-recorder, which was needed by our technical team in New York. The plaster around my right foot and leg was still wet as I tried to load the machine into the car, and I had to call for assistance from my wife Sue. She said the whole thing was total madness, particularly as my driving foot was not only encased in wet plaster, but was several times larger than it should have been. On my arrival in New York, John Mahoney, the ITN Foreign Editor, who had come out from London to oversee things, nearly had a heart attack as he saw his American correspondent arriving to cover a major story on crutches. The crutches and my injured leg could easily be kept out of camera shot, but mobility is everything when covering a big story, and I clearly could not move with my usual speed. I had not told London about my accident, fearing that I would be banned from covering the Convention, and that is precisely what John Mahoney now attempted to do. I argued with him, and told him that he could send me home if I failed to do my job properly, and he agreed to let me stay.

Somehow or other I managed to get through the week, caught up in the hubbub and the excitement of the Convention, at which the Democrats picked Jimmy Carter as their Presidential candidate. In the subsequent election, America as a whole chose this unusual man to be its leader. It did not work out. The American people did not warm to him, and his White House staff of Southerners was completely unable to handle the great machinery of government in Washington. Relations with Congress quickly broke down, and Carter's single-term Presidency eventually ended in 1981 with the failed attempt to rescue the American hostages held in Iran.

Over five years, I had reported on Watergate and an American Presidential election. A correspondent in Washington could hardly have wished for two more absorbing stories to cover. As one of our American friends told me when we eventually prepared to leave the United States, 'You sure as hell picked your time to be here.' But my job was not just to report the high politics of America. Part of my brief was to cover any major story that broke, not just in the United States, but throughout North, Central and South America too. There were not many days, during the years when Washington was home base, when I was not reporting something from somewhere.

CHAPTER FIVE

The Prince and the Train Robber:
Across the Americas

The USA is a vibrant place. Its great cities are famous around the world, but it is also made up of hundreds of thousands of small towns, as well as strange rural communities like those in the mountains of West Virginia or the Bayou country of Louisiana. There are great tracts of the country with truly distinctive characteristics, like New England, California and the Deep South. There are smaller but no less distinctive areas which are often associated with religious sects – the homelands, for example, of the Amish in Pennsylvania and the Mormons in Utah. In between are the tremendous regions of mountain, swamp or desert. The United States of America was always likely to produce news or good feature stories. I went to Louisville, for example, for the Kentucky Derby, which Princess Margaret was attending, where I had an embarrassing public run-in at a press conference with Lord Snowdon, who was still her husband at the time. An American magazine had just published a detailed account of what it said was the true state of their marriage, and I tried to raise the matter with him. He cleverly turned the tables on me, inviting me to give some details of what the magazine had reported. Fortunately, I saw the trap, and mumbled something about suggestions that their relationship was not in a particularly happy state. It is just as well that I went no further. The diplomat from the British Embassy who was travelling with Lord Snowdon told me later that he would have sued me for libel if I had repeated any of the allegations contained in the article.

In Memphis, Tennessee, in the heart of the Bible belt, I discovered that a group of Southern ladies were being taught belly-dancing. Off we went, and brought back the pictures to prove it, which not only filled more of an ITN bulletin than they rightly should have, but ultimately led my American friends to hire a belly-dancer to perform at my farewell party in Washington. There were visits to the North Slope of Alaska, during the perpetual daylight of the Arctic summer, to cover the story of BP's exploration for oil and gas, and later to report on the controversy over the way a gigantic pipeline to bring the oil south was being constructed.

There were countless trips to New York, to cover events at the United Nations, and in the city generally, especially as the controversy raged over whether Concorde should ever be allowed to land there. In that city above all, but throughout the country too, I quickly discovered how articulate most Americans are. They are, in the nicest possible way, the world's loudmouths, with a view on everything and ready to express it. Street interviews were a joy. In Britain, so many people you would approach for so-called 'vox pop' interviews (from the Latin *vox populi*, the voice of the people) would lower their heads and scuttle by, muttering, 'I haven't got time' or 'I don't know anything about it.' That happened very rarely in America. Most people would give you their views about anything and everything, and, if required, at length. When they realised you were British, they would often want simply to chat – sometimes just so they could hear 'that lovely English accent'.

Once again, I covered various royal tours, in America itself and in Canada and Mexico. At the pre-tour briefing for one of them, the Queen's Press Secretary at the time, the normally imperturbable Ronald Allison, was thrown into total confusion by an American journalist who wanted to know if the Queen delivered her speeches exactly as they were printed in the advance copies. He, like the rest of us, was convinced that he had failed to hear aright when the questioner asked, 'Sir, is the Queen a textual deviant?'

I joined Prince Charles on a tour of those immense areas of Canada which lie deep inside the Arctic Circle. Conditions in the high Arctic produced all kinds of problems. Not only did the cables of our camera gear snap like twigs in the extreme cold, but the Prince's plane broke down, and he had to transfer to the aircraft which had been assigned to the journalists travelling the long distances with him. That night, he was due to take part in an informal concert at the tiny settlement we had reached, and he and his detective wrote a spoof version of the hymn 'Almighty, invisible, God only wise'. It contained the lines 'O where, may I ask, is the monarchy going, When Princes and pressmen must share the same Boeing?'

It all meant a great deal of travelling, because we would almost always film the story ourselves, rather than expect, as happens nowadays, to use someone else's footage. In any case, the early and mid-1970s were still the technical Dark Ages in British television news. Though the Americans were beginning to move into what became known as Electronic News Gathering (ENG), and were already using the first examples of electronic cameras and satellite links, ITN did not make the change until 1980.

Most of my work, therefore, was still done on film, which was flown back, undeveloped, either to Washington or to London. Fortunately, planes in the States have always operated more like British trains and buses. Travelling around on them was made even easier by far less stringent security than is now required, and by a wonderful system that allowed you to write your own ticket for any domestic flight on special blank coupons, for which you paid later. Provided you turned up at the boarding gate five minutes before departure time, you could usually expect to get a seat. As a result, I became an expert at reading airline timetables, and at finding a route home, usually via New York, where I would deliver my film cans at the very last minute for shipping to London on the overnight flight.

Sometimes, however, getting film from A to B was far from easy. During 1976, America had celebrated the Bicentennial, its 200th birthday, and the highlight of the year-long celebrations was a great gathering in Philadelphia on Independence Day, 4 July, where the original Declaration of Independence had been signed precisely two centuries earlier.

I was still on crutches after my accident in Puerto Rico. So, as it happened, was my regular cameraman, an extraordinary character called David Haylock, an American normally based in Miami who worked almost exclusively for ITN and used to join me at various locations around the United States. The Americans could not believe their eyes, as we joined the official press contingent in Washington for the helicopter trip to Philadelphia, when they saw a British television company being represented by two disabled characters on such an important state occasion which the President himself would attend.

But more difficulties were to follow that day. I had to take the film of the historic events back to Washington for processing, editing and what in those days was a rare satellite feed to London, which meant breaking away from the official transport arrangements for the press. To make the feed from Washington in time, I had arranged for a small charter plane to pick me up at Philadelphia airport. I had not, however, reckoned with the fact that the historic centre of Philadelphia, where the ceremonies were to take place, had been completely sealed off, and that, as a result, there was no easy means by which I could reach the airport.

It was a very hot day, and my right leg was beginning to swell quite severely inside its plaster case. Somehow, I managed to hobble to the edge of the restricted area, where I waited at a set of traffic lights in an attempt to find some means of transport. There were no taxis to be found, the drivers having wisely decided to give downtown Philadelphia a wide berth on such a day, and take-off time for my charter was getting dangerously close. Eventually, a huge Harley-Davidson motorcycle, with a giant of a man in the saddle, stopped at the red light. In desperation, I asked him for a lift. He took one look at me and, more to the point, at the crutch I was using, and let out a huge guffaw. 'Hey, man,' he snorted, 'what is this? Some kinda joke?'

I tried to assure him that it was anything but a joke, and, to prove it, offered to pay him whatever he wanted for the ride, pulling $40 from my back pocket, all the cash I had, to reinforce the point. That did the trick. 'Yeah, well, you'd best git yerself on board, man,' he said, in words that were music to my ears, though doing so proved easier for him to suggest than for me to accomplish. ITN's Washington correspondent was a weird sight that day. A pillion passenger in a crash helmet roaring through the suburbs of Philadelphia, a crutch wedged under one arm, a bag full of film cans under the other, and a leg encased in white plaster, stuck out at an angle which suggested a constant right turn. Somehow, though, it all worked out, and I not only made the flight to Washington, but the satellite feed too.

Other assignments with my cameraman David Haylock proved less wacky, but even more extraordinary. In September 1973, for example, we were both asked to go to Chile, to cover the rebellion there that had resulted in the death of the President, Salvador Allende. Along with roughly a hundred other journalists from around the world, we got as far as the Argentinian capital, Buenos Aires, where we waited, in growing frustration, for the border with Chile to open. David was a restless character at the best of times, but, after a couple of days of inactivity, he was at screaming point, and said that he was determined to charter an aircraft in which we would simply try to fly into the Chilean capital, Santiago.

Somewhat reluctantly I agreed to support him, in what was clearly an extremely foolhardy exercise. Not only would we be running the gauntlet of Chile's air-defence system, but we would have to fly across the Andes mountains, which rise in that area to well over 20,000 feet. That last consideration meant that nothing less than a large aircraft would be suitable, though not even I was contemplating what David then came up with.

He eventually told me that Aerolineas Argentinas, the national airline of Argentina, was prepared to charter to us a Boeing 707 airliner for $25,000, provided that we paid up front, in American dollars and in cash. 'Perfect,' declared David. 'We can split the cost with the BBC and the American networks.' The BBC, however, proved less than enthusiastic about the scheme. Having contacted her London headquarters, the local BBC representative said that she had been told, in no uncertain terms, that she was to have nothing whatsoever to do with such a madcap exercise.

David, ever contemptuous of bureaucracy, then hit on another idea. We would organise the whole thing ourselves, by selling seats on the plane, for cash, directly to the waiting journalists. Most of them were staying in the same hotel, and word quickly spread that a charter flight was being arranged. Having armed ourselves with a receipt book, we did brisk business from my hotel room issuing 'tickets' at $200 a time. The pile of greenbacks grew steadily and rapidly, most of it in notes of quite small denominations. We quickly raised not just what the airline needed, but a little more. To David's intense disgust, I later insisted on sharing out the profit during the flight, which, to my utter astonishment, and after a last-minute hiccup at the airport, did actually take place.

The Chilean authorities agreed to admit a party of foreign journalists, and Aerolineas Argentinas, spurred on by the prospect of this instant and unexpected boost to their cash flow, arranged the necessary air-traffic-control clearance. The main airport in the Chilean capital was still closed, so our flight was diverted to a military base near the city. As we prepared to land, the military authorities showed a marked reluctance to switch on the runway landing lights, and, once they had done so, our pilot discovered that the runway was an extremely short one, resulting in one of the most frightening landings I have ever experienced. Nevertheless, we made it – though, after running an instant air charter company for two or three days, covering a South American revolution seemed rather tame stuff.

In February 1974, I was in South America once more. This time, the setting was Brazil, and the story, though very different from the coup in Chile, was even more extraordinary.

For nine years, there had been constant interest in Britain concerning one of the so-called Great Train Robbers. Ronnie Biggs was one of a gang of men who had held up a mail train some fifty miles from London one night in August 1963, and had stolen two and a half million pounds. For that he had been sentenced to thirty years in jail, but he had escaped from Wandsworth prison in July 1965.

Early in 1974, the London *Daily Express* had learnt that

Biggs, after living for some time in Australia, had finally settled in Rio de Janeiro. They also learnt that, weary of life on the run, he was seriously thinking about giving himself up. As a result, the *Express* did two things. They contacted Biggs, promising to pay him handsomely for his story. But, without telling Ronnie Biggs, they also contacted Scotland Yard. The story of Biggs' whereabouts therefore broke at the same time as the news that Detective Chief Superintendent Jack Slipper was travelling to Rio to arrest Biggs, and to bring him back to Britain. I was immediately sent from Washington to cover the story.

Throughout, I laboured under some difficulties. To save money, ITN had decided not to send my regular Miami-based cameraman, David Haylock. The powers-that-be in London, ever anxious to save a bob or two, had been delighted to find that a crew from Southern Television, the ITV station which in those days held the franchise for the South of England, was already in Rio, waiting for the arrival of the competitors in a round-the-world yacht race. So a money-saving deal was struck, and I was told to work with them.

They were not, however, much used to covering hard news, and were employing a technical system entirely different from ITN's that involved the sound being recorded on a separate, reel-to-reel tape recorder. News cameras at the time combined picture and sound on the reels of film so as to keep the two properly synchronised, or, as the jargon had it, 'in synch'. There was also another problem. Our rivals, the BBC, had a local, and bilingual, correspondent in Rio, a young woman called Jan Rocha. None of us, however, spoke Portuguese, the local language. We asked our hotel to find us an interpreter, and an extremely aristocratic lady later presented herself. Over the next few days, she struggled on with us, but it soon became obvious that chasing around various Brazilian jails and courthouses was very far removed from her normal line of duties.

If I had my problems, however, they were as nothing compared with those about to hit Chief Superintendent Slipper. No doubt, despite his hangdog looks and melancholy air, he was a fine detective in London, but the impression he gave in Rio was more that of Inspector Clouseau, the bumbling detective so famously played by Peter Sellers in the *Pink Panther* films. He had left a freezing London at short notice, and, still clad in a good British suit, was clearly finding the Brazilian heat more than a little troublesome. Still more difficult was the impenetrable Brazilian bureaucracy, which eventually defeated him entirely. It was clear that Scotland Yard and the British authorities had not done the homework necessary for Biggs' speedy extradition. Indeed, they gave the constant impression of believing that it would simply be a matter of arresting Biggs, expressing a few quick thanks to the Brazilians and hauling him on to the next plane to London.

It was not to be. The Brazilians decided to hold Biggs in custody while they sorted a few things out, first at a local police station and later at police headquarters. This was in the same building where Chief Inspector Slipper was arguing the case for taking Biggs straight back to London. Consequently, a large crowd of British and local reporters, photographers and camera crews, myself among them, was camped outside.

The delay was Biggs' salvation. He had learnt from another prisoner that if he was the father, or the likely father, of a Brazilian child he almost certainly could not be extradited, and it so happened that his girlfriend, Raimunda, had just told him she was pregnant. Secondly, Biggs was furious at what he regarded as a double-cross by the *Express*. He had wanted to try and strike some kind of bargain with the British police over giving himself up, which the paper had now blown apart. He therefore told the Brazilians that he had been 'betrayed'. A betrayed Englishman with a pregnant Brazilian girlfriend was excuse enough for the authorities to do what they would almost certainly have done anyway, which was nothing – at least for the moment. It could all wait till tomorrow, or next week, or next month.

After some time, a distinctly downcast British policeman emerged from the headquarters building. Ahead of the pack, I managed to reach Mr Slipper to ask him, 'Chief Superintendent, *are* you taking Biggs back with you?' 'No,' came his scarcely audible reply – confirmation that his mission had failed.

The Brazilians soon decided that such a complicated matter as the extradition of a foreign prisoner could only be handled in the capital, Brasilia, 600 miles away, where there was a special prison for such people. There, the press pack reassembled to bombard the prison authorities with so many requests for an interview with Ronnie Biggs that they eventually agreed to a press conference – of sorts. In true Brazilian fashion, it was to be a press conference like no other.

Perhaps to protect his own back, the police chief decided that the whole thing should technically be a photo-opportunity, since Biggs' Australian wife, Charmian, was coming to visit him. There was just one problem. He decided not to tell either Mr or Mrs Biggs about the plan. Our strict orders were, therefore, to wait in the car park of the detention centre at eight o'clock on the appointed evening, but at all costs to keep well out of sight, so that Charmian Biggs would suspect nothing. Failure to do so could mean the cancellation of the arrangement.

Mrs Biggs eventually arrived, very late, after getting lost in a city which seemed to boast no street names or numbers. With her was an Australian journalist who believed that he had the exclusive rights to the story of her visit, just as the London *Daily Express* still hoped that Ronnie's story was all theirs. Both were to be abruptly disappointed. Within minutes of Mrs Biggs' arrival, the rest of us were summoned from our darkened cars. We crept across the car park to be led inside the detention centre. Suddenly, we all burst in on what was supposed to be a moment of tender, and private, reunion between Ronnie and Charmian. Understandably, both were extremely angry. To Ronnie, this was yet another double-cross, this time by the Brazilians. Charmian burst into floods of tears. In the end, realising that they had little choice in the matter, they both agreed to talk to us.

I was now at something of an advantage. I had realised, once the rendezvous at the detention centre had been arranged, that we would need some lights in order to be able to film inside it, and I had managed to borrow a set from the local television station. By sitting directly in front of the two of them, holding the lights in one hand, and a microphone in the other, I was able to behave rather in the manner of a secret police interrogator, and to turn considerable chunks of a rambling and chaotic press conference into what amounted to an exclusive interview. The BBC, represented by their correspondent Jan Rocha and her locally based crew, had one other disadvantage. Jan had little experience of directing television crews, least of all a crew who were expected to film a press conference conducted in English, a language which they did not understand. Because they had no idea of what was being said, they managed to miss most of the juiciest quotes.

Juicy they most certainly were, especially when it came to the matter of Ronnie Biggs and his relations with the *Daily Express*. I asked him how the plan to give himself up had all been arranged. 'The only person who knew,' said Biggs, 'was the chief of that shitty newspaper.' He spotted Colin Mackenzie and Bill Lovelace, the *Express* reporter and cameraman who had interviewed and photographed him just ahead of Inspector Slipper's arrival, but who both claimed that they had not been told of their paper's decision to tip off Scotland Yard. Turning to them, Biggs declared, 'You're two nice guys. But you work for a grubby organ. And organ's the right word.'

Ronnie Biggs was pleased to have got that off his chest, and I was pleased with what I had in the camera. We parted on the best of terms, with my giving him the paperback I was reading at the time, Frederick Forsyth's *The Odessa File*, to help him while away the long hours in jail. The *Daily Express* was far less pleased. As I left the detention centre, Colin Mackenzie took me aside to ask, 'Any chance of taking those nasty remarks about the *Express* out of the film before you send it to London, Mike?' I made it clear that there was no chance whatsoever.

At the time, I spoke more boldly than I knew. Anxious to get my report back to London as quickly as possible, I took the first available flight from Brasilia to Rio early the next morning, which happened to be a Sunday. I needed to use the facilities of the main television station there, TV-Globo, to process and edit the film, since the story had been judged worthy of the colossal cost of a direct satellite feed. I had reckoned without the rules governing Sunday working at TV-Globo. It was almost completely deserted. Eventually, after promises of overtime, to be paid out by me in cash, some technicians were located and agreed to come in and help. But, as Shakespeare said, troubles come not as single spies, but in battalions. Now, the difficulties of working with the Southern Television crew, rather than a regular ITN team, began to assert themselves.

Once the film had been developed, it was clear that the Southern TV crew had done a magnificent job of shooting the pictures of Ronnie and Charmian. However, following their usual practice, the sound was on a separate reel of magnetic tape which would only run 'in synch' with the pictures by means of a special electronic signal. Needless to say, all that equipment was entirely incompatible with anything within TV-Globo. Voltages, running speeds, pulse tone signals – all were completely different.

Fortunately, one young technician working at the station regarded all this as the greatest possible challenge to his skill. He was determined to crack the problem. Somehow he managed to transfer the sound from the magnetic tape to another piece of film which could run alongside our pictures. Precisely how he did it, I have no idea, but it seemed to involve the insertion of a screwdriver into some part of our own recorder-player so as to alter its running speed. At the same time, the pictures were projected on to a makeshift screen, and our technician friend then made an educated guess as to whether the lips of Mr and Mrs Biggs were moving at approximately the same time as the sound which was issuing forth from the tape recorder, or vice versa. In London, they were a little puzzled by the eventual result, though they declared it usable – just. What had happened, they asked? We spared them the details, merely explaining that we had encountered one or two minor problems. Anyway, we were a long way away, and surely it was something to do with the quality of the satellite feed, wasn't it?

Sadly, it all had to come to an end. I count myself lucky that I was a foreign correspondent at a time before the accountants began to rule the television roost. They now declare all too often that it is much too expensive to have journalists and camera crews roaming the world, getting stories for themselves, when so much is available, at the flick of an electronic switch, from news agencies and television stations around the globe. In covering a story, though, nothing ever beats actually being there, even for newspaper and radio journalists. The chance to sniff the air, to get the smell and feel of a story, to talk to eye-witnesses and officials and victims, adds something to reporting that reading news agency reports and watching someone else's videotape can never provide. If nothing else, five years away from London had surely proved that.

CHAPTER SIX

'Is That Quite Clear?': Encountering Margaret Thatcher

As my time in America came to an end, the prospects awaiting me in London were limited. To be more blunt, there was no job lined up in London which, in my view, could equal the excitements of living and working overseas. The best I could hope for was a return to what is known in the trade as 'general reporting', a blanket title given to all those areas of journalism not covered in any news organisation by the 'specialist' reporters who concentrate on politics or business or health and so on. It has one essential requirement – that you must be prepared to do anything or go anywhere at a moment's notice, and to take on an assignment about which, initially, you know very little.

I was not exactly out of practice when it came to this kind of journalism. My time in Washington had included a good deal of such general reporting, as well as the big stories like Watergate and the Presidential election, both in and beyond the United States. Now, as I returned to London in 1977, there was the additional compensation of being more at the centre of what makes your own country tick than is ever possible when you are away from headquarters as a foreign correspondent. The political upheavals in Britain of the

81

1970s, for example, and particularly those of 1974, with its two general elections in the space of a year, had largely passed me by, especially since those events had been little reported in a United States convulsed by its own political problems.

I think my superiors at ITN would have been perfectly happy for me to stay in Washington for a very long time, but I had been determined to return, not least because the boys' schooling had reached a critical point. We had wondered how my younger son Robin would fit into a school in London after five years in the American system. He had never been to a British school. He had a marked American accent and had been used, for example, to beginning every schoolday by standing with his fellow pupils, hand on heart, and pledging allegiance in the traditional way to the American flag. We need not have worried. After just one day at his new British school, he had realised that being part of the crowd was essential. When we asked him at the end of that first day if things had gone well, he replied, with a thick London accent, 'Yeah, Oi think Oi'm goin' to loike it there.'

As his father at work, however, I was rather less happy. In those days, ITN had very few overseas postings, and there were no vacancies in any of them, even if I had wanted another spell abroad. At home, too, all the specialist correspondents' jobs were filled, and there were no immediate vacancies in prospect in that area. There was nothing for it. I would have to go back to the 'taxi rank' of general reporters.

Many of my colleagues later told me that they had been astonished that I had agreed to move from ITN's top foreign posting without the guarantee of a senior position in London. But I have never been greatly concerned with the business of status. That is not false modesty, but a genuine dislike of the sort of internal bickering over status and 'who does what' which, over the years, I have seen corroding many colleagues' careers. So I decided to roll up my sleeves and make the best of what, after all, was not a bad job at all – general reporting for one of the world's top news organisations.

In one of the bizarre quirks which are the hallmark of journalism, one of my very first assignments, once I was re-established in London, took me straight back to America. Sir Freddie Laker had just won the right to set up the very first 'no-frills' airline – his Skytrain service to New York. The lack of frills meant that the press, like everyone else, was expected to queue up for tickets at Gatwick Airport: part of the revolutionary nature of the service was that it started out as a 'turn up, pay and fly' operation. To be sure of seats on the inaugural flight, we showed up twenty-four hours or so before the plane was due to leave. Freddie Laker would occasionally come and scan the queue, grinning as he saw a large number of journalists being treated for once like ordinary members of the public.

At this stage, I had no more than a general interest in political reporting. That, as I shall describe, came a little later. I was not, for example, present at the Conservative Party conference in October 1977, and it was therefore only with the natural interest of a general reporter that I was aware of a speech by a young man called William Hague that had set that conference alight. He had expounded a thoroughly Thatch-erite view of things, although it would be another two years before Mrs Thatcher began to put them into practice. He had declared that the people of Britain, and particularly the young people of Britain, 'don't want to go to Callaghan's promised land, which must surely rank as the most abhorrent and miserable land ever promised to the people of a nation state'. And he had raised much laughter as, gazing out at the audience in front of him, he had declared, 'It's all right for some of you. Some of you won't be here in thirty or forty years' time.'

The speech had, of course, been extensively reported in the papers and on TV and radio, not least because Mrs Thatcher herself, with smiles of approval at the exposition by one so young of her way of thinking, had led the platform in a standing ovation. It was on the Monday following the speech, however, that William Hague and I met for the first time. After his moment of fame, it was time for the sixteen-year-old schoolboy to resume his daily routine and to return to his lessons at Wath-upon-Dearne comprehensive school near his home in South Yorkshire.

ITN decided that it wanted coverage of it all, and I headed straight for the Hague family home early that Monday morning. Indeed, it seems that I made rather too eager a start to things, since, as William Hague has told me since, his mother suddenly found an ITN camera peering at her through her glass-panelled kitchen door as she prepared breakfast for William and his father. She was not best pleased, by all accounts, because she was still not quite fully dressed and was in her housecoat at the time, and for several days afterwards went around declaring, 'I cannot believe that Michael Brunson would do such a thing!'

Looking at the film more than twenty years on, it is a miracle that we recorded any pictures at all. In those days, the quality of the colour film we used was not very good at the best of times, and a particularly foggy Yorkshire morning didn't help. No images of Mrs Hague in her housecoat appear to have survived, but William is seen tucking into a hearty fried breakfast, with a copy of *The Times*, open at the political page, spread out on the table beside him. The headline reads 'Ministers fire early shots in what may prove campaign for the next general election' – *The Times* did not exactly go for racy headlines two decades ago. In a brief interview before boarding the school bus, William reveals that his day will be taken up with 'economics, history, English and politics', and shyly

A London school photograph – taken when I was seven. Much else may have changed, but my hairstyle, it seems, has not.

One year on, and into the short-trousered uniform of my new school – Goldington Road (now Castle Lower) in Bedford.

Aged 14, and now in long trousers after winning a scholarship to Bedford School, something of which my mother was immensely proud.

Undergraduate madness – helping to haul an Austin Seven into Queen's College, Oxford for a production of Jean Anouilh's *Time Remembered*.

A decidedly serious young graduate in 1963 – just down from Oxford, with a BBC traineeship agreed and a spell as a VSO volunteer in Sierra Leone immediately ahead.

At work as a BBC Radio reporter in 1965. Interviews were recorded on the reel-to-reel tape recorder, to be edited later using a razor blade.

It's a hard life – beside the pool in Miami and on the phone to London while waiting for the tansatlantic oarsman, John Fairfax, to arrive.

As a young reporter outside ITN's former Wells Street headquarters near Oxford Circus in London. I was soon ordered to replace the glasses with a more fashionable pair – and I did.

Covering the Indo-Pakistan War in 1971. The ancient-looking film camera, with cables stretching between the cameraman, the sound recordist and myself, was still the standard equipment for television crews at the time.

On the border between India and Pakistan in 1971. The extraordinary climate in the region required heavy protection against the early morning cold, and the gradual shedding of layers of clothing throughout the rest of the day.

A restaurant in Reggio di Calabria in southern Italy became an unofficial press club in July 1970. Scores of European journalists were covering the riots in the city – though the trouble always stopped in time for lunch.

The strangest of many makeshift sound recording booths constructed in a hotel bathroom to blot out extraneous noise during the royal tour of the Far East in 1972.

Sue, Jonathan and Robin at our house in Washington in 1973. The TV Times photographer from London wanted all the American clichés – hence Sue's cowboy hat, my football helmet and Jonathan's baseball glove.

A stroll with the family in Washington in 1973, in between the hectic days spent reporting the Watergate scandal.

Meeting President Gerald Ford during the 1976 American Presidential election. The interview was filmed in the observation car of his campaign train as it crossed his home state of Michigan.

Meeting Jimmy Carter during the 1976 American Presidential election.

agrees that, when it comes to politics, he may already be able to speak with a certain amount of experience.

We went ahead of the bus to the school, where the presence of our cameras meant that most of the arriving pupils decided that it would be far more interesting to stay outside and see what was going on rather than entering the building. We recorded another interview with one of his fellow pupils. 'He's always been like this,' he told us, 'since he was about thirteen. People keep on saying he's going to be the next Prime Minister. Well, not the next, but he will be in time.' When young William arrived, it was to a rousing, if not especially respectful, greeting from 500 of his schoolmates. All very embarrassing at the time, no doubt, but useful early training, perhaps, in both handling a crowd and dealing with the media, for the future Leader of the Conservative Party.

In June 1978, I went to Zaire, the former Belgian Congo, where civil war had broken out once again. The capital, Kinshasa, was a city in an all too familiar state of African chaos, gripped, for example, by hyperinflation. The only effective means of changing money was through the services of a black South African Jew, who would do the rounds at the Intercontinental Hotel, carrying a large case filled with local-currency banknotes. Payment for services at the hotel consisted of depositing wads of this currency, still with wrappers or elastic bands around them, on the cashier's counter like so many Lego building blocks – if, that is, you could prise the cashier away from his television set. World Cup football was under way at the time.

Chaos also reigned at Kinshasa airport, from which we needed to travel some 800 miles south to Kolwezi, where a particularly brutal massacre had taken place. There were no scheduled civilian flights to southern Zaire, and the only way to travel there was to try and hitch a ride. Most flights to the south left around daybreak, so you had two choices. You either snatched a bit of sleep on the tarmac, listening for signs of activity as a plane was being prepared, or got to the airport very early in the morning. In both cases, you simply asked the various pilots for a ride south. Once in Kolwezi, there was no accommodation available, since the town had been heavily shelled and was all but deserted. An ad-hoc peace-keeping force was also in the town, so we bedded down in a wrecked motel, alongside a number of Belgian paratroopers and a company of the French Foreign Legion. I slept on the stage of what used to be the ballroom, wrapped in a discarded silk parachute.

We travelled backwards and forwards to Kolwezi on a variety of planes. One journey was made in a Belgian Air Force transport aircraft, carrying thousands of gallons of petrol in a number of enormous, though rather fragile-looking, rubber tanks. They were stowed in the very cabin that we were travelling in, and wobbled alarmingly like giant, sinister jellies throughout the flight. On another occasion, we hitched a ride on an Argosy, an ex-RAF transport plane, which was being flown by two young British pilots for a German company engaged in some highly secretive rocket and missile work in Zaire.

A number of other reporters from Europe and America were also covering the story, most of them hardened members of that exclusive if unofficial club of international war reporters. They are by nature a tough bunch, but they are also exceedingly competitive, none more so, on this occasion, than a BBC reporter called Simon Dring, who was spurred on to new heights of aggressive behaviour by the sight of myself and an ITN camera crew.

Our reports were still being shot on film, which meant that the cans containing the unprocessed rolls had to be hand-carried back from the south to Kinshasa. Simon Dring, along with the rest of us, was therefore having to travel backwards and forwards on whatever flights we could find between Kolwezi and Kinshasa airport. There, under a procedure that is now specifically banned for security reasons, a helpful passenger on one of the scheduled international flights would be approached and asked to carry the film to somewhere in Europe for us. From that point, it could be collected and forwarded to London. Such arrangements were the only way of getting our reports back to ITN, since the local air-freight service in Kinshasa, even if it existed, could certainly not be relied upon.

I was therefore relieved to note that on one occasion Simon Dring appeared to be safely installed in the Kinshasa Inter-continental Hotel for the night. I assumed that he and his crew would be joining us on a rare official press trip to the south, arranged for the next day. For once, we would not have to bother about hitching a ride, though I was puzzled and alarmed, once on the flight the following morning, to discover that there was no BBC crew and reporter on board. The reason became clear on our arrival in Kolwezi. As we rode into town in a couple of army trucks, we saw Simon Dring and his crew by the side of the road, giving us a smug wave. Simply to prove the point that they did not have to rely on official press arrangements, they had slipped out of the hotel in Kinshasa in the middle of the night and hitched a ride south, so as to get to Kolwezi ahead of the rest of us.

Perhaps it was this spell of war reporting, challenging though it was, which reinforced my growing conviction that my future lay in specialist reporting in Britain. After my return from Washington, I grew increasingly aware of the likelihood of a general election. I could see how precarious the fate of the Callaghan Government had become, only kept in office for a

time by the Lib–Lab pact and beset by the problems of
inflation, unemployment, devolution and relations with the
trades unions. It was within this context that I was offered a
lifeline.

I was called in for a meeting with the Editor, who knew of
my disappointment at simply being returned to the 'taxi rank'
of general reporters. He told me that, when the election came,
ITN would not be setting about things as it had during past
elections, but would be operating in an entirely different way
in organising its campaign coverage. 'Target teams', each
consisting of a reporter, a producer and two camera crews,
would be attached to the three main party leaders, James
Callaghan, Margaret Thatcher and David Steel, for the whole
of the campaign once the election had been called. Those
teams would follow the leader to which they had been
assigned on a round-the-clock, day-by-day basis as he or
she travelled the length and breadth of Britain. Even though
the election might be up to eighteen months away, the Editor
wanted me to know that the 'target team' reporter assigned to
cover Margaret Thatcher would be myself.

Looking back, I can identify that moment, with great
clarity, as the starting point for what was to become, much
later, my full-time occupation as a political correspondent.
Not that I realised it at the time. I accepted the assignment as
the one bright spot at an otherwise rather gloomy point in my
career, and without any great expectation that it would lead
to anything very remarkable in the short term. The day-to-day
reporting of Mrs Thatcher's performance as Leader of the
Opposition was, after all, the responsibility of our team at
Westminster, and I could not immediately see that I would
have very much to do in that regard until the election was
actually called.

I was wrong, for two reasons. One was the very nature of
the lady herself, who throughout her political life has been a

lightning conductor, attracting attention and generating headlines, whatever she does and wherever she goes. The second
had to do with my own nature. I had never been one to sit
back and simply let the opportunities come to me. If I was to
be Mrs Thatcher's campaign reporter, I would see whether
she was already waging some kind of campaign and, if she
was, I would start reporting it well before the general election.

I did not have to wait long. At the end of January 1978,
Mrs Thatcher gave a wide-ranging interview as Leader of the
Opposition to Granada Television's current affairs programme *World in Action*, during which she was asked about
the ever sensitive issue of immigration. She replied with what
she later described as some 'extremely mild remarks'. What
she actually said was this: 'People are really rather afraid that
this country might be rather swamped by people with a
different culture.' Others immediately found her remarks,
and particularly her use of the word 'swamped', to be anything but mild, hearing in them an echo of Enoch Powell's
notorious 'rivers of blood' speech almost exactly ten years
earlier. The Liberal Party leader, David Steel, called Mrs
Thatcher's remarks 'really quite wicked', and, from the
Labour Party, Denis Healey accused her of 'cold-blooded
calculation in stirring up the muddy waters of racial prejudice'.

The following day, Mrs Thatcher was due to conduct a
morning's campaigning for the Conservative candidate in a
by-election in the Ilford North constituency to the east of
London. On the schedule for her flying visit was a concluding
news conference and I suggested to the News Editor that I
should go and cover it. I found the Conservative campaign
headquarters right on the border of the constituency, and
close to the notorious Gants Hill roundabout, to which all
roads to the east of London seem to lead. The building itself
turned out to be the disused, though still appropriately

named, Seven Ways Restaurant. The news conference was to be held in a large and unusually depressing room, hung from floor to ceiling with the faded maroon curtains which had presumably once, in its heyday, been the establishment's glory. This, then, was the unlikely setting for my first-ever meeting with the Iron Lady.

It turned out to be an explosive encounter. The news conference was surprisingly poorly attended, with no more than five or six other journalists present. I was therefore able, at an early stage, to ask about the previous evening's *World in Action* interview. Given the reaction that her remarks on immigration had produced, and the accusation that she had been deliberately stirring up racial hatred, I thought it perfectly natural to ask whether she did not now regret having raised the issue. A volcanic eruption followed. She had not *raised* the matter. How could I possibly say that she had *raised* the matter? She had simply been asked a question, and she had replied to it in a perfectly honest and straightforward manner. What on earth was I talking about? How could I possibly put such a question to her?

Stunned into silence, I left it to others among the equally astonished press corps to take up the running, and they quickly turned to local issues. The news conference drew to a close and I assumed that that was the end of the matter. But I was wrong. During some closing remarks, the volcano erupted again. Mrs Thatcher announced that she wished to say a word or two about the media. What President Mitterrand was later said to have described as 'the eyes of Caligula' swivelled menacingly in my direction. Mitterrand also referred to the 'mouth of Marilyn Monroe', but it had now assumed an altogether firmer set. She wanted journalists to know that she always did her homework, and that if we were to be regarded as true professionals she expected us to do ours. Of course, she wanted good relations with the media, and she was perfectly prepared to answer any and every question. She always had, and she always would, with one proviso. They had to be accurate questions, properly based on facts. 'Is that clear?' she concluded, before sweeping from the room.

At the time, I felt pretty shell-shocked. Was this the woman that I would have to deal with during the rigours of the forthcoming general election campaign? I quickly came to realise, however, that it had been an exceptionally useful experience. It had given me, at our very first meeting, the clearest possible insight into what made Margaret Thatcher tick, and into the way in which she operated. It was all to stand me in good stead not just during the election, but during the many times over the following years when we were to meet again.

That morning in Ilford had shown me the strength of her combative approach to politics. In private, or in public matters that did not involve political argument, she could be as charming, courteous and gentle a person as you could ever hope to meet, always aware of the interests and concerns of others. But, once that switch marked 'politics' was flicked on in her head, she became, not a different person, but a different kind of person, always ready to challenge everything, to worry at an issue like a dog with a bone, to test an argument to its limits by ruthless questioning. That was her way of proving to herself that, as she took up a position on a given matter, her stand was well founded, and that, once that stand had been taken, she was right not to be shifted from it.

Our encounter in Ilford had also shown me in an instant how strongly she believed in the old adage that the best form of defence is attack. That morning, she had seized the opportunity which I had given her, by the use of some careless language, to turn the focus away from those who were attacking her, by herself attacking the press for what she claimed was misrepresentation. She later admitted that she was 'taken aback' by the furore her answer on immigration had caused, but there was not the slightest suggestion, either at the time or later, that she had any regrets about what she had said. Indeed, quite the reverse was the case, for she later claimed that the whole episode had helped to clarify and strengthen the Conservative Party's position on immigration as it was eventually set out in the 1979 manifesto.

I also saw that morning in Ilford how she would always try to find the ammunition for her attacks in some weakness or failure on the part of her adversary. She would pounce on the slightest mistake or inaccuracy. Much later, during a terrible day in the House of Commons for Neil Kinnock, I watched as she destroyed him by simply picking away at the facts. Then, having won the argument against him, she turned, witheringly to tell the House, 'I fear that the Right Honourable Gentleman is not the master of his brief!' As very many people, not just in the opposition parties or the media, but in her own Cabinet, Government and party were to learn, it was always a good idea to master your brief, and to master it to the letter, before confronting Margaret Thatcher.

Margaret Thatcher, however, did not, at that time, have a monopoly when it came to difficult relations with the press. The Prime Minister of the day, James Callaghan, could be equally difficult, often belying his nickname of 'Sunny Jim'. I had very few face-to-face encounters with him, but one of my first jobs, years earlier, had involved meeting him. I was still working, at that time, on the BBC *24 Hours* programme and I was asked to go down to Westminster to see him safely installed in a studio there so that he could be interviewed 'down the line' by the presenter, Michael Barratt. Barratt was the Jeremy Paxman of his day, known for his tough questioning and aggressive manner, and, as contact was made to establish the link with Lime Grove studios in West London, I heard the Prime Minister say, 'Now, Mr Barratt, none of your nonsense, please. Let's just have straightforward questions, if you don't mind.'

Later, during the 1979 election campaign, there was to be a spectacular row with ITN's David Rose, which led to Callaghan cutting short a pre-recorded interview on the ground that it was unfair to question him only on the subject of industrial relations. A compromise was reached and a second interview was recorded, on condition that the first should not be broadcast. The Prime Minister's temper was not improved when news of the altercation quickly became public. The first version of the interview, complete with his demands that it should be curtailed, had been broadcast by mistake in the United States.

It was clear, therefore, in the run-up to the 1979 election that neither Margaret Thatcher nor James Callaghan had the monopoly of prickly relations with the media. What was equally clear, however, was that, of the two, Margaret Thatcher began to work harder at the whole business of handling the press, and above all of how to deal with television.

It is hard to grasp, now that television has come to dominate British as well as American campaigns, how many British politicians despised television until comparatively recent times. After all, it was not until February 1988 that the House of Commons voted to allow the televising of their proceedings, and then only for an experimental six-month period that began in November 1989, though at the end of it the arrangement became a permanent one. As Mrs Thatcher came to power, however, many politicians still seemed to take the view once expressed by Winston Churchill, when he explained why he had decided to appear on television. 'I am sorry to have to descend to this level,' he said, 'but we all have to keep pace with modern improvements.' Even in the late 1970s, that view still found many an echo in the corridors of power. A 'them and us' attitude still prevailed – we are here to get on with governing, and they are here simply to report what we say and do. Occasionally, television, like the press in general, might be of use to us. Otherwise, we can perfectly well manage without it.

For many years, political reporting of all kinds on radio and television had been bound by the most draconian rules, designed to prevent any supposed contempt of Parliament. Until 1957, no issue that was likely to be the subject of Parliamentary debate could be reported or discussed on radio or television during the preceding fourteen days. This extraordinary rule had been formulated during the Second World War, but had become a 'gentleman's agreement' between the BBC and the politicians in 1947. Worse than that, it had been debated in Parliament in 1956, where a majority of politicians had spoken in its favour, and it only collapsed the following year under the weight of media pressure surrounding the Suez crisis. Even more astonishingly there was, until 1958, no radio and television coverage of what was happening on the ground during any election campaign in Britain, though the parties had begun to make increasingly innovative use of party political broadcasts at election time. The ban on campaign coverage once again resulted from a self-denying ordinance by the BBC in the early days of television. The Corporation had decided, with the warm approval of the politicians, that only by having no coverage of a campaign at all could complete impartiality be guaranteed. It was the start of ITV, and the birth of ITN in 1955, which began to change that extraordinary view.

Change came swiftly as a result of a by-election being called in the Lancashire town of Rochdale in 1958. Lancashire was in what was known as 'Granadaland', the area covered by one of the most enterprising of the new ITV companies. Granada announced that, whatever the custom and practice had been in the past, it would be covering the by-election in its local news bulletins. The BBC issued a statement saying, 'We do not intend to depart from our usual practice in by-elections that we do not influence voters nor report the campaigns in news bulletins.'

The Editor of ITN at the time was Geoffrey (later Sir Geoffrey) Cox, and he took up the challenge at national level. He commissioned the first-ever national coverage of an election campaign, amid dark threats that, by so doing, he might lay himself open to all kinds of penalties, up to and including a spell in jail. It was, by modern standards, low key stuff about the local candidates going about their canvassing, with a description of what the candidates stood for, since it did not contain actual excerpts from their speeches. Geoffrey Cox did not want to push his luck too far, but what he achieved by his decision was a huge step forward in political broadcasting. As the late Kenneth Allsop wrote in the *Daily Mail* at the time, 'Television is established as the new hub of the hustings.'

Yet, as the 1979 general election campaign approached, things had not moved vastly further forward. Campaign coverage was, and still is, subject to detailed legislation known as the Representation of the People Act (RPA), which imposes on broadcasters rules designed to secure impartial coverage, to which the rest of the press are not subject. Over the years, custom and practice has meant that things have become a little easier. Broadcasters no longer encounter problems on the scale of those that faced me in 1970, for example, when I covered Enoch Powell's general election campaign in Wolverhampton. My reporting was held up for two days as I tried to find the Communist candidate, because the RPA was felt to require, at the very least, that we should include pictures of all those who were standing, if we had shown pictures of any single one of them. In fact, the Communist candidate in Wolverhampton had decided that he was not going to engage in any active campaigning at all, and in the end we got away with a brief shot of him driving off in a battered old Volkswagen Beetle.

But, despite some relaxation of the rules, television coverage of politics in general, and elections in particular, was by 1979 still pretty heavy going. That was something that Margaret Thatcher was determined to try and change, because she believed it would produce political dividends.

She began with herself. She accepted the advice of her media adviser, Gordon (later Sir Gordon) Reece, that she needed to work on the way she looked and sounded on television. She agreed, on his advice, to lower her rather shrill, almost schoolgirlish voice, which had grated on so many MPs when she first took up her duties as Leader of the Opposition. He also gently suggested a softer hairstyle, and some cosmetic work on her teeth. Like Tony Blair and his team almost twenty years on, Margaret Thatcher and Gordon Reece also turned their eyes across the Atlantic, to see what lessons about campaigning could be learnt from the United States.

To that end, Gordon Reece asked me to meet him soon after I had returned from America, and my assignment to the Thatcher campaign had been announced. Gordon was an engaging man, who had something of a reputation as a 'high liver'. Indeed, Mrs Thatcher herself described him as 'a man whose principal diet was champagne and cigars'. He always reminded me of that star entertainer of the 1950s, Arthur Askey. He had the same short height as the comedian and, I thought, something of the same 'cheeky chappie' manner. I was invited to meet him at his club, Buck's, the home of Buck's Fizz, which we proceeded to consume in liberal quantities as he explained that he wanted to learn what he could from me about campaign coverage in the United States.

I was somewhat on my guard, not wishing to compromise my own position as an objective reporter by appearing to be offering active help to a particular campaign, so I decided to turn the meeting as much to my advantage as to his. I stressed to Reece the completely crucial role which television, and particularly television coverage of the campaign, had played in the 1976 American Presidential election. In particular, I outlined the way that the virtually unknown Jimmy Carter had used television to establish his identity. He had not, for example, waited for the traditional start of campaigning in the New Hampshire primary in early 1976, but had used television coverage of a big political event in late 1975 known as the 'Iowa caucus', to great effect. I also stressed that one of the key elements of all American campaigning was the easy access the media had to all the candidates, and how their schedules were shaped around the main television news bulletins of the day. I added that I thought it might be to everyone's advantage if the same sort of relationship could be built up between the politicians and the media in Britain.

He said that much of what I had told him confirmed his own thinking about the way the Thatcher campaign should be run. He said he was particularly aware of the need for greater media access to the party Leader than was traditionally the case in British election campaigns. He was also well aware of the problems we faced in getting our material back to the 'feed-points' where it could be edited and sent to London in time for the various bulletins.

During the next few months, he began what was effectively a trial run of his general election strategy. A number of campaigning visits were arranged, even though no campaign was formally under way. I often covered them and, to my considerable surprise, was frequently able to get my reports of them shown on ITN's bulletins. It was unusual in those days for political coverage to move very far outside the confines of Westminster, but Mrs Thatcher still had, at that time, considerable novelty value, particularly as she began to exploit that new phenomenon of British electioneering, the photo-opportunity. Looking back on our coverage, I think we fell far too easily for the Thatcher–Reece game plan, both in the run-up to the 1979 election and during it. But offering interesting and different pictures to television news producers is like offering Mars bars to someone addicted to chocolate. Both find what is on offer very hard to resist.

So, in the pre-election period, we trooped round unlikely places like a vast cement works near Dartford in Kent, which has since closed down, as have a very large number of the factories I once visited in Mrs Thatcher's company. At the cement works, I remember being struck by, and filming, the extraordinary speed at which she rattled round the place, her short, quick footsteps kicking up little clouds of cement dust around her ankles, as though her feet were constantly causing a series of minor explosions. She also visited a firm of steeple-jacks in Fulham, in West London, and began, in answer to the photographers' entreaties, to climb an iron ladder attached to what I suppose must have been the chimney in the yard on which the steeplejacks trained. Here the coquettish, almost flirty side of her nature came to the fore, as she realised that a skirt was not the most advisable piece of clothing to be wearing for such an occasion. Although she was scarcely high enough up the chimney to have suffered any embarrassment, she turned to us all, fluttering her eyelids, and commanded, 'Don't look!'

It was during a day of similar campaigning that one piece of news that everyone had been waiting for failed to happen. Most people, including Mrs Thatcher, believed that James Callaghan would call the general election in the autumn of

1978, and would not take the risk of waiting until the end of his full five-year term the following year. He himself had teased the Trade Union Congress in early September that year, by singing to them the old music-hall song which began, 'There I was, waiting at the Church'. Even so, there was a widespread belief that the waiting would last only two more days, until the Cabinet meeting on Thursday, 7 September.

Mrs Thatcher began that day at a factory in Gloucestershire which made photocopiers. I was there, with a small contingent of other reporters, crews and photographers, all of us knowing that we would have to stick with her until an announcement came. In what turned out to be a useful rehearsal of a typical day during the later general election, we trailed after her up the M5 motorway to the outskirts of Birmingham. Eventually, we ended up at a small hotel, still awaiting the news, though Mrs Thatcher herself had been given a private warning during the course of the day that the election would not be called.

The Prime Minister told the Cabinet that he was going to wait, and an official announcement was made that there would be no autumn election. We now know that he had reached that decision in principle by about the middle of August 1978, after taking soundings among some of his senior Cabinet colleagues. Broadly speaking, he had weighed the fact of an economy on the mend against the certain prospect of trouble with the unions over pay restraint. What seems to have finally convinced him to place his faith in the improving economic situation, and to soldier on, was evidence that an autumn election would have produced a result in which Labour had no clear majority, a prospect that he simply could not stomach.

Out on the road with the Leader of the Opposition, Mrs Thatcher's travelling office had been set up in a tiny bedroom in the small Midlands hotel we had finally reached, and I interviewed her about Callaghan's decision. Though by that time we had switched from film to electronic cameras, we were still travelling with a full complement of technicians. We therefore had some difficulty in squeezing her, one or two of her aides, myself, the cameraman, the sound recordist and the lighting engineer around the bed, but somehow we managed it and the interview got under way. She spoke of her sense of disappointment and frustration that the Prime Minister had not dared to face the country.

In due course, and after a period of strikes and industrial unrest which is now known as the Winter of Discontent, James Callaghan did face the country and he lost. Ever since people have spoken of his greatest mistake in not going for an autumn election. It was a mistake, but such a judgement can be made now with all the benefits of hindsight. At the time, it was a closer call. Even Margaret Thatcher later admitted that, if she had been forced to fight an election in the autumn of 1978, she might have 'scraped in with a small overall majority', and that just one or two mistakes in a Conservative campaign that autumn could have ruined even that small chance.

Throughout the winter, the lorry drivers' strike caused massive disruption, strikes by hospital workers meant that operations on seriously ill people were delayed, and a strike by council workers in Liverpool meant that some of the dead could not be buried in that city. The Opposition made the most of it all, and the Government's position was harmed still further by some unfortunate remarks by the Prime Minister, as he returned from a summit meeting on the Caribbean island of Guadeloupe. Pictures of him enjoying the sunshine there had already caused offence in shivering Britain, and, once again, it was a question by David Rose of ITN that touched a raw nerve. He asked him about the growing sense of chaos in Britain while he'd been away. The Prime Minister bridled, and replied, 'I don't think other people in the world will share the view that there is mounting chaos.' By the following morning, that had become the *Sun*'s famous headline: 'Crisis? What Crisis?'

Ultimately, a true crisis brought about the change of government. At the end of March 1979, Labour lost a vote of confidence in the House of Commons, by just one vote. A general election was immediately called, the first time a government had been forced to go to the country in that way for fifty-five years. The specific issue was Scottish devolution, but the Government was in deep trouble on a whole number of fronts, which foreshadowed a lively battle between the parties before polling day on 3 May. Both ITN generally and I in particular were relieved and excited – relieved that the waiting was over, and excited by the chance to put into practice all the plans we had worked on for far better coverage of a British general election campaign than had ever previously been seen.

For me personally, this really was a case of the first time being the best. In time, I covered five general election campaigns, but none of the later contests compared with that first one in 1979. Although the Conservatives eventually won with an overall majority of forty-three, such an outcome was never a foregone conclusion. The opinion polls swung this way and that during the seventeen days of formal campaigning, as the country came to terms with the fact that, if they chose Mrs Thatcher, they were going to vote in a leader who represented radical change in almost every way.

Most immediately, from my point of view, she was going to do things very differently in the way she fought the election. For a start, she hit upon what was then regarded as the novel idea of hiring a 'battle bus'. This was a coach fitted out as a travelling headquarters and mobile office – though, since so much of the technology we now take for granted was in its infancy, the office equipment aboard the bus consisted of a number of typewriters and an unreliable mobile phone.

It was also clear that the style of campaigning which had been tried out in the previous months, with its heavy emphasis on the photo-opportunity, would now be used in spades. Our two travelling cameramen never lacked for a picture. The Leader of the Conservative Party tasted chocolates in Birmingham, butter in Aberdeen, and tea, without milk or sugar, at a tea factory in Newcastle. She had wires stuck all over her as her heart was checked in Milton Keynes, and she waved two shopping bags around in Halifax – to show, she said, how much a pound had bought under the Tories six years earlier, and how much less it was now buying under Labour. Most famously of all, she cuddled a calf in a field near Ipswich. It was that last incident which came to symbolise the whole new approach to campaigning. It was all meant to tie in with whatever the theme of the day was supposed to be, presumably something to do with agriculture. But the whole operation seemed so outrageously over the top that it produced plenty of criticism that it was simply a picture for the sake of the picture alone.

It certainly made an impact. During her tour of the farm in question, she came to a field, where the farmer proudly presented the young calf, born a matter of hours previously, for Mrs Thatcher's inspection. Not only did she inspect it, but she also scooped up the startled creature and sat down in the field with it. The automatic drives on the cameras of the stills photographers began sounding like a volley of rifle fire, as they held their fingers firmly on the shutter buttons, intent on capturing every last frame. The television cameras held their gaze steadily upon the scene, as Mrs Thatcher not only posed, but also began to answer questions with the young animal still clasped to her bosom. In my commentary later, I described the event, with considerable understatement and with not a little irony, as probably the first time that a major British politician had ever conducted a news conference in the middle of a field while holding a farm animal. So agitated did Denis Thatcher become that he was heard to remark, 'If we're not careful, we'll have a dead calf on our hands.' Indeed, for several days afterwards, I and several other of the travelling reporters made regular phone calls to the farm, enquiring about the calf's health, in the hope of an even more spectacular denouement to the whole business, but it was not to be. The calf, in the true spirit of Thatcherism, survived.

In all of this, the fact that we were using the new electronic cameras was of tremendous assistance. Until a year or two previously, the reporting of most news events outside the studio depended on the use of colour film. Once it had been shot, the magazine containing the exposed film had to be taken off the camera and its contents transferred into film cans. This was done inside a special black 'changing bag', into which the magazine, the cans and the cameraman's arms were inserted. The strange shape of the bag, with its dark colour, zip fastenings and two long and elasticated sleeves led to it being known in the trade as 'Queen Mary's knickers'. In Scotland, an elderly matron once spotted an unfortunate BBC cameraman as he sat performing this strange transfer ritual, with the black bag draped across his lap. Seeing suspicious movement taking place in an area adjacent to the man's groin, the Scottish lady assumed the worst and set about him with her umbrella, as she denounced him as a filthy pervert. The operation, usually completed without such a hazard, meant that the precious film, by now transferred into cans, was taken, often by a dispatch rider on a motorbike, to a film laboratory to be processed, either at our own premises in London or at another ITV station.

Now this tedious process had been eliminated. Film had been replaced by videotape, and though the new cameras and, more to the point, the separate video recorders were heavy and cumbersome, the whole operation of shooting, editing and transmitting to London became immeasurably faster, with the ending of the need for film processing. This gave us the opportunity to develop entirely new techniques.

Traditionally the big set speeches at the evening rallies had required the use of an outside broadcast unit, a vast travelling circus of cameras and other equipment which would lumber into position hours ahead of the event and take ages to set up, and to dismantle later. Now, my 'target team' and I worked out a system by which our two small cameras would be quickly set up on their tripods in different positions in the hall. By using radio microphones, the two cameras could pick up the same sound feed as they covered either the whole speech, or the newsworthy sections of it. In that way, we were able to get to and cover the evening speeches far more quickly and to greater effect than we could ever have done on film. Editing was also far quicker and easier since we could speedily cut together the different pictures of the same speech, as recorded by the two cameras, into one visually interesting package.

Mrs Thatcher's itinerary was extensive. After holding a morning press conference in London, she would often dash to Gatwick where her campaign plane – another first – would be waiting. The travelling press would also be waiting, already aboard the same plane, and we would all then fly off to a local airport somewhere. On arrival, Mrs Thatcher would climb aboard her pre-positioned battle bus, and most of the press would board the waiting press coach.

My producer, Mike Nolan, an Australian of few words but a brilliant organiser, had worked out that, most of the time, the press bus was not for us. This was an especially wise decision, not only because the bus frequently got lost, but because we would often need to dash off somewhere on our own, to edit our packages and to feed our efforts to London. He therefore asked ITN to make sure that a large car with a driver would be waiting for us, and our equipment, at whatever airport the Thatcher campaign plane was due to fly to. This had the added advantage of allowing us to get away quickly, and to arrive at the first location well ahead of Mrs Thatcher and her entourage.

This arrangement, though highly convenient, frequently produced considerable confusion. The waiting car was usually a large limousine which had just formed part of a funeral cortège, with the driver still in full chauffeur's uniform. One of our cameramen, Chris Squires, developed a regular ritual, designed to change the driver's sombre mien. He would first tell the man to take his peaked hat off, and, if he so desired, his chauffeur's jacket as well. He would then ask him to turn on Radio One, very loudly. Most of the drivers were more than happy to do so, but professional pride would usually overtake most of them as we approached our various destinations, and the jackets and peaked caps would go back on. As a result, the local bigwigs would regularly assume that the large black limousine bearing down on them, complete with uniformed driver at the wheel, contained the revered figure of Margaret Thatcher. They were often considerably put out to discover that the contrary was the case, once they had sprung forward to open the car door. The airways would suddenly resonate to a blast of Radio One, and out would clamber four scruffy members of ITN.

Mrs Thatcher did not win the election on the simple basis of photo-opportunities, but they underlined one of the most important reasons for her eventual victory. They were a symbol of the important fact that she represented great change, a different way of doing things. That appealed to enough of the voters to allow her to record, at that time, the biggest swing from one party to another since 1945. The greatest shift was among skilled workers – the so-called blue-collar vote. Many of them had been disgusted by the Labour Government's attempt to hold down wages through its prices and incomes policy. Many had also been equally appalled by the chaos and disruption caused by the militant tactics of some of the unions during the Winter of Discontent.

There was also the matter of the personality of Mrs Thatcher herself. She was the ultimate individualist, who could no more stomach what used to be called the 'corporatism' of old-style socialism than she could, later, the 'community politics' of New Labour. Her whole political philosophy was founded on the bedrock of her belief that the individual was responsible for his or her actions and well-being. That was what she was trying to say in her notorious remark some years later when she told an interviewer, 'There is no such thing as society. There are individuals, men and women, and there are families.' Therein, too, lay her instinctive mistrust of so much of what governments got up to. That mistrust was widespread; it included, for example, a strong distaste for the state-running of British industry, soon to be reduced through her programme of privatisation. It also coloured her view about what was happening on the continent, where, behind her campaign for 'my billion' and her many other battles with Brussels, lay her belief that what was really going on was the creation, by stealth, of a United States of Europe.

In her very first speech of the 1979 campaign, she had declared in Cardiff, 'I am a conviction politician. The Old Testament prophets did not merely say, "Brothers, I want consensus." They said, "This is my faith and vision." ' After the years of Harold Wilson and James Callaghan trying to strike a deal with the 'Brothers' of the trades unions, Mrs

Thatcher's campaigning promise of strong 'I know best' leadership struck a chord with a sufficient number of the voters for her to win through handsomely. Britain was, for good or ill, now going to live with that vision of hers for the next eleven years.

CHAPTER SEVEN

'You Are Not Welcome Here': On the Diplomatic Beat

The 1979 general election marked the end of my time as a general reporter. I did not, however, move immediately into political reporting, but became a foreign affairs specialist, first as a London-based European correspondent and then as ITN's Diplomatic Editor. Again, I was lucky. Just as I moved into this area of journalism, a lot began to happen. NATO entered into a major confrontation with the Soviet Union over the stationing of new missiles in Europe. At the same time, Britain's new Prime Minister began an epic battle on many issues with what was then still called the European Community (EC) or, more usually, the Common Market, most particularly over the question of how much Britain should contribute to the EC budget.

Mrs Thatcher decided from the start that this country was contributing far too much, and that she wasn't going to have it. Contributions to Brussels were, and still are, worked out on the basis of each country's receipts from VAT and import duties. A small percentage of its total VAT take and all its import duties are paid into the European pot. From that pot, cash is paid out to Europe's farmers under the Common Agricultural Policy (the CAP), and to the member states for projects like the construction of major roads and the rebuilding of town and city centres, which are seen as benefiting Europe as a whole.

A serious problem had arisen in Mrs Thatcher's eyes, because Britain was predominantly an industrial country whose economy was founded, above all, on its trading links, not just with Europe but with the rest of the world. That meant that we were paying into the EC's coffers far more than we were getting back, for example, in support for British farmers. She reckoned that we were out of pocket to the tune of around a thousand million pounds a year, which she wanted back in the form of a rebate. The headlines soon had it in punchy form: 'Maggie: My Billion' was their concise version of all this complicated arithmetic.

She began the struggle within weeks of winning the general election, at the first of many European summits she was about to attend. There were then three meetings of the leaders of Europe each year, though the number has since been cut back to two. Mrs Thatcher's first was held in the historic French city of Strasbourg, which, positioned as it is just across the Rhine from Germany, had quickly become a powerful symbol of European union.

The host, President Giscard d'Estaing, was delighted that a fellow conservative had been returned to power in the United Kingdom, and he made quite a fuss of the new British leader. An elaborate photo-call was arranged at which all the Leaders formed a long line across a street near Strasbourg cathedral. They advanced down it, in line abreast and a great show of unity, for the benefit of the television cameras, our own among them. The unity was not to last, but at this early stage Mrs Thatcher did not want to be the party-pooper. She merely registered the fact that the matter of the British contribution would have to be sorted out, and that she would be insisting on a solution. So began a period of turmoil and upheaval in Britain's relations with Europe which was to occupy a great deal of my time as a correspondent, and which would increasingly tear the Conservative Party apart over the course of the next twenty years.

Having bitten her lip at Strasbourg, Mrs Thatcher did raise the question of Britain's budget contribution, devastatingly, at the Dublin summit held just before Christmas, six months later. I was one of the many journalists who waited, hour after hour, in the cramped area reserved for us inside Dublin Castle, for news about what was actually happening. Enough information, however, was already seeping out from the various delegations for us to realise that a major row was in progress between Margaret Thatcher and the rest.

At these summits, news often emerges in the most curious of ways. This time, the first confirmation that things had gone seriously wrong came when ITN's Political Editor at that time, Julian Havilland, managed to get hold of the Belgian version of the draft communiqué. He happened to have been brought up in South Africa and had learnt Afrikaans, which is not so very different from Flemish, and he was therefore able to give us a rough translation of the Flemish text. Despite the unorthodox way in which we had discovered it, the huge difference of opinion between Mrs Thatcher and the other leaders was quite easy to discern. When the European leaders finally broke up, a few of us managed to corner the West German Chancellor, Helmut Schmidt, in a doorway to ask him for the details. Normally the most polite of men, despite his generally gloomy view of life, he also gave us a further indication of how badly things had gone by simply elbowing his way through us all, grunting angrily that he was already 'deeply behind schedule', and refusing all further comment.

Finally, Mrs Thatcher called us all in for her end-of-summit press conference. I had been used to seeing her looking exhausted at the end of long days of election campaigning, but I had never seen her look as drained as she did then. Her face was drawn and ashen, and her voice was weary with fatigue. She had plainly had very little sleep. Much of the night had been spent working with her officials after she had begun the battle for 'her billion' over dinner and the talks held later the previous evening, though a story that Helmut Schmidt was so bored by it all that he had fallen asleep was officially denied.

There was no gainsaying the fact, however, that the Germans and the French were outraged by what they saw as a barefaced British attempt at bending the EC's rules. Then, and for many years afterwards, their view was that if you joined the club, you had to abide by its regulations, even if it meant that the outcome appeared to be unfair. West Germany at that time did even worse than Britain under the financial arrangements and was the biggest net contributor to the funds of the EC by far. However, Britain, despite being far poorer, was about to replace Germany as the country paying in the largest amount and getting the least back, which fuelled Mrs Thatcher's indignation all the more.

What added extra colour to the argument, and still does, was the political dimension. Helmut Schmidt took the view that Germany's large contribution was money well spent if it led to the success of the EC and the resulting unity of Europe. Europe, and indeed the world, would never again suffer the risk of German domination and the two world wars which had resulted from it, if his country was a member of a trading bloc which also brought with it a considerable degree of *political* union. War between European countries which were members of the same club was simply unthinkable, and would remain so. It was an argument strongly carried forward by Helmut Schmidt's successor Chancellor Kohl, who, years later, worked hard to bring about a single currency in Europe because he saw it as providing a clear path towards ever greater political union.

But, at the summit in Dublin Castle in December 1979, Margaret Thatcher served clear notice that, as British Leader, she would tolerate none of that kind of talk. As to the events of the meeting itself, she explained that the Dutch had been particularly helpful in trying to broker a settlement, but that nothing had been achieved. Indeed, the row was not to be finally settled for a further five years.

An interim agreement, lasting for three years, was eventually reached at Luxembourg in 1980, but the matter came bubbling to the surface again, with France once more holding the EC Presidency, at the summit held in the magnificent surroundings of Fontainebleau in 1984. Once again, I had an insight into the way things work at the top.

Summit meetings are usually deeply frustrating for television correspondents like myself, who like to have good pictures to work with, as we attempt to liven up our reporting of negotiations that are often very heavy going. Yet it is normally very difficult at such summits to get any decent pictures, despite the fact that the surroundings in which the leaders meet are often deliberately chosen to show off the glories of their respective countries. You tend to end up with lots of shots of the leaders' cars arriving at the various locations chosen for the talks, and of the leaders themselves getting out of their vehicles, waving and smiling and saying nothing of any importance whatsoever. These are supplemented by what are called 'pool pictures' of moments such as the opening of the sessions themselves, or of the lunches and dinners, and even, on occasion, the breakfasts, at which the leaders continue their discussions, and to which only a limited number of cameramen are admitted. These 'pool pictures' tend to be even more boring.

Imagine our delight, therefore, at the 1984 Fontainebleau summit when my crew and I managed to break free and found ourselves on a raised terrace overlooking a garden in which we noticed the French and German Foreign Ministers were strolling. In those days, no decisions at any of these get-togethers were ever reached unless the French and German Governments approved of what was going on, and it was often left to their Foreign Ministers to hammer out the details. There they were, heads down and deep in conversation, apparently unaware of our presence. We shamelessly decided to try and eavesdrop, and pointed towards them a kind of microphone that is very good at picking things up at quite long distances. The British and French authorities were not best pleased when they found out later that I had included a snatch of the recorded conversation in my coverage, and access to some hitherto unrestricted areas at the summit was curtailed as a result.

We discovered that M. Cheysson and Herr Genscher had overcome the language barrier by speaking English, and that they had been discussing Mrs Thatcher and what kind of deal she would accept to settle the row over the British budget contribution. It was clear from their conversation that the prospects for a deal being struck were not particularly good, because Mrs Thatcher was putting up a real fight. 'So what's she going to do?' we heard Cheysson asking his German opposite number. 'Suppose she blocks it?' At that point, they lifted their eyes, and were horrified to spot us. Although they immediately ended their conversation, we knew that a fearsome battle would rage on until something was finally agreed. And so it turned out, a fact that we soon had confirmed through another of the strange practices that marked these summits.

Leaders of the smaller countries, most notably the Irish and the Dutch, had relatively few of their own journalists to deal with, and would often spend time with British journalists like myself. On this occasion it was the Dutch, speaking with their customary fluent English, who helpfully confirmed for us, on

114

an off-the-record basis, that Mrs Thatcher had indeed accepted a permanent formula of a two-thirds rebate of Britain's VAT payments, which finally settled the 'my billion' row.

Interviewing the Prime Minister after the summit, I asked her if the deal meant the end of the everlasting row with Europe over the British budget rebate. Putting on her sweetest voice, she replied, 'I believe so. It has been exasperating and frustrating, but in the end each of them knew that, if they had been in the same position, they would have put forward the same arguments.' It was the classic Thatcher case over Europe – that even those ardent pro-Europeans, the French and the Germans, would always be French and German first and Europeans second if they wanted something badly enough, and that she was only playing the same game.

Any idea, however, that Fontainebleau would henceforward set Britain on a course of harmony with the rest of Europe was, of course, wide of the mark. In Britain itself, Margaret Thatcher's deep feelings of antipathy towards the European ideal, and her way of handling her country's relations with Europe, were matters which many of her colleagues, and indeed many of the members of her own Cabinet, found difficult to stomach. Among those who seemed to cope with it better than most was Lord Carrington, the first of the three Foreign Secretaries with whom I came into close contact.

Peter Carrington had several things going for him. He was a man of immense charm, the sort of person you instinctively liked. Despite his hereditary peerage and his somewhat strangulated upper-class vowels, he was never, for a single moment, patronising or 'hoity-toity' with anybody. Quite the reverse was the case, as he often insisted, with mock seriousness, that his real name was Smith. He would then explain, with a broadening grin, that the first Lord Carrington had indeed been called Smith, before being ennobled at the end of the eighteenth century, though he did not add that the Smiths were a family of rather successful bankers.

Despite the charm, which is a particularly useful gift for a Foreign Secretary to possess, Lord Carrington could display flashes of sharp temper. There was a particularly ghastly meeting in Nigeria, during one of that country's rare periods of civilian rule, when he was invited to address the Foreign Affairs Committee of the Nigerian Parliament in front of the television cameras. After his own remarks, he was subjected to a long and intemperate tirade by various members of the committee on the subject of students' fees in Britain, which had recently been raised for students from foreign and Commonwealth countries who were studying in Britain. He endured it stoically, before leaving as quickly as he could at the end of the session. 'Bloody cheek,' he hissed, though unfortunately out of camera range, as he passed me on the way out.

Lord Carrington's other advantage was that Mrs Thatcher always liked aristocrats, real or imagined, and particularly those who did not go in for a lot of anguished theorising. Peter Carrington was nobody's fool, but he was, at heart, a soldier and a somewhat bluff Tory of the old but liberal school within the Conservative Party. Although he was instinctively pro-European, for example, he and Margaret Thatcher could work together, largely because she could rely on her Foreign Secretary to get on with the job without making a fuss.

It was entirely typical of Lord Carrington's character that he felt compelled to resign after the invasion of the Falkland Islands by Argentina at the beginning of April 1982. Though the invasion itself came as a considerable surprise to everyone, there had been some clear warning signs of serious trouble. However, his difficulties were compounded by the fact that, just four days before it happened, he had decided to go ahead with a visit to Israel, though he was soon forced to make a hurried return to London. One of his chief concerns during his time as Foreign Secretary had been the possibility of a peace settlement in the Middle East, and it was to pursue that aim that he had left the country. But his decision to go ahead with such a visit, rather than remain at his desk in London, did much to reinforce the view that, when it came to the Falklands crisis, the Foreign Secretary's eye had been off the ball.

He immediately realised the enormity of what had happened. I conducted a joint interview with him and the Defence Secretary, John Nott, on the day of the invasion, and his discomfiture was plain for all to see. 'Carrington looked ghastly; all his usual spark gone', my notes for the day record. The day after the invasion, there was a rare Saturday debate in the Commons, in which his position was made still more difficult because, as a member of the House of Lords, he could not take part in it. Despite the fact that Mrs Thatcher used the debate to announce that a British Task Force would sail to reclaim the islands, he realised that both Parliament and the public were demanding a whipping boy – 'a righteous anger which I felt I had to assuage.' he said later – and he offered his resignation. Over the weekend, Mrs Thatcher tried to persuade him to stay; she believed that his experience and his international standing would be needed more than ever before. But Lord Carrington and two of his fellow Ministers at the Foreign Office resigned on the Monday.

Given the national mood, his departure was inevitable, but he did not, in the end, wait to be forced from office, as happened with so many of the Ministers who got into trouble in later years. His was the last old-style resignation on a point of honour from a British government, and it hurt him deeply. It hurt his wife Iona even more. I passed her on the grand staircase in the Foreign Office, which leads to the Foreign Secretary's office, on my way to conduct a post-resignation interview. I muttered a word or two about how sorry I was about what had happened. 'It's all your fault,' came Lady

Carrington's swift reply. It was, I soon realised, a sharp reference, not to me personally, but to the exceedingly hostile press which her husband had received.

His successor was Francis Pym. However, as attempts were made to try and find a diplomatic settlement to the crisis, relations between Mrs Thatcher and her new Foreign Secretary quickly began to deteriorate. I had always found him an easy and pleasant person to talk to, while realising that he was constantly ready to see the difficulties and problems in any situation. It was, however, an approach to life that Mrs Thatcher simply could not abide.

At the outset, as the Task Force set sail, the focus of attention was as much on the diplomatic as on the military efforts. Within a week, the American Secretary of State, Alexander Haig, had become deeply involved, and had started a round of shuttle diplomacy by visiting the Argentinian capital, Buenos Aires, in an attempt to broker a settlement. His return to London on the Easter Monday Bank Holiday, to report to the British Government, resulted in one of the longest waits outside an event – known in the journalistic trade as a 'doorstep' – that I was ever involved in.

As any reporter who has stood there for any length of time will tell you, Downing Street itself is a dismal place, where there are no facilities whatsoever for the waiting press. You simply stand there for as long as it takes. In this case, the vigil took almost thirteen hours, as Mrs Thatcher and her War Cabinet argued, line by line, over the proposals which General Haig had brought back from Buenos Aires. After much discussion, Ministers found the proposals unacceptable, but the diplomatic efforts for a solution continued, only to reach a point twelve days later when Francis Pym and Margaret Thatcher were in serious disagreement over the possibility of a settlement. Things came to such a pass, she recorded later, that had her Foreign Secretary's view prevailed, she would have resigned as Prime Minister.

In the event, the War Cabinet backed her position and not Francis Pym's, but it resulted in serious and long-term damage to their working relationship. Suddenly, however, our attention switched to the military situation, rather than the tensions within the Cabinet, as the news arrived that British forces had recaptured the outlying island of South Georgia. After careful checks by the Prime Minister's office as to the exact time of ITN's late news bulletin that Saturday evening, Mrs Thatcher and the Defence Secretary John Nott appeared live during the course of it, as they emerged together from the front door of Number Ten. Mr Nott gave the news about South Georgia, but the reporters present began to ask him further questions about the whole conduct of the military campaign, to Mrs Thatcher's clear irritation. She immediately interrupted. 'Just rejoice at that news and congratulate our armed forces,' she declared, adding a further 'rejoice' for good measure. Thus was another famous headline born.

In the immediate aftermath of the invasion of the Falklands by Argentina, John Nott had also offered to quit. He was promptly told by Mrs Thatcher that she wasn't having her Defence Secretary resigning with the Task Force already at sea. So he stayed, and became responsible for one of the worst examples of the mishandling of government public relations.

The regular announcements of the military situation were made by a civil servant called Ian McDonald, the official spokesman at the Ministry of Defence. He had a markedly soulful look, as though he was permanently depressed, not just by the Falklands War, but by life in general. That was coupled with a rather high-pitched voice, which was both gloomy and annoyingly precise and pedantic. Everyone came to dread his announcements. If they contained news of setbacks, like the loss of HMS *Sheffield*, he would preface them with some such phrase as 'I am afraid that I have some bad news.' The nation would hold its breath, expecting the worst, though even the good news, when it came, was delivered in the same flat, deadpan style.

It took a long time for anyone to realise in Government that presentation really does matter. McDonald was not the right man to do that job, and he should have been swiftly replaced, but he continued to do it, simply because, within the civil service hierarchy, he was down to do it. That attitude persisted for a very long time within the Government Information Service. It is why most journalists held most government press officers in such low regard, and why the shake-up in the Service, insisted upon by the Blair Government, was both necessary and long overdue.

After victory in the Falklands, John Nott remained in the Cabinet until the September 1985 reshuffle, and decided to leave Parliament for good at the 1987 election. Francis Pym's departure from the Cabinet was an altogether more difficult affair. He was sacked, after the differences between himself and Margaret Thatcher continued to grow and were finally demonstrated in public.

It is not often that the strained relationships within a government are clearly on display, though in recent times Michael Heseltine's storming out of Cabinet and high-profile resignations by Nigel Lawson and Geoffrey Howe have given us visible evidence that those clashes of personality are often there. During the 1983 general election campaign, when I was once again covering Mrs Thatcher's activities, I saw for myself how her relations with Francis Pym had broken down.

At the launch of the Conservative manifesto, the Foreign Secretary was asked about the aftermath of the Falklands War, and in a spirit of reconciliation, he seemed to suggest that talks might be reopened with the Argentinians. 'But not about sovereignty,' Mrs Thatcher suddenly snapped. Watching the video pictures later was like reading a textbook of Thatcherite body language. Her putdown of the hapless Pym was accompanied by a sharp, bird-like thrust forward of head and neck, swiftly followed by a terrible glare in his direction. Thus prompted, he indicated that, of course, sovereignty could not be discussed. 'No,' the Prime Minister repeated, in case anyone had missed the Foreign Secretary's climb-down. A firm nod of her head followed, just to show who was really in charge. Back in the cutting room, we played and replayed the dreadful moment – our two cameras at the launch had captured it all. A little later in the campaign, Francis Pym said that he did not think that huge majorities were a very good idea for governments, and he was slapped down in public again. After two such humiliations, his post-election return to the backbenches came as no surprise, except perhaps to him. In the months and years that followed, he made no secret of his belief that he had been treated in a disgraceful and shabby way.

The 1983 campaign did indeed produce a thumping Conservative win. Mrs Thatcher used the same campaigning tactics that she had employed in 1979, and her days out on the road were designed, as before, to produce as many telling photo-opportunities as possible. Once again, such occasions were not entirely hazard-free.

We all got stuck, for example, in a very muddy, indeed waterlogged, field on a farm in Cornwall, despite being issued with wellingtons by the thoughtful farmer. ITN's cameraman had to be hauled from the mud to safety by the Prime Minister herself. We caused chaos when she stopped for lunch at Harry Ramsden's fish-and-chip shop in Leeds, where tables were overturned and startled diners pushed aside in the scramble for pictures by a press pack that was not on its best behaviour. There was a bizarre last day, when in an apparent attempt to blow what remained of Conservative campaign funds our

Central Office minders loaded us all into a fleet of helicopters. We descended on Salisbury in a sort of re-creation of the famous scene in *Apocalypse Now*, the American movie about the Vietnam War, when the screen is entirely filled with menacing helicopter gunships. We then moved on to the Isle of Wight, which Mrs Thatcher, in her turn, appeared to invade, standing in the open bow door of a giant hovercraft, as it came up out of the water and up a large slipway. All in all, it was another huge success for the Conservative campaign machine. Mrs Thatcher was returned to Downing Street with an overall majority of 144.

The election over, I returned to my duties as Diplomatic Editor, which meant a good deal of contact with the newly appointed Foreign Secretary, Sir Geoffrey Howe. He remains, in my view, a greatly underrated figure in recent British politics. His quiet manner and his thoughtful delivery famously earned him the nickname 'Mogadon Man', derived from a well-known brand of sleeping pill. But if Lord Carrington's charm was an asset at the Foreign Office, so, to a far greater degree, was Howe's sharp mind, and his patience in understanding and seeking to negotiate his way through the many diplomatic difficulties at the time in our relations with Europe and the rest of the world.

Things did not, however, always go entirely to plan. On a visit to Saudi Arabia, he was asked to meet the King at what was, apparently, the latest and newest of his palaces near Riyadh airport – so new that neither the local British Embassy staff nor the Saudi officials in the motorcade knew exactly where it was. Suddenly, the road we were on came to an abrupt end and all that stretched before us was mile after mile of desert. A miffed Foreign Secretary climbed out of his official car. The look on his face showed that he was well aware that I was about to put together a story, with the pictures to prove it, of the 'Howe's mission runs into the sand' variety.

His most spectacular setback came towards the end of his time as Foreign Secretary, when he embarked on a mission to South Africa at a time when that country's apartheid regime was still firmly in place. Britain had held the line against full economic sanctions at the Commonwealth conference in the Bahamas in October 1985 – a difficult conference to cover, incidentally, since all our discussions took place alongside a particularly inviting and extensive beach.

By the middle of 1986, a Commonwealth mission to South Africa had also failed to bring about any change there. In one last attempt and before a number of crucial international meetings later in the year which were bound to demand the imposition of full sanctions, Geoffrey Howe agreed to see what he could do. He decided to begin his mission with a visit to two of the so-called front-line states, South Africa's near neighbours, and he took with him a number of correspondents, myself among them, aboard his RAF VC-10. Our first stop was the Zambian capital, Lusaka, to see President Kenneth Kaunda, one of Africa's longest-serving leaders and an emotional man at the best of times. On the subject of South Africa and apartheid, he was particularly emotional, and he was never afraid of displaying the fact.

The President was in the habit of greeting his guests in a large reception room at his official residence, with the television cameras present, before taking them off for private talks. We were unaware of this, and when we arrived in the room we saw that it was set out as though for the formal talks. We were therefore surprised to be invited to sit down, together with Sir Geoffrey Howe and all his officials at a large table. The reason soon became apparent. In walked the President, dressed as usual in his dark safari suit, and carrying in one hand, as always, a large white handkerchief. He sat

123

down at the head of the table, and fixed the British Foreign Secretary with a cold stare. 'You are not welcome here,' he told him bluntly, before explaining at some length the shortcomings of Britain's policy on South Africa. Then, in a reference to the fact that he had once danced with Mrs Thatcher at an earlier Commonwealth conference, he said that he had only agreed to see Sir Geoffrey out of respect for 'my dancing partner', but then criticised her for 'dancing with apartheid'. I could scarcely believe my eyes and ears, my senses heightened by the knowledge that our camera was recording every word. At the end of it all, Howe managed a reply of some kind, before mercifully escaping to the privacy of the talks proper.

We moved on to Harare in Zimbabwe for a meeting with President Mugabe, and then on to Maputo, the capital of Mozambique, where we stayed overnight in an immense, crumbling hotel by the sea, which had clearly once been a place of great colonial luxury. Everything had gone to rack and ruin as a result of the civil war, and, as a result, we all had to queue for hours to use the one working telephone. The Foreign Secretary then returned to London, while I went back to Harare, where a meeting of the heads of all the front-line states was due to take place.

We began our filming at Harare airport, recording the arrival of the various delegations. Many of the front-line states, including the host nation, Zimbabwe, had decided to show their solidarity with the freedom movement in South Africa by replacing their national anthems with the freedom song 'Sikolele Africa', which the anti-apartheid movement had adopted as its own. This ensured, as the delegates arrived for the meeting, extremely frequent repetition of the song by the military band. It often had to be played twice per arrival, since it was in most cases the anthem of both the arriving leader and the host country. It is a beautiful song, which is just as well, since hearing it sixteen times during the course of the morning would otherwise have been a little hard to take.

The conference itself ran late, and the time difference with London meant that I was going to be very pushed to include even President Mugabe's opening speech in my report for that night's *News at Ten*. I decided that we should record only the first few minutes of the speech and then make a dash for the television station, which was some way from the centre of Harare. There I would edit and feed my report. My crew and I got out of the building where the summit meeting was taking place and raced across the car park just as the light was fading in the African dusk. To the watching security guards, three white men running from a building in which an international conference was taking place could mean only one thing – that we had planted a bomb inside it. They promptly, and understandably, detained us, and by the time we had satisfied them that we were not terrorists it was too late to send a report to London. A classic case of more haste, less speed.

A few days later, Sir Geoffrey Howe resumed his mission in South Africa itself, beginning with talks with the South African President, P. W. Botha. After the first, difficult session, the President said that a second meeting would not be possible for another six days, which meant that we had a problem. What were we all going to do with ourselves? Thus began Howe's Magical Mystery Tour. The VC-10 became a sort of holiday charter aircraft, as a number of visits to neighbouring countries were quickly arranged. 'Onward, ever onward, even unto the sands of Botswana, Sir Geoffrey Howe continues his mission like a kind of diplomatic Flying Dutchman,' I said in a somewhat overblown commentary at the time. Not only did we go to Botswana, we went off to Swaziland and Lesotho too, and a second visit to see President Kaunda in Zambia was also put on the schedule. In retrospect, Sir Geoffrey probably wished that such a return visit had not been arranged.

Arriving at President Kaunda's residence for a second time, we were once more shown into the reception room and invited to sit around the large table. I muttered to a colleague that I couldn't believe that the President, having already humiliated Sir Geoffrey in this room on the first visit, was about to do so again. Unfortunately, lightning did strike twice. President Kaunda proceeded to denounce him in precisely the same terms as on the earlier occasion, and again with the cameras present. He told him that he was no more welcome on his second visit than he had been on his first, and he coupled it all with further sharp messages for his 'dancing partner' in London.

During a television interview after the talks were over, I suggested to Sir Geoffrey that he ought to have got up and walked out. His answer was typical of his patient, low-key but determined style, coupled with an unbelievably thick skin, which Margaret Thatcher ultimately found so infuriating. 'Walking out', he told me, 'would have been quite wrong. I think that's absolutely the wrong kind of diplomacy. Diplomacy isn't a series of walk-outs, but talk-throughs.' That may normally be the case, but on this trip all the talking, both in South Africa and outside it, had brought about no change whatsoever.

Working the diplomatic beat often meant travelling around the world with the Prime Minister and the Foreign Secretary. There were frequent visits to the world's capitals for the increasing number of summits, and two visits to Beijing and Hong Kong as the deal was struck to hand back the colony to the Chinese. And, on one occasion, there was the chance to use the Foreign Secretary's visit to gain access to a country which would otherwise have been impossible.

The early part of 1985 had seen the growth in Poland of the liberation movement called Solidarity, which had grown out of the shipyard strike at Gdansk, led by one of the electricians there, Lech Walesa. News of the strike, and of Solidarity's struggle with the Communist Government in Poland, had been getting out by a number of circuitous routes. I had first become involved in the reporting of it by monitoring Polish television broadcasts in London. These transmissions could be picked up on the Swedish island of Bornholm, off the Polish coast in the Baltic Sea, and from there they were transmitted by Swedish television to the rest of Europe. I also made contact with the large community of Polish exiles in London, who were receiving messages from Poland, including copies of Solidarity's underground newspaper and, on occasion, amateur film of events there, especially pictures of what was happening in the Gdansk shipyard. At one stage, there was enough such material available to allow me to put together a report in London every night for a month, but clearly this was no substitute for actually going to Poland.

My chance came as the result of a visit there by Geoffrey Howe. He was in Warsaw for three days in April 1985, primarily for talks with the Polish military leader, General Jaruzelski. But, as often happens on such occasions, the bureaucracy which produces the visas in London for such trips means that they cover a longer period than that of the official visit. That had happened on this occasion, and I decided to stay in Poland after Sir Geoffrey had left.

It was a remarkable time to be there, as General Jaruzelski struggled to accommodate what amounted to a popular, national uprising within his own hardline Communist regime, and all against the background of possible invasion by what was still known as the Soviet Union. His dilemma was mirrored in the attitude of the Polish authorities towards journalists, both their own and those from foreign countries like myself and my crew. On one occasion, the visas in our passports were cancelled at the immigration office by means of large red annulment stamps, and we were about to leave for the airport. At the last moment, they relented. The annulment stamps were themselves annulled, and we were allowed to stay.

I was able to remain in Poland for a full month. The weather was bitterly cold, which meant a trip to a Warsaw department store to try to find some warm clothing. The sparse choice, and the complete absence of some basic foods, underlined that life for ordinary Polish people was a distinct struggle. Everywhere, for example, we would see the daily queues outside the bakeries for bread. The Solidarity movement, at the very least, held out the possibility of change. I was able to see, for example, the offices in Warsaw where its immensely popular underground newspaper was unfailingly produced night after night, ready for distribution across the country through a network of the movement's supporters.

In Gdansk, I met and interviewed Lech Walesa, and saw the rudimentary printing works where thousands of posters, calling together protest meetings, were produced by hand on a silk-screen printing frame, and hung up on long lines to dry. Each contained the distinctive Solidarity emblem, the Polish word 'Solidarnosc' combined with the Polish flag, and was produced in the national colours of red and white. Later I attended some of the packed meetings and rallies the posters had announced, where speaker after speaker demanded change and greater freedom.

In our Warsaw hotel, I listened as the first radio broadcast of a Roman Catholic Mass for many years was transmitted. This came about as the result of a further concession by the Government to Solidarity, and I watched as the hotel staff stopped at intervals during their work that Sunday morning to join in the service. Finally, towards the end of my stay, I was able to report that General Jaruzelski's Government had decided to give Solidarity official recognition. I had witnessed a major step along the road towards Poland's full independence, and the eventual break-up of the Soviet empire. I had truly seen history being made.

CHAPTER EIGHT

Lobby and Gallery:
The World of Westminster

In the autumn of 1986, I was suddenly tossed into a new
and very different world, with my appointment as ITN's
Political Editor. I believed that it was a world that was
not going to be so very strange to me. I had, after all, covered
two general elections as a campaign reporter, and during my
time as Diplomatic Editor I had met many of the leading
politicians and had come into close contact with the Prime
Minister and the Foreign Secretary. I thought that such
experience was as good a preparation as any for my new
appointment, and I was wrong.

What I needed to learn was a different kind of journalism.
Even during my time as a diplomatic correspondent, my
reporting was often simply a matter of laying out the facts
that were in front of me. Often, that is all a television reporter
is required to do. A very experienced political correspondent
sensed the problem straight away, knowing that I had no
track record as an investigative journalist. With brutal frank-
ness, he told me within days of my taking up my new post,
'You'll never be any good at your new job. You're too bloody
smooth!' He might have put it rather more elegantly, but I
soon appreciated what he meant. Political reporting can never

be just about the polished presentation of what's going on in front of your nose. As a fledgeling political analyst, I needed to learn the absolute necessity of never accepting any apparent political fact at face value, but rather to get to the bottom of what was really going on, in order to form a properly informed and reasoned judgement.

That may sound blindingly obvious, but it was a lesson I learnt the hard way at the first of the 1986 party conferences. Even the tiniest details had to be mastered. The Liberals, as they were then still called, were holding their assembly in Eastbourne. It was never to be referred to as a conference, I was immediately told, since the Liberals believed in a truly participatory democracy, which the word 'assembly' more accurately described. The learning curve over names and titles was to continue at the Conservative conference within the month, where I learnt that there were no such people as delegates, only 'representatives'.

In 1986, the arguments over the extent and nature of the alliance between the Liberals and the Social Democratic Party were as pointed and difficult as they had ever been. The so-called 'Gang of Four', Roy Jenkins, David Owen, Shirley Williams and Bill Rodgers, had founded the SDP in 1981. The new party had succeeded in appealing not just to those many thousands of voters who, like its founders, had become deeply disillusioned with the Labour Party, but to many thousands more 'political novices', people who found in the SDP's policies and approach to politics something refreshingly new and attractive. But, despite considerable popular support – the Alliance had, in December 1981, briefly reached 50 per cent in the opinion polls – the SDP had found it difficult under the 'first past the post' system of British general elections to gain seats at Westminster. At the 1986 SDP conference, a speaker had asked, 'What have the Liberals got that we haven't got?' Back came a shout from the audience, 'Members of Parliament!'

David Owen had replaced Roy Jenkins as the SDP leader in 1983, and his appointment had always caused many Liberals considerable difficulty. Despite the fact that the Liberals and the SDP had agreed to an alliance, many Liberal Party members considered David Owen far too right-wing, especially on the issue of defence, and it was on that issue that the storm was about to break at Eastbourne.

David Owen addressed the Liberal assembly on its opening day and was politely, if not very enthusiastically, received. That was in sharp contrast to his appearances at previous Liberal Party gatherings, during which he had been booed and heckled. Now, with all the arrogance of a newcomer to the world of political reporting, I suggested that all would be well in the crucial defence debate on the Wednesday, largely on the evidence of the reception David Owen had received. It was my belief, I declared, that David Steel, the Liberal Leader, would win support for a defence policy which would allow for the retention and possible use of a limited British nuclear deterrent, which was also the firm policy of the SDP. My judgement proved to be entirely wrong.

In a chaotic vote at the end of the debate, the Liberal leadership was defeated, albeit by just twenty-seven votes, but defeated nonetheless. Against David Steel's wishes the party had voted for a non-nuclear defence policy, and, after the vote, he came to our makeshift studio to do a single interview for all ITN's programmes. It was agreed that I should conduct it, with the Political Editor of *Channel Four News*, Elinor Goodman, sitting close by, on the floor of the cramped cabin, listening in. I concentrated solely on the defence issue, to Elinor's increasing exasperation. As I drew things to a close, Elinor could contain herself no longer and said to me, in a loud whisper, 'Ask him about the future of the Alliance with David Owen, for God's sake!' I quickly sought to repair an obvious and serious omission in the line of questioning.

'Who's actually conducting this interview?' asked David Steel, with some justification, having heard Elinor's prompting. It was all an early, and valuable, warning not to run before I could walk in this new world of political reporting.

For such a newcomer as myself, the Labour Party conference in Blackpool the following week had at least one clear advantage. There was a distinct and obvious story to be told – the unveiling of the party's new 'Red Rose' image, and the emergence into the limelight of the mastermind behind it all, Peter Mandelson. On the first day, when the new platform, dominated by the rose emblem, was in full use for the first time, I ran into Barbara Castle at the back of the hall and asked her what she thought of it all. 'It reminds me', she said, 'of what happens sometimes in people's homes. You put a new set of doors on the front of the kitchen cupboards, and everyone thinks you've got a new kitchen. But the truth is, nothing's really changed. It's the same here. Labour's just got itself a new set of cupboard doors.'

At the time, she wasn't far from the truth. The old left-wing forces within the Labour Party could still count on a great deal of support, especially at the conference. The issue of defence dominated the week's agenda, with Labour still clinging to a non-nuclear defence policy. In the foyer of the Imperial Hotel, Denis Healey told me that Britain's retention of nuclear weapons was helping to contribute to the worldwide risk of radioactive contamination – the 'nuclear winter' he called it. In his speech to conference, Neil Kinnock strongly defended the party's defence policy, with the words, 'I am prepared to die for my country, but I don't want my country to die for me.' At the end of the conference, Neil and Glenys Kinnock stood on the platform throwing roses at the delegates, something Tony Benn later described as a 'disgusting spectacle'. The party's image had changed. Much else about it had not.

Neil Kinnock was a mercurial figure, capable of great warmth, yet also of fiery anger towards those he dealt with, especially political journalists. He could fly into a temper in an instant, and begin denouncing any one of us in front of our colleagues. When I began my time as ITN's Political Editor, he was still holding a briefing every Thursday evening in the Shadow Cabinet room, but he soon ended the practice. He let it be known that he had come to regard the sessions as a waste of time. He believed that, whatever he said, we would all go away and write anything we wanted about him anyway, especially those correspondents who worked for newspapers which traditionally supported the Tories.

Our right to criticise him was something that he found difficult to live with, and during the early years of his leadership he was meticulous in seeking to correct even the smallest mistakes in our reporting. Mistakes can and do occur, but setting the record straight is something that party leaders normally leave to their staff, unless it is a very serious matter indeed. Even the tiniest error, however, could produce a personal letter from Neil Kinnock. I received one from him that resembled a seismograph recording a major earthquake, his handwriting, in the thick black felt-tipped pen he always used, scored across the page. Later, the job of chief castigator of the media fell to Peter Mandelson, as his Campaigns and Communications Director, who kept up a constant flow of telephone calls to us all. The messages were not just to correct mistakes, but to offer his views on what we had or had not said in our reports, and the prominence, or lack of it, which our respective editors had given them.

Yet Neil Kinnock was capable of immense friendliness and good humour. He was not a man to whom I ever got close, which made, perhaps, those moments when his sterner side gave way to something different all the more striking. In an interview at the end of one Labour Party conference, I had put to him the criticism, voiced by the Tories, that he was not up to the job of Prime Minister. I asked him point-blank if he was. His answer was forthright. 'I am fit and ready for Number Ten,' he declared. He went on to set out, with remarkable clarity, why he felt all the personal criticism of him was unfounded. At the end of it, we both realised that the interview had, somehow, gone very well – it had taken off, as they say, and had broken new ground. Suddenly he got up and went to a desk in the corner of his temporary office and found a copy of a book of poems by his favourite Welsh poet, Idris Davies. The felt-tipped pen was produced once more, but this time the ink was campaign red, and, on the title page, he wrote a dedication and signed it. It was his way of expressing his satisfaction at how things had gone.

Back at Westminster, after the 1986 party conference season, I set about learning the way things worked in and around the House of Commons. As I did so, I became more and more depressed, and, at one stage, I seriously considered a return to general reporting.

Even today, the Commons is a formidably difficult place for new arrivals. The atmosphere of the gentleman's club pervades it, and with it goes the unwritten rule, especially among the journalists who work there, that you are not truly admitted to its workings until you have somehow proved yourself. Information seeps out of the woodwork, and what formal notice there is about what is actually going on, even about such simple things as the calling of briefings or the timing of press conferences, is completely haphazard. You come to rely on a mutual back-up system, exchanging information with your colleagues to make sure that you know what is really happening.

That is the downside of what is known as the Lobby system. The title derives from the fact that while all journalists covering the House of Commons are admitted to the Press Gallery, perched high above the Speaker's chair at the end of the Commons chamber, most, though not all, of those journalists also have access to the large open area just outside the swing doors at the other end of it. The name given to that space, the Members' Lobby, has transferred itself to the journalists concerned, who are known as a result as the Lobby.

Opponents of the system describe the Lobby as a pernicious and anti-democratic closed shop. They would like everything that governments tell journalists to be on the record, and to be recorded or carried live on radio and television. In fact, no government in the world operates such a system, and, even if it did, off-the-record briefing for individual journalists would still continue.

In Britain, there has been one recent and significant change. All Lobby briefings by Number Ten are now on the record, attributable to the Prime Minister's Official Spokesman, though they cannot be recorded for use on radio and television. This was one of the first changes Alastair Campbell introduced after Labour's 1997 election victory. It provides, in my view, a useful halfway house between open-to-all briefings and the old, closed, secretive system of the past. It helps to guard against any abuse of the system by the Government, and it means that contact between Government and the press can take place in a more relaxed and business-like atmosphere than if every word uttered was available for radio and television transmission. In a further safeguard, following an enquiry by a Commons Select Committee, a tape-recording of the briefings made by Number Ten is now kept for a short time.

The Lobby system is also criticised for encouraging 'pack journalism' – everyone clubbing together to write an agreed version of the story. There is a certain amount of comparing of notes among correspondents, but the Lobby is a fiercely competitive place. Those with genuinely exclusive stories will always try to keep them to themselves until they have been published or broadcast, but news of major scoops often begins to trickle out by word of mouth among the other members of the Lobby. That is usually because the politicians, or those who work for them, have also got word that something is going on and start talking about it to other journalists. The Lobby system is very easy to criticise, but the plain fact is that, if you are not in the loop at Westminster, you can be at a considerable disadvantage. As a new boy, I was discovering that fact for myself.

There was also the problem of the complete lack of facilities for television correspondents. Although the House of Lords had voted in 1985 to admit the cameras, there was still considerable resistance to the idea in the Commons, where television coverage did not begin until November 1989. I had always been used to working with pictures in compiling my reports, and suddenly there were next to none available. Until shortly before my arrival, coverage of the Commons had usually consisted of a correspondent sitting in a studio telling the viewers what had happened, and even that had not been without its problems. There are no studios inside the buildings that make up the Houses of Parliament. At the time of my arrival, a simple studio, with a single camera in it, was located in what used to be Scotland Yard, the headquarters of the Metropolitan Police. These premises, some 300 yards from the Palace of Westminster, had been renamed the Norman Shaw Building and turned largely into MPs' offices, with a very small amount of space allocated to the broadcasters. One of my predecessors, Julian Havilland, was famous for never making the dash to this studio to deliver his report until the very last minute, and had, on one occasion, failed to realise that a heavy rainstorm was in progress. As a result, steam could clearly be seen rising from him during his broadcast, as the studio lights began to dry out his soaked clothing.

As I struggled to put together my early Parliamentary reports, I did at least have the small advantage of the audio tape of the Commons proceedings. A sound feed had been made available for broadcasting since early 1978, and this could be included in my packages, illustrated by a picture of the relevant MP. But it was clearly an unsatisfactory way of covering the Commons, and the fact that the House came to appreciate that was one of the reasons for their eventual decision to allow the cameras in.

Has that decision been good for the Commons or not? I believe that it has, and that we would now find it very strange indeed if the proceedings of the Commons were not televised. Early fears about MPs playing to the cameras have proved ill founded, even if one or two of them still ham it up a bit, by waving things like posters or newspapers or by wearing silly badges, to try to 'get themselves on the telly' or to reinforce their point at Question Time or during a debate.

At the start a significant minority of MPs were against the idea of televising the Commons. They were certain that the House would be changed for ever, and for the worse. Not long after the cameras were admitted, Mrs Thatcher button-holed me and the BBC Political Editor, John Cole, at a drinks party at Conservative Central Office and proceeded to tell us both in forceful terms, and at some length, how much she regretted the decision. Her point was that it was no longer possible to sustain a reasoned argument in a speech because of the number of interventions from the backbenches – members jumping up to interrupt so as to get their faces on television.

Mrs Thatcher was a well-known opponent of televising, and, as our conversation showed, she found the presence of the cameras difficult to accept for quite some time. Her argument about the number of interventions was not well founded. They had always happened, in any case, and if there was a slight increase immediately after the cameras were introduced, it proved to be a short-lived problem. But Mrs Thatcher's opposition was a minority view, and MPs quickly came to live with the cameras and, indeed, to forget that they were there at all.

I believe that televising both Houses of Parliament has been a power for good. I said before they were introduced that I thought that Ministers would be the main beneficiaries, as the public watched important announcements that affected their lives being made in the Commons and the Lords. Reports of such ministerial statements, and the immediate reactions to them, quickly began to form the bulk of our Parliamentary coverage on the main news bulletins. Other important occasions, such as the State Opening of Parliament, the Budget, resignation speeches by Ministers, and major debates on, for example, the decision to commit British troops to the Gulf War, quickly began to receive much wider coverage than had been possible before the introduction of the cameras. The decision to let people see for themselves what their MPs actually said and did at Westminster was, in my view, an important enhancement of the democratic process. The wonder is that it took so long for it to happen.

In 1986, as I took up my duties at Westminster with the decision to admit the cameras still three years off, the lack of pictures from the Commons was far from my only problem. I had no proper facilities close at hand for compiling my edited television reports, whether there was anything visually interesting in them or not. Just before my arrival, ITN decided to station a crew on a permanent basis at the Norman Shaw studio, but there was insufficient room inside it to install any editing equipment. We hunted high and low for alternative premises, and the best we could come up with was a tiny storeroom on the second floor of the Red Lion pub, a short distance along Whitehall. When the struggle to operate our equipment among the cans of cooking oil and the brushes and the brooms finally became too much to bear, we negotiated the temporary use, on a day-by-day basis, of the landlord's bedroom, until we all got heartily sick of the inconvenience which that caused to all concerned. After a time, we discovered that the new Queen Elizabeth conference centre opposite Westminster Abbey had been constructed with space for a number of television studios in its basement, but that they had never been built. ITN, and a number of other broadcasters, were able to install facilities there, which served us well for several years.

As I gradually found my feet at Westminster, the pace of political reporting began to speed up. It was widely expected that Mrs Thatcher would go to the country in June 1987, after four years of her second term of office, and eventually she did so. In the meantime, there was extensive speculation about the election date, particularly as the polls indicated that, this time around, it would be no walkover for the Tories. Both Labour and the Liberals had enjoyed by-election successes during 1986, and the Liberal–SDP Alliance was shortly to receive another boost at a by-election in Greenwich.

The question marks over the Conservatives' prospects, and the fact that Greenwich is only fifteen minutes by train from Central London, meant that I covered the campaign there far more thoroughly than usual. The SDP candidate, Rosie Barnes, seemed to typify so much of what that party stood for. She admitted at the start of her campaign that she was very much one of those political novices who were such a feature of the Social Democrats' membership. Her fresh-faced appeal was reinforced throughout by constant references to her local roots and knowledge of the constituency, as councillor, housewife and mother.

To the consternation of a Government that was contemplating going to the country in four months' time, she ended up taking the seat by an astonishing six and a half thousand votes. There was just one small hiccup. At one of her last campaign meetings, Mrs Barnes had allowed herself a foretaste of the victory that seemed almost certain to be hers. She was wearing a dark-grey shirt, and, as she raised both her arms in jubilation above her head, it was immediately apparent that her underarm anti-perspirant had failed to a very significant degree. Unfortunately, for months afterwards, it always seemed to be that shot which emerged from the ITN library when television pictures of her were required.

In marked contrast to the 1983 general election campaign, with its 'Falklands Factor', the battle that got under way in early May 1987 was a much more difficult affair for the Conservatives. Stresses and strains at Central Office troubled it throughout. Mrs Thatcher, unhappy with the way things were going, expected the Deputy Chairman of the Tory Party, Lord Young, to keep an eye on Norman Tebbit, the Chairman, who was officially running things. At one stage during that campaign, I talked privately at Central Office to Harvey Thomas, the wonderfully extrovert man who was in charge of making the actual arrangements for Mrs Thatcher's campaign out on the road. Shaking his head, he complained that he had no real idea which of the chiefs he was supposed to listen to at Central Office, 'since there are two campaign programmes being worked out here, one by the Chairman and one by the Deputy Chairman'. In fact, with all the experience he had gained from running religious crusades for the American evangelist Billy Graham, Harvey Thomas simply did his own thing anyway, despite the ups and downs of the campaign. A week before polling day, an opinion poll had cut the Tory lead to 4 per cent, and, on what became known as 'Wobbly Thursday', news of a serious Thatcher–

Tebbit row, over the way the campaign was being run, soon leaked out.

It seemed clear to many of us what the problem was – that so much of what the Conservatives were proposing for their third term in office had been poorly thought out. The manifesto was itself a curiosity, despite being described by Mrs Thatcher later as 'the best ever produced by the Conservative Party'. It came in a plastic wallet, containing two booklets the size of pocket airline timetables. One booklet was entitled 'Our First Eight Years', designed to set out the record of Tory achievement. In the other was the manifesto proper, specifically designed to show that, after eight years, the Tories had not run out of steam, and that they were putting forward new and radical proposals. One such proposal was for what amounted to the return of the old grammar schools, which, by a particular irony, had been abolished in record numbers by Mrs Thatcher during her time as Education Secretary under Edward Heath. Under the new proposals, a number of schools were to be given a very high degree of independence within the state sector, and were to be known as 'grant-maintained' schools.

At one of the Tories' regular morning press conferences, three days after the launch of the manifesto, I began to question Mrs Thatcher closely about those proposals, which seemed particularly vague on the details of how the new schools would operate. How would the pupils who would attend these grant-maintained schools be chosen? Would they be specially selected for them? How would that selection operate? Was she contemplating a return to the old 'Eleven-plus', the examination that used to send children to different kinds of secondary schools on the basis of a single examination?

She and I got into something of a public argument, as we batted the issue to and fro. With the tone of her voice sharpening, and its volume rising, she was dismissive of my questioning. 'Schools already do select,' she declared, in a reference to the way in which some state schools interviewed parents before admitting pupils. 'These enormous problems which you mention simply don't arise!' But that was not the end of the argument.

At large press conferences, it is very easy for the questioning to range backwards and forwards over a number of subjects in an uncoordinated way. On this occasion, we all began to smell blood, as Mrs Thatcher's answers on the new schools seemed unusually vague and confusing. Others, notably the BBC's Political Editor, John Cole, continued to press hard for answers, especially on the question of whether parents would be expected to pay fees of some kind. It did not go well and, immediately the press conference was over, Mrs Thatcher began a fearsome post-mortem upstairs. It was not the first during the 1987 campaign – and nor was it to be the last, but those around her noticed very little change in her own behaviour as a result of them. Twenty minutes or so after most of the discussions, she was already off in her battle bus, or heading for the airport, to begin campaigning somewhere around the country. Any problems with the press were quickly forgotten the moment she was out on the road.

By contrast to the problems at Central Office, Labour's campaign gave the appearance of running on tramlines, and was as far removed from the disaster of their 1983 campaign as it was possible to imagine. Neil Kinnock, as suspicious as ever of the Lobby and the London-based press in general, decided to hold most of his morning press conferences outside London, speaking in whatever part of the country he had chosen for that day's campaigning. This created some difficulties for the Westminster-based political editors, who needed to be in London to listen to the other party leaders, as I discovered for myself. After two elections in which I had been out on the road with one particular campaign team, this was the first during which I was to spend most of my time in London, and to take part in that curious ritual of British general elections, the early-morning dash.

By tradition, the first appointment of the day for the leaders of the three main parties, or another of the high-powered members of their campaign team, was to hold a press conference in London. The tradition also meant that the conferences followed each other in rapid succession, but in different buildings. In 1987, Labour was still making use of its former headquarters at Transport House in Smith Square, which was almost opposite Conservative Central Office. After they had finished, it was a simple matter of crossing the road to listen to, and to question, the Tories. It was not quite so simple, however, actually getting into Central Office. After the IRA bombing of the Grand Hotel in Brighton during their annual conference three years earlier, the Conservatives had, understandably, put a strict security operation in place, which took a considerable amount of time to negotiate.

At this election, the Liberals and the Social Democrats decided that they would hold joint press conferences. They were, after all, fighting as an Alliance, but each morning, it seemed, the event only served to underline the tensions between the two parties, and particularly between the two leaders, David Owen and David Steel. One week into the campaign, Steel talked of cutting down on what he called their 'Tweedledum and Tweedledee' appearances together, but they continued nonetheless. Owen came across as the tougher and more authoritarian of the two, especially on defence, the issue which had split the parties at the Eastbourne assembly, and on the question of whether or not the Alliance would ever sustain a Conservative government in office. There was no blazing public row, but the image of two men ill at ease with

145

each other was reinforced after one morning press conference had come to an end. Both leaders emerged to board their respective campaign coaches – by now a battle bus had become part of every British political leader's standard campaign kit. In full view of the cameras, Dr Owen turned right towards his vehicle, declaring, 'I'm off to Birmingham.' David Steel turned left towards his, announcing, 'I'm off to Bristol.' The pictures, and the sound, of two leaders heading in different directions told the true story – that this was a deeply uneasy alliance.

The Liberal–SDP conferences were held at the National Liberal Club, a rambling and faded pile, built in the days when the Liberals had actually formed governments in Britain and could support a club of their own in London. This building, not far from Charing Cross Station, was some distance from Smith Square, where both the other main parties were operating. In order to encourage attendance at their own event, while still allowing us to cover the rest, the Alliance arranged for a shuttle bus, which often turned out to be an open-top double-decker normally used to ferry tourists past Big Ben. The Liberal Democrats continued this curious practice at the next election, though by 1997 they had wisely decided to move closer to the action, by hiring a large room in Church House, Westminster.

At the 1987 Labour press conferences, the party's Campaign Director, Bryan Gould, was left to deal with us all in Neil Kinnock's absence. At these occasions, too, defence kept coming up, as questions persisted about Labour's non-nuclear defence policy, particularly after Mr Kinnock had said that British troops would 'take to the hills' and fight a guerrilla campaign if necessary, were the British Isles ever to be attacked and occupied. After one morning conference, I interviewed Gerald Kaufman, the party's defence spokesman. During my later, two-minute report, I made space to show that I had asked him three times whether or not he would press the nuclear 'button' to use the missiles aboard Britain's Polaris submarines. Clearly uncomfortable with his party's position on defence, he had repeated, three times, that the party had a clear policy, and that was that. It was some way off Jeremy Paxman's later record of fourteen identical questions to Michael Howard, but the message that came across in both cases was the same – that an interviewee was in some difficulty with the answers he was having to give.

For the most part, however, Labour's campaign went well, typified by one of the few party political broadcasts ever to stick in the memory. It was instantly dubbed 'Kinnock – the Movie'. It was made by the *Chariots of Fire* director, Hugh Hudson, with the simple aim of presenting Neil and Glenys as the ideal couple for the age. It did so by showing them everywhere – at home in their kitchen over breakfast, out on the campaign trail, or, in the most memorable sequence, shot from a helicopter, as they walked along a cliff-top path, hand in hand, to the strains of uplifting music. It may have been magnificent – so much so that, by popular demand, it was shown on television for a second time – but, like the campaign as a whole, it did not win the war. The defence issue, and the continuing public doubts about Neil Kinnock, which the Hugh Hudson broadcast had failed to dispel, meant that Mrs Thatcher won her third term easily. She re-entered Downing Street with an overall majority of 102.

CHAPTER NINE

Defiance and Tears: The End of a Premiership

B y the middle of 1987, having won her third term in office, Margaret Thatcher seemed, to use a word that later became loaded with meaning, unassailable. As I watched her return to Central Office on election night, crushed in among hundreds of cheering supporters, there seemed every chance of her famous prediction of going 'on and on and on' being fulfilled. By contrast, Labour was demoralised and the Alliance of the Social Democrats and the Liberals began to collapse. Overall, the two Alliance parties had lost just one seat, but the SDP had done especially badly. The number of its MPs had been reduced to five, and one of the party's founders, Roy Jenkins, was among those who had lost their seats.

Immediately, there were proposals for a Liberal SDP merger, and, a little later, talks about such a merger began. Much of my time that autumn was spent in reporting those tortuous negotiations, which ended in a draft agreement just as *News at Ten* was about to go on the air. In such circumstances, ITN's technical engineers are normally a tower of strength, quietly establishing sound and video links back to base from all kinds of seemingly impossible locations. But on this occasion they were, for some reason, experiencing terrible difficulty in getting things set up in time for a live interview with Shirley Williams, the SDP President, outside the party's headquarters in Cowley Street, not far from the House of Commons. In the end, it went ahead at the very last moment, with Mrs Williams clamping an earpiece to her ear with her right hand. On the ground in front of her, and only just out of camera shot, was a kneeling technician, offering up to her, like a plate of terrible grey spaghetti, a tangle of connecting wires. Only his steady hand prevented the earpiece from being pulled from Shirley Williams' grasp. Had that happened, all communication with her interviewer would have been instantly cut off.

In the end, a majority of Liberals and Social Democrats voted for a merger, after bitter debates at two specially convened conferences. The Liberal vote took place at a particularly grim hotel on the outskirts of Blackpool, famously christened some years earlier by one journalist the 'Colditz of the North'. Outside the wind howled; inside the vote was held in a vast and bleak concrete hangar, more usually the setting for trade exhibitions. The distance between the speakers at the rostrum and our camera was so great, and the platform on which that camera was perched so insecure, that the resulting pictures suggested we had been aboard a storm-tossed liner throughout.

Working conditions were better at the SDP conference in the Crucible Theatre in Sheffield, but the debate in that party was even more acrimonious. Once again, a majority voted to merge, but, as a result, many members decided to soldier on, under David Owen's leadership, as a continuing and separate party. It all came to a sad end three years later, after the SDP candidate in the Bootle by-election got fewer votes than the representative from the Monster Raving Loony Party.

At first, the newly merged party called themselves the Social and Liberal Democrats, though they attempted to stop broad-casters like myself calling them the SLD. The Conservatives enjoyed themselves by employing a feeble joke and constantly referring to the 'Salads', even though the Government's own problems were beginning to grow. One of the first of those problems involved a seemingly trivial event. A reporter from Central Television had, at ITN's request, located the Health Minister, Edwina Currie, as she did a spot of Saturday-morning campaigning in the Midlands. ITN, as it often did, had asked the reporter to doorstep the Minister, not knowing in advance whether she would answer any questions, because a number of stories had appeared suggesting that there was a problem over whether eggs were safe to eat.

I was in ITN's London headquarters, and I watched in the newsroom as the pre-recorded interview was sent down the line to us. Not only had Mrs Currie agreed to talk, but, astonishingly, I heard her say, 'Most of the egg production of this country, sadly, is now infected with salmonella.' Whether or not it was true, it was clearly an extremely serious statement for a minister to have made, and, after the interview was shown three times that Saturday, public panic broke out, with egg sales plummeting. The country's egg producers insisted that what Mrs Currie had said was inaccurate, but, appearing before the cameras during the course of her ministerial duties three days later, she refused to take back or even modify her words, though she was persistently invited to do so. A fort-night after making her original remarks, she was forced to resign.

Ministerial resignations played an important part during the last three years of the Thatcher administration as the problems grew, and there has been much criticism of political journalists like myself for not having spotted the seeds of Mrs Thatcher's downfall during the 1987 election campaign. Most particularly, it is said, we should have paid more attention to the disastrous promise in the manifesto to introduce the notorious poll tax in England and Wales – it was already due to replace the old domestic rating system in Scotland. In mitigation, I can only use that old plea of the daily journalist, that it did not look quite like that at the time.

The Conservatives' policy proposals *had* come under very close scrutiny during the campaign, but attention had focused on other highly contentious areas, above all their plans for the reform of state education. In addition to the proposals for grant-maintained schools, there were plans for the introduction of a national curriculum in England and Wales. There was also a proposal for the abolition of the much criticised Inner London Education Authority (ILEA) – all of which later generated plenty of heat in both Houses of Parliament, as the proposals eventually became law. In addition, the Conservatives' decision to go for what amounted to a trial run of the poll tax in Scotland had already been agreed by Parliament some six months before the election, even if that decision had not attracted much attention south of the border.

At the time, I had tried to bring the issue of the poll tax to wider public attention with what is known in television journalism as a 'backgrounder', a report that deals, not with the hard news of the day, but with topical issues of a more general nature. I am told that at the BBC they were known, hideously, for a time as 'BEXPOs' – shorthand, apparently, for Brief Explanatory Offerings. There was some reluctance at ITN to tackle what appeared to be the arcane subject of what was about to replace the rates in Scotland, on the reasonable grounds that it was a purely Scottish story, and therefore of no interest to viewers south of the border. I argued strongly that what was about to happen in Scotland, through the introduction of a new Bill, was a clear blueprint of the poll tax which would happen soon enough in England and Wales, and that we should say so. As a result, both my explanatory package the day before the Scottish Bill's publication and coverage of that event the following day did, in the end, secure a slot on *News at Ten*.

It was important that they did, because the poll tax represented a major departure in British taxation, which had always been roughly based on the principle of ability to pay. In the case of income tax, there was a direct relationship between what you paid and what you earned. In the case of the local rates, which the poll tax was designed to replace, there was a rough equivalence, since the amount paid by each household was determined by the size of the house in which that household lived, and, for the most part, it was the wealthier people who lived in the larger houses. Now, although there was to be a banding system, everyone living in a particular house was required to pay the new tax, at least in part, with the result that a large number of adults living in a relatively modest property could find themselves collectively paying the same amount as someone living alone in a very large house indeed – 'the Duke paying as much as the dustman', as we all began to express it. The tax was also politically motivated, based on the belief that if it forced people to realise that their local council was wasteful or inefficient – and in the Conservatives' eyes most councils controlled by any other party were precisely that – then local residents would vote such councils out of office.

To emphasise that idea, and to minimise the 'Duke and dustman' charge, Mrs Thatcher insisted, to the last, that the new tax should be called the community charge, and she would sharply correct each and every Opposition MP, journalist or anyone else who tried to call it the poll tax. Long after she had left office, she was still claiming in interviews with myself and others that, given time, it could have all been made to work. But the poll tax went against one of the rules of thumb for the conduct of government that she had set herself,

153

and which she liked to call Thatcher's Laws of Politics. This rule was that you must always work with the grain of the people, and never against it. Another rule was that in politics the unexpected always happens. Three years later, it did.

The poll tax was a key element in Mrs Thatcher's eventual departure from office. From the moment of its introduction, it began to do her political damage. There was an immediate and extensive revolt against it in Scotland, organised in a movement which quickly became known as the 'Can't Pay, Won't Pay' campaign. The revolt against it in the rest of the country may have been slower to materialise, but, when it came, it was even more serious.

The Bill to bring in the poll tax in England and Wales was introduced in the Commons in the autumn of 1987, and, from the start, it attracted a considerable number of Tory rebels. People like the former Minister Sir George Young and the backbencher Michael Mates led a campaign to try to change the tax and make it fairer. At a vote on what became known as the 'Mates amendment', thirty-eight Conservatives in all, including eleven former Ministers, voted against it.

There was a similar revolt in the House of Lords, led by an unlikely rebel, Lord Chelwood, better known from his days in the Commons as the MP Sir Tufton Beamish. However, the Conservative whips called up the Tory backwoodsmen to ensure the Bill's passage through the Lords. Our cameras hovered outside Chancellor's Gate, the main entrance to the Upper House, to watch them arrive. Four of the more infirm peers were in wheelchairs. In all, seventy Conservative hereditary peers who seldom, if ever, attended Lords debates turned up to help vote the measure through. Lord Chelwood was just one of the many broad-minded Tories, often called 'One-Nation' Conservatives, who were outraged by the poll tax. Another was an MP called Robert Adley, to whose

154

constituency, Christchurch in Hampshire, I went to report on grass-roots reaction.

Robert Adley, who sadly died in May 1993 at the early age of fifty-eight, was chiefly known at Westminster for his great love of trains, especially steam trains. He took photographs of them and he wrote books about them, and was known to many as 'Puff-puff' Adley. He was a mild-mannered man who, while he always knew his own mind, was not among the usual roll-call of Tory rebels. Nonetheless, as we went around Christchurch together, his angry concern for the large number of retired people among his constituents was clear. Many of them were living in homes which had increased in value over the years, while their incomes had remained fixed. Under the plans for the poll tax, retired couples were particularly at risk of having to pay far more than they had under the rates, since each individual in a household was required to pay the new tax. Together, we met a number of such people, both in their homes and in the streets. It was clear that the local MP was getting support for his stand from members of all the political parties in his constituency, and not just from his regular Conservative supporters.

It was the reaction in constituencies like Robert Adley's that was gradually fuelling more and more resentment among ordinary people towards the Conservatives in general, and Margaret Thatcher in particular. It grew and grew, and came to a head in a night of serious rioting in Central London in March 1990, a matter of days before the poll tax was due to come into effect. But, for me, it was another demonstration that had taken place earlier the same day which brought home the extent of that public anger.

The Conservatives were holding a meeting of their Central Council in Cheltenham, where Mrs Thatcher was addressing the party activists who make up that body. But, even as she spoke, a huge anti-poll-tax march was taking place outside

155

the hall on the streets of that attractive town. Those taking part in it were not, for the most part, members of extreme left-wing groups like the Socialist Workers Party. Nor were they the sort of people who, later that day, turned the march in London into vicious rioting. The demonstrators on the streets of Cheltenham – itself a powerful symbol of Middle England – were clearly ordinary but angry people, some with their children in pushchairs, protesting against what they simply saw as an unfair tax. Estimates of the amount people would actually pay had been rising steadily. Now, with most councils having set the amount of the tax, it was clear that many people would indeed be paying far more than before. As a result, the Cheltenham march was just one of many which had become a regular feature in Britain's cities and towns each weekend.

Alongside public resentment, trouble was growing among Conservative MPs and peers at Westminster. It was the MPs who mattered above all. Until the rules were changed much later, the position of Leader of the Conservative Party, and thus the position of Prime Minister, lay in their hands, and their hands alone, for as long as a Conservative government remained undefeated between general elections on an issue of confidence. Among many Tory MPs, the poll tax was a clear source of annoyance, even though relatively few of them were prepared to defy the whips and vote against the Government. As a political journalist, you soon learn that bravery in the voting lobbies is not a particularly conspicuous virtue among most MPs. But there was also growing annoyance about Mrs Thatcher's dealings with Europe, and resentment about the way she seemed to be ignoring opinion within the party at large, and among backbench MPs in particular.

Some months earlier, the party Chairman, Kenneth Baker, had suggested that the Prime Minister really was about to change her ways. A number of senior backbenchers had been invited to lunch at Downing Street, and in an unusual interview afterwards Baker told me that the backbenchers had suggested to Mrs Thatcher that she needed to 'get her act together' and to pay rather more regard to their opinions. Things would be different from that day forward, Kenneth Baker suggested. The Prime Minister would be changing her ways. The effect of that message was rather diminished when, just a few days later, Mrs Thatcher said that she had heard reports about what had been said to her, but that no such words had been used. Indeed she wondered, given the descriptions of it, whether she had even been at the lunch in question. There was, in fact, no change in the Thatcher way of doing things, either on the poll tax or any other issue. It all helped to produce a serious rift, behind the scenes, between the Prime Minister and two of the most senior members of her Cabinet – the Foreign Secretary, Sir Geoffrey Howe, and the Chancellor, Nigel Lawson.

I personally found the Chancellor a somewhat remote and forbidding figure, not the sort of Minister you could ever simply pass the time of day with if you happened to bump into him. Though he was perfectly civil on those occasions when we did meet, there was always a somewhat intimidating aura about him. He had the air of someone possessed of an especially formidable intellect. His analytical approach to government had brought him to the firm conclusion by early 1989 that it was in Britain's interest to join the European Exchange Rate Mechanism (the ERM). Both he and Geoffrey Howe believed that British membership of the ERM, so long promised by the Government 'when the time was right', would help to end the increasingly isolated position which Britain occupied in Europe. They argued that such a move would strengthen, rather than weaken, Britain's case against full economic and monetary union and that ERM membership would also help to restore financial discipline in Britain, with great benefits in the fight against inflation.

In conditions of great secrecy, Nigel Lawson and Geoffrey Howe worked on a memorandum, which they presented to the Prime Minister just ahead of the summit of European leaders in Madrid in June 1989. The document set out the two Ministers' views and recommended that the Prime Minister should commit Britain to joining the ERM in three years' time.

It caused a huge row. There was an angry meeting with Mrs Thatcher in Downing Street six days before the summit. Lawson and Howe sought another meeting with her during the weekend before the summit began. She indicated at first that she would call in to see each of them individually – Nigel Lawson at his official country residence in Buckinghamshire, and Geoffrey Howe at his official London home in Carlton Gardens – on her way back from Chequers. The two men, however, were not falling for divide-and-rule tactics of that sort, and a second meeting was arranged in Downing Street instead. In the course of it, both the Chancellor and the Foreign Secretary threatened to resign if their demands were not met. Mrs Thatcher had little alternative but to announce in Madrid that Britain would be joining the ERM, though at a date of the British Government's choosing.

Mrs Thatcher was clear in her own mind that it was Howe, rather than Lawson, who had been the driving force behind what she regarded as a pre-Madrid conspiracy against her. Her revenge was swift. In an extensive reshuffle, just after the Madrid summit, Geoffrey Howe was sacked as Foreign Secretary and appointed Leader of the House of Commons. Reshuffle Day – 24 July 1989 – was a classic example of how often television reporting, with its emphasis on visual evidence and its reliance on pictures, can fail to tell the true story of what is actually going on. By the time I came to report on that day's events for *News at Ten*, we knew a little more of the background – word had leaked out, for example, that the ex-Foreign Secretary had been offered and had turned down the job of Home Secretary – but not the full story. Later conversations with Sir Geoffrey's friends and colleagues, however, served only to emphasise how little of what had really happened I had been able to relate at the time.

Geoffrey Howe was clearly not unaware of the risk that he might be removed from the Foreign Office. His wife Elspeth had quietly warned one of their luncheon guests at Chevening, their official country residence, a week or two earlier that it might be a good thing to take up her husband's offer of a tour around the house 'because I don't know how much longer we're going to be here'. When the axe fell, however, at the start of the reshuffle, Sir Geoffrey was deeply shocked. He was a man who was very far from given to displays of emotion, but one of his closest advisers told me later that it was the nearest he had ever seen him come to tears.

After a meeting on the morning of Reshuffle Day – the first of two with the Prime Minister – he had returned to Carlton Gardens in such a state of despair that he drafted a letter of resignation from the Government. He had indeed been offered the Home Office, but had decided that he couldn't face the prospect of taking on that particularly difficult department. As he thought things over, however, he characteristically decided on a 'stay and fight' policy, and his second meeting with the Prime Minister in the afternoon focused on how that could be achieved.

Still smarting from what she saw as her defeat over the Madrid summit, she told Sir Geoffrey that he could have any job in Government he wanted 'apart from Nigel's'. Having been Chancellor once before, it was not a job he was likely to want in any event. He suggested, and she agreed, that he should become Deputy Prime Minister and Leader of the

House of Commons (with which came the title of Lord President of the Council) and that he should also have responsibility for co-ordinating campaign strategy for the next general election.

It may all have looked and sounded good, but it was a situation that simply could not last. For a start, in the immediate aftermath of the reshuffle, there was clear briefing from Number Ten against Sir Geoffrey. It was made very obvious to me and other members of the Lobby that the position of Deputy Prime Minister was one that Mrs Thatcher now held to be of no account whatsoever. That was despite the fact that, just a few years previously, the title had been held, and used to considerable effect, by Willie Whitelaw, one of her most trusted advisers. Stories also appeared suggesting that there had been a row over houses. As Foreign Secretary, Sir Geoffrey Howe had hugely enjoyed the use of Chevening, where, as my wife and I can personally attest, he was extremely generous with his hospitality. However, he has always insisted that the idea that he should be allowed to use the Chancellor's residence, Dorneywood in Buckinghamshire, as a replacement for Chevening was entirely Mrs Thatcher's. What angered him, however, when the stories about the supposed row over houses appeared, was the suspicion that Number Ten was quietly encouraging a whispering campaign against him.

There was, in addition, soon to be another severe blow to any attempt at preserving Cabinet unity. On 26 October 1989, the Chancellor of the Exchequer, Nigel Lawson, resigned. This time there had been rather more advance evidence of trouble ahead, with Mrs Thatcher's decision to reappoint Sir Alan Walters, an economics professor with decidedly right-wing views, as one of her special advisers. Sir Alan, for example, believed that the whole idea of the European Monetary System, which the Chancellor had forced Mrs Thatcher to sign up to, consisted of what he called 'half-baked' economics, and he had said so. Lawson had also been forced to endure a withering attack in the Commons on the question of who was really running the Government's economic policy, delivered by the Shadow Chancellor, John Smith, at his sarcastic best. Later Nigel Lawson was overheard at a dinner telling his old ally Geoffrey Howe, 'Geoffrey, I cannot go on like this. It's simply absurd. It's impossible.'

In the wake of his resignation, Margaret Thatcher was forced to endure the embarrassment of being lectured by a resigning minister on how government should be conducted, and on her failings in that regard. In his resignation letter, the Chancellor told her that economic policy could be properly conducted only if those in charge of it were in complete agreement, and that such a situation could not obtain 'so long as Alan Walters remains your personal economic adviser'. In his resignation speech in the Commons, he said that Prime Ministers had to appoint Ministers they trusted and then let them get on with carrying out policy.

When it came, however, to that heady mix of issues – economic policy and Europe – Margaret Thatcher was simply incapable of sitting back and letting others make the running. She made that abundantly clear to those of us who covered the European summit that followed Madrid, held in Strasbourg in December 1989. The Strasbourg summit took an important first step towards the introduction of a single European currency by deciding that there would be a special summit of all the leaders to agree how it should be introduced. The President of the European Commission, Jacques Delors, had already drawn up a master plan, and the summit had agreed to implement the first stage of it, though that involved little more than some initial exploratory moves. At the end of the meeting, however, the host, President Mitterrand of France, hailed what had been achieved as a decision of historic proportions, adding that he hoped Britain would

161

soon show 'good common sense' and join wholeheartedly in the whole single-currency project.

Nothing could have been calculated to annoy Mrs Thatcher more – she had already signalled that the single currency was something that she would never, ever sign up to. She was hardly in the best of moods anyway. At the same summit, every other member country except Britain had voted to accept a package of measures known as the Social Chapter. But it was on the single-currency question that she let fly during an end-of-summit interview with me. 'I will *not* see the pound abolished,' she declared. 'No! Certainly not! I'm not here to preside over the abolition of the pound sterling.'

'No ecus replacing pounds, then?' I prompted her.

'No!' she replied. 'That's stage two and three of Delors, and I made it perfectly clear that no major party in the British Parliament will accept that.' Her forthright answer seemed plain enough. In case it was not, she decided to make sure that, once the camera had been switched off, everyone who had come into the room for the recording of the interview would be leaving it without a shadow of doubt about her own personal feelings on the matter.

At the Prime Minister's side during that interview were a number of officials, and they included not only her regular advisers, but also some of the British diplomats based in Brussels, just the sort of people who, in Margaret Thatcher's eyes, ran the risk of 'going native'. I had the distinct feeling that it was as much for their benefit as for mine that, having completed the recording, with its brief comment on the single European currency, Mrs Thatcher's eyes began to swivel around the room as she prepared to speak. 'Do you think', she eventually thundered, 'that I have been elected Prime Minister to see the Queen's head removed from the United Kingdom's notes and coins? Most certainly not! Never! Never!'

*   *   *

Mrs Thatcher's presumption in appearing to speak at the summit for every major political party in Britain, let alone for every member of her own Cabinet, in declaring that Britain would never join the single currency hardly served to improve her relationship with Sir Geoffrey Howe. Inevitably, things went from bad to worse. There were increasingly frequent reports about the way that the Prime Minister was putting him down in front of colleagues, even during Cabinet meetings. One Minister told me at the time that things had become so dreadful that 'Margaret can scarcely bear to be in the same room as Geoffrey, let alone speak to him.' Finally, the inevitable explosion occurred.

The direct cause of that explosion was, equally inevitably, Europe, an area of policy which had already given the Conservatives years of grief, and which would continue to do so. As events surrounding the Madrid and Strasbourg summits had confirmed, Geoffrey Howe was a thoroughgoing, though far from starry-eyed, Euro-enthusiast. Margaret Thatcher was not. Nonetheless, as someone who believed it was better to fight from within rather than to surrender to any great displays of principle, he had remained publicly loyal, even when he was privately in almost total disagreement with his Leader. He had profoundly disagreed, for example, with the speech that Mrs Thatcher had delivered in Bruges in September 1988, in which she had sharply criticised the institutions of the European Community. As Foreign Secretary at the time, he had been sent a copy of the first draft. After reading it through, he had flung it down on his desk in a rare display of total fury, shouting, 'This is preposterous.' Publicly, though, he had held his peace. Now, however, things reached the point where he was able to do so no longer.

On Tuesday, 30 October 1990, Mrs Thatcher came to the House of Commons to report on the latest gathering of Europe's leaders. A special summit meeting had been held in Rome the previous weekend to discuss the future direction of Europe and, crucially, the next moves towards the introduction of the single currency. Word had already leaked out that Mrs Thatcher had said quite categorically, during the course of the deliberations at that summit, that Britain would never, ever agree to join such a currency. However much that echoed her private thoughts and opinions, as she had expressed them to me, for example, at the conclusion of the Strasbourg summit the previous December, her declaration in Rome meant that she had finally taken up a public position which went well beyond any agreed Cabinet policy.

There was, therefore, more than usual interest in Britain in what Mrs Thatcher would tell MPs about the Rome summit on her return from it, not least among those of us who were in our places in the Commons Press Gallery to hear it. Her prepared statement, delivered with Sir Geoffrey Howe sitting alongside her on the Government front bench, was moderate enough in tone. However, it only required a highly critical response to that statement by the Leader of the Opposition for that tone, and indeed her whole attitude, to change, almost in an instant. As she began her response to Neil Kinnock's remarks, we all sensed a very considerable change of gear. She openly attacked the President of the European Commission, Jacques Delors, a popular hate-figure among Tory Eurosceptics, since he was the author of the document which set out how the single currency would come about. It was, however, on plans for the political future of Europe, which Delors had also mapped out, that Mrs Thatcher most fiercely attacked the Commission President. He wanted three things, she said: the European Parliament to become the EC's democratic body, the Commission to be its executive, and the Council of Ministers to be its Senate. To such proposals, she had a simple reply: 'No! No! No!'

The Tory benches erupted with repeated shouts of 'Hear!

Hear!' and the waving of order papers, the wild enthusiasm of the sceptics easily cancelling out the clear discomfiture of the pro-Europeans. I watched Sir Geoffrey Howe. His face, I could clearly see, was frozen into a mask of horrified disapproval. Mrs Thatcher's 'No! No! No!' and the scenes in the Commons which they produced were immediately replayed again and again on every news bulletin, and formed, of course, a major part of my report on that night's *News at Ten*. Sir Geoffrey quickly sensed that his Leader had tapped what he regarded as a highly dangerous vein of hostility to Europe, which in his view would do irreparable damage if it were allowed to continue. He told a colleague, 'She'll get away with this if we don't stop her.'

Sir Geoffrey Howe decided, finally, that the only way of stopping Margaret Thatcher was to resign from the Government. He had come close to resignation three times before. He had considered it over the question of sanctions on South Africa, which Mrs Thatcher had refused to support. He had openly threatened the Prime Minister with his resignation in the run-up to the Madrid summit, and he had actually drafted a letter of resignation after he had been sacked as Foreign Secretary. Now he decided that it truly was the only course open to him. There was, however, a problem over when, exactly, he should resign. Parliament was about to go into recess before the start of a new session, and as Leader of the House of Commons he typically felt that he had a responsibility to see through the completion of all the outstanding business of the session. It was, therefore, two days after he had decided to resign that he actually did so.

Even then what happened would have been farcical had it not been so serious. At the end of each Parliamentary session, there is a formal, but very brief, ceremony called prorogation, by which proceedings are brought to a close, and which most

MPs ignore. As a result, it was possible on the day in question to see, in an almost completely deserted chamber, the Leader of the House of Commons, sitting silently on the government front bench beside the Prime Minister, with, unbeknown to her and the rest of us, a resignation letter in his pocket. Prorogation over, there was a meeting of the Cabinet at which Sir Geoffrey was forced to endure another humiliation, as Mrs Thatcher ticked him off in front of the rest of his Ministerial colleagues over preparations for the legislation to be included in the forthcoming Queen's speech.

With Cabinet over, Sir Geoffrey tried to arrange a private meeting with her, but was told that no such meeting was possible, even to discuss what he said was a personal and extremely important matter. It was only later, after an official in his office contacted an official in hers, explaining that the Deputy Prime Minister was about to resign and that he thought he ought to tell the Prime Minister why, that a meeting was finally arranged between them and he was able to do so.

Both of them quickly realised that there was nothing that could be said or done that would prevent his going. How bad things had become was later confirmed in Mrs Thatcher's memoirs when, giving her account of the events of the day, she wrote: 'In the Cabinet he was a force for obstruction, in the Party a focus of resentment, in the country a source of division. On top of all that, we found each other's company almost intolerable.' In his own memoirs, Sir Geoffrey gives a characteristically low-key version of events, in which he recounts how Mrs Thatcher had asked if there was anything she could do to make him change his mind. He replied by saying that he 'thought not', and records that 'the point was not seriously pursued'. Hardly surprising, in the circumstances.

As a result of the traditional short break which the Commons takes before the Queen's speech, it was not until almost a fortnight later that Sir Geoffrey exercised the right that all MPs have to make a personal statement to the House of Commons. It was, perhaps, just as well. In the interval, he lost his voice, and our cameras caught him outside his London home silently mouthing his unwillingness to talk. In fact, he turned down all requests for interviews, as he worked on his resignation speech.

What a speech it turned out to be – chiefly remembered for its references to 'broken bats' and the use of other cricketing terms in its savage criticism of Margaret Thatcher. It later emerged, however, that she herself had put the idea of using such phrases into Sir Geoffrey's head, because she had used similar terminology herself the night before. He had become aware of that after watching *News at Ten* the evening before he spoke in the Commons.

Until the programme was abolished, the timing of the speeches at the annual Lord Mayor's Banquet in London was always an advantage to ITN. Those speeches rarely begin until late in the evening, usually after the BBC's bulletin at 9 p.m., but in time for what was still our own main news bulletin. On this occasion, I had shown a defiant Prime Minister at the banquet, dressed in a full-length black and white dress, with a huge collar, which made her look like Queen Elizabeth I. In her speech, she insisted that she was 'still at the crease, though the bowling has been pretty hostile of late' – a clear reference to her Deputy's decision to quit, and the reasons for his departure that he had set out in his letter of resignation. She went on, however, in defiant tone: 'There will be no ducking bouncers, no stonewalling, no playing for time. The bowling's going to get hit all around the ground.'

In their London home, as Sir Geoffrey and his wife watched *News at Ten*, the cricketing terminology was certainly not lost on Lady Howe. She had not only played cricket at her school,

Wycombe Abbey, but had captained the school team and had continued to play the game as an active member of Reigate Ladies' Cricket Club. She remarked to her husband on Mrs Thatcher's turn of phrase. 'Ah, yes,' Sir Geoffrey had replied, 'but she's using a broken bat.'

In the Commons the following day, the thought re-emerged during his sustained attack on the Prime Minister. Once again, the chamber was absolutely packed, and so was the Press Gallery. Mrs Thatcher was in her place, after answering Prime Minister's Questions. She had been warned in general terms about what was coming next, and she stayed in her place to hear it. She was unable, however, even if she had wanted to, to turn to see Sir Geoffrey, who was speaking from the backbenches behind and to the right of her.

He began slowly and calmly, recalling what he and the Prime Minister had achieved together, but he soon moved to the question of Europe, and the way in which he believed Britain's dealings with Europe should be conducted. 'It is here', he said, 'that the Prime Minister risks leading herself and others astray in matters of substance, as well as of style.' The cricketing phraseology was soon used, to devastating effect. Sir Geoffrey turned to the handling of economic policy and suggested that the Prime Minister had constantly undermined the Chancellor and the Governor of the Bank of England in their conduct of it. 'It is rather like sending your opening batsmen to the crease,' he said, 'only for them to find, the moment the first balls are bowled, that their bats have been broken before the game by the team captain.' Later, I checked through the television pictures from the Commons. I noticed that David Sumberg, one of the Tory MPs sitting immediately behind Sir Geoffrey, could be seen to wince as those words were uttered.

As I watched the delivery of the speech from the Commons Press Gallery, I realised that the MPs below us were not the

only ones who had gasped at that phrase. Like my fellow
journalists all around me, I could not believe that the normally mild-mannered Sir Geoffrey was prepared to go this far
in attacking the Leader of his own party. My mind went back
to those scenes in Lusaka, when, severely provoked not once
but twice by President Kaunda, he had still remained calm.
Now, it was clear, Margaret Thatcher had goaded him
beyond endurance. He himself, I learnt later, had told his
advisers, as he worked on the speech, that it would only be
interpreted in one of two ways – as a damp squib or as a
savage attack. 'Let's go for savage attack,' he had told them.

How savage became even clearer as he continued to deliver
it. He spoke of the 'tragedy' that had resulted from Mrs
Thatcher's attitude to Europe, which had put Britain's future
more and more at risk. To an increasingly astonished House,
he declared that he had tried to uphold the idea of true
Cabinet government, or, as he put it, government by persuasion. 'I realise now that the task had become futile; trying to
stretch the meaning of words beyond what was credible, and
trying to pretend that there was a common policy when every
step forward risked being subverted by some casual comment
or impulsive answer.' That was immediately recognised not
just as a reference to the private battles around the Cabinet
table, but as a direct attack on the way Mrs Thatcher had
behaved at the European summit in Rome and in the House of
Commons after it. Finally, he spoke of the conflict between his
instinctive loyalty to his Prime Minister and his loyalty to his
country. He ended with these words: 'The time has come for
others to consider their own response to the tragic conflict of
loyalties, with which I have myself wrestled for perhaps too
long.'

The thoughtful, bitter and almost sorrowful end to the
speech left the House stunned into silence. Then a great
hubbub broke out, as everyone began comparing his or her

reactions with everyone else. My commentary on that night's *News at Ten* has, I believe, stood the test of time. 'So ended', I said, 'a truly astonishing speech – astonishing because the criticism of a serving Prime Minister was so clear, so savage. MPs with twenty-five years' or more experience are saying tonight', I continued, 'that they have never heard anything like it, and it is certain that many of them are rethinking their position concerning the Prime Minister, and what they will do in any leadership election.' The immediate thought was there – that Margaret Thatcher's position as Prime Minister had been put in extreme danger.

Among the journalists at Westminster, there was instant agreement on one point – that it was totally out of character for Sir Geoffrey to have behaved in such a fashion. Only the extent of the humiliation and hurt that Mrs Thatcher had heaped upon him, we believed, could explain the speech. In the light of the well-known antipathy between his wife and Margaret Thatcher, some commentators later called it 'Elspeth's Revenge', and suggested that Lady Howe had been behind the decision to make it. In fact she had, at first, gently counselled her husband to go quietly.

In any case, to seek such explanations is to misunderstand what lay behind the whole affair. Of course, he was angry at the way in which he had been treated, indeed humiliated, by Mrs Thatcher, but he was also convinced that Britain was being improperly governed, especially when it came to the question of our dealings with Europe. In his view, the Prime Minister's attitude meant that, as Europe began to rethink its future, Britain once again risked missing an historic opportunity to be part of the process. That, he believed, could profoundly damage the country. In a speech at the Conservative Party conference just weeks earlier, and in an interview with me at the time, he had used the familiar metaphor of the European train, once more leaving the station without Britain on board. For that, he placed the blame squarely at Margaret Thatcher's door, and he had no longer been able to prevent himself from saying so.

So often, in the years since those events, I heard people say that it was Michael Heseltine's challenge that brought down Margaret Thatcher. That is technically true, since it was his decision to oppose her for the leadership of the Conservative Party that led to her departure from Number Ten, but it was how all the leading pro-Europeans in the Party, and especially, those in the Cabinet, conducted themselves over a number of years that prepared the ice on which she would finally slip and fall. Michael Heseltine's resignation during the Westland affair started the process, and his eventual decision to challenge her in a leadership ballot completed it. However, with Mr Heseltine on the backbenches during the intervening period, it was Geoffrey Howe, working first with Nigel Lawson and then on his own, who played a role that was, in my view, ultimately more significant and decisive than Michael Heseltine's in bringing Margaret Thatcher down. The die was cast once he concluded that she had to be reined in and brought to account. At first, he tried, as always, to work from within. Sticking to his own high ideals and standards, he attempted to turn her back to traditional, middle-of-the-road, pro-European Conservatism. When that attempt finally failed, it was like watching a machine that was out of control. The public eruption of bitterness in his resignation speech set the wheels spinning. They could not be stopped until Margaret Thatcher resigned.

However, as Mrs Thatcher herself had acknowledged in her speech at the Lord Mayor's Banquet, with its reference to the 'fast bowling' she was facing, it was not just the problems of Europe which were crowding in upon her in the autumn of 1990. Since the general election, the deep public anger over the poll tax had grown and grown, and showed no signs of diminishing. Inflation and interest rates, and hence the cost of mortgages, had soared, as the so-called 'Lawson Boom' had been replaced by a serious downturn. In addition, Britain was once more at war, this time in the Gulf, after the invasion of Kuwait by the Iraqi leader Saddam Hussein, who had also taken a number of British hostages.

Mrs Thatcher had already faced one unprecedented challenge to her leadership of the Conservative Party, and thus to her position as Prime Minister. Under a set of recently revised rules, there was provision for such a challenge to take place at the beginning of every new Parliamentary session, and in the autumn of 1989 just such a challenge had been mounted. In the event, she easily saw off the bid to replace her by a stalking-horse candidate, the Tory MP Sir Anthony Meyer, by 314 votes to 33, though a further twenty-four ballot papers had been spoilt, and three votes had not been cast at all, including Michael Heseltine's.

Ever since, all eyes had been on Heseltine, still a backbencher after the Westland affair four years earlier, to see whether he would make a move against Mrs Thatcher. He continued to travel what is known as the 'rubber-chicken circuit', endlessly doing the rounds of Tory Party functions at constituency level, with the risk of being served a great deal of poor-quality food as he did so. The Tory faithful had not forgotten his annual bravura performances at the party conferences, and his travels were intended to keep that memory bright, against the day when he might need grass-roots support in any leadership bid. Every time, however, we asked him whether he *would* challenge the Prime Minister, he resorted to a carefully formulated stock answer, declaring that he could not foresee a situation in which that could possibly arise.

Now, in the aftermath of Sir Geoffrey Howe's resignation, that situation *had* arisen. Less than twenty-four hours after Sir

Geoffrey had spoken in the Commons, Michael Heseltine announced his intention to stand, which triggered the first ballot in another, and far more serious, leadership contest.

It is astonishing to realise now that, within the space of twenty-eight days, Britain had a new Prime Minister. Margaret Thatcher failed to win the first ballot of the leadership contest by just four votes. She was immediately persuaded by a majority of her Cabinet colleagues that she would not win the second ballot. John Major did win it, and succeeded her. The Conservative Party never recovered from the shock of getting rid of its most successful peacetime leader, and, looking back on the rush of events during that month, two impressions remain uppermost in my mind.

The first is how poorly organised the Thatcher campaign was, and how very different things might have been if she, and those who were in charge of it, had fought a better one. If just two people had voted for *her*, rather than for Michael Heseltine, in the first ballot, she would have survived, and would, at least, have had the chance of winning round her opponents during another year in office. Perhaps, though, the rot had set in too deeply. During a long interview, a year after she had ceased to be Prime Minister, I asked her about the leadership campaign, and why she had not made a much greater personal attempt to gather in the required support among backbench Conservative MPs. Her reply spoke volumes about what had gone wrong. 'Did they really expect me to go around begging for their votes?' she said. The answer is 'Yes, they did,' if only because they wanted assurances from her, personally, that things really would change.

Matters were left instead to her campaign managers, George Younger and Peter Morrison, who simply failed to mount the energetic campaign on her behalf that was required, or to give, on her behalf, the sort of assurances about the future that were needed. Mrs Thatcher herself did no canvassing in person in the Commons tea-room or the lobbies. She was clearly expecting that her record over eleven years would carry her through, supported by the instinctive loyalty of most Tories towards a Conservative Prime Minister. That certainly seems to have coloured her 'business as usual' decision to spend three days in Paris, at a summit meeting on European security, at a time when Michael Heseltine was seeking out every last vote. However, as Sir Geoffrey Howe's speech had specifically made clear, such instinctive loyalty towards her among Tory MPs, and any automatic respect among them for the fact that she was Prime Minister, could no longer be taken for granted.

My second and most lasting impression of events at that time is the sheer speed with which they moved, once Mrs Thatcher had failed, by four votes, to get the necessary margin of victory in the first ballot on the evening of Tuesday, 20 November. She herself had rushed out into the courtyard of the British Embassy in Paris to confirm that she would stand in the second round. Back in London on the Wednesday, she had paused on the steps of Number Ten, on her way to the Commons, to declare, 'I fight on, I fight to win.'

But by then she was in serious trouble. I spent a good deal of that Wednesday in the Members' Lobby, just outside the doors of the Commons chamber itself, talking to any and every Tory MP I encountered. Opinion was still divided as to whether she could, or indeed should, survive, but it was not difficult to find Conservative MPs ready to face our cameras, and to suggest that Margaret Thatcher should now step down. Michael Mates, Michael Heseltine's campaign manager, told us that Tory MPs who had voted for Mrs Thatcher in the first ballot were now promising to switch their votes to Heseltine in the second.

Ministers started the day by agreeing to stick to a line in public that they would support her if she fought on. That very morning, however, one former member of the Cabinet, who was still very much at the centre of things, told me that he felt support was simply ebbing away from her by the minute. One of Mrs Thatcher's entourage, Norman Tebbit, explicitly told me that 'some colleagues' were saying to her, 'Look, this is just too awful. You shouldn't have to go through this and we would entirely understand if you were to walk away from it.' But he immediately rejected any suggestion that he himself was being disloyal. There was, he said, a problem. If there was to be a second ballot, was there a candidate who could defeat Heseltine? In his view there was not, and that meant that support should flow back to Mrs Thatcher, 'because, actually, you see, the party doesn't want Mr Heseltine.'

With hindsight, it is now clear that he was right about Heseltine, but wrong to hope, or expect, that Mrs Thatcher could survive simply because of the lack of a suitable candidate to oppose her. Other Tories, whose views I respected, told me throughout the day that she could and would survive in any case. Heavyweight support did still seem to be there. Douglas Hurd had agreed to propose her in the second ballot, and John Major, suffering dental problems at his home near Huntingdon, sent a handwritten note out to our reporter waiting in the road outside confirming that he would be seconding her if she decided to stand.

Gradually, though, word began to leak out that Mrs Thatcher's position was increasingly being questioned within the party. She was indeed talking to 'colleagues', as Norman Tebbit had suggested. She was, in fact, taking soundings from each member of the Cabinet about her chances. That led me to say on *News at Ten* that night: 'Mrs Thatcher is, indeed, for now, fighting on, but she is also continuing to take her own soundings, throughout the party, about her position.'

Just before 9.30 a.m. on Thursday, 21 November 1990, Margaret Thatcher resigned. I was on my way into Westminster with the car radio on when the newsflash came through. I nearly drove off the Hammersmith flyover as a result. It is easy to think now that I should not have been so surprised, given the fact that Mrs Thatcher had taken the decision to go, in principle, the night before, and that my opposite number on the BBC, John Cole, had already hinted at her departure. But news of her face-to-face meetings with the members of the Cabinet had only emerged slowly. Things did not leak from the Thatcher Downing Street to anything like the same extent as they did under subsequent occupants.

With the official news of her resignation, the ITV network took a brave and unusual decision. Plans had been made for some time, under the code-name 'Operation Open Ender', to switch the entire network to ITN for continuous live broadcasting in the case of a major national event, which, indelicately but practically, we always assumed would be the death of the Queen Mother. Now, suddenly, ITN was to go 'open ended' to cover a major political story as it unfolded.

One of ITN's political correspondents, Jackie Ashley, was already on duty at Westminster, and, as we went on the air at 10 a.m., it was she who appeared from our 'live' position on Abingdon Green, a patch of grass just across the road from the Commons, which the BBC and many MPs insist on calling College Green. ITN had rushed an extra news editor, Sandy Macintyre, to Westminster from our Gray's Inn Road headquarters in Holborn to help out on what was plainly going to be a very hectic day. As Jackie kept things going during the opening minutes of the broadcast by repeating the few details we had from Number Ten, Sandy set off to scour the area for possible interviewees. What followed was a wonderful reminder that, even at moments of high seriousness, moments of high farce are never far away.

Sandy spotted a distinguished-looking gentleman emerging from St Stephen's entrance, which allows public access to both the House of Commons and the House of Lords. He looked vaguely familiar, at least, to Sandy who was pretty certain that he was a Tory MP. He certainly looked the part, and on that basis Sandy swiftly told him the news of Mrs Thatcher's resignation, and asked him whether he would agree to an immediate live interview. 'Well, if you really want me,' came the reply. 'I'm a Conservative peer, you know.'

During the short walk from St Stephen's to Abingdon Green, the interviewee-to-be gently mentioned his status in life twice more to Sandy Macintyre. Sandy, however, mindful that Jackie Ashley's solo performance could not last much longer, was not going to let some tiny detail like the interviewee's precise identity stand in the way of getting someone else, indeed anyone else, in front of the camera. Thus it was that, once his Lordship was wired up to enable him to hear the questions that would be put to him from the studio, he could also hear the programme director shouting down the line, 'Who is he? Does anyone know? Isn't he that Tory MP Sir Marcus Fox?'

'They seem to think I'm Marcus Fox,' our increasingly bewildered guest said to Sandy Macintyre, still standing beside him on Abingdon Green. 'Let me give you my card, so that you've got the details of exactly who I am.' With just seconds to go before the interview began, Sandy glanced down at it and decided it was going to be simpler to leave both the programme director and indeed the nation in blissful ignorance as to why we had selected this particular interviewee. On the card were the words 'Lord Newall, Chairman, British Greyhound Racing Board'.

We reported the rest of that day's events without further hiccups, during some six hours of continuous live broadcasting. There was much to tell. There was all the reaction, as the nation's politicians, and many others, responded to the enormity of what had happened. There were also all the events that were still taking place in Downing Street and, later, in the House of Commons.

After an emotional Cabinet meeting, John Wakeham, who just the day before had been appointed Margaret Thatcher's campaign manager in readiness for a second-ballot contest, came out into Downing Street to confirm that she had indeed met most of the Cabinet face to face the previous evening. 'The one thing that is certain', he said, 'is that every member of the Cabinet would have voted for her in the next round, but there were differing views as to what her chances of winning the ballot were. She listened to them all, and decided that this was the best way forward.'

I asked John Wakeham, 'Was she told point-blank that she could not hope to win?' 'By some people certainly,' he replied. 'But some people thought she could win, and some people thought it was her duty to stay on. She listened to them all, and came finally to this conclusion.' The Environment Secretary at the time, Chris Patten, was one of those who told ITN that he would have voted for her on the second ballot, but had advised her that she would not win it.

Later, Mrs Thatcher herself emerged into the street, which was packed as never before with journalists and photographers, cameras and microphones, as she left for an audience with the Queen before her appearance in the House of Commons. Even though she had effectively announced her resignation by making it clear that she would not stand in the second ballot, that resignation would not take place until her successor had been chosen. That meant that there would not be the usual instant and brutal changeover of Prime Ministers at Number Ten, which is normally one of the curiosities of British political life. It was decided that she would not actually leave office for another six days. She was therefore in the Commons that afternoon, not just for the regular Thursday session of Prime Minister's Questions, which were still held twice-weekly at the time, but also to speak in a 'no confidence' debate, which had been secured several days earlier by the Opposition.

Once again, less than two weeks after the high drama of Sir Geoffrey Howe's speech, the chamber and the Press Gallery were packed to capacity, to witness another extraordinary event. An Ulster Unionist MP said that he knew what she was going through 'because we know what betrayal means'. Neil Kinnock said that by stepping down she had shown 'that she amounts to more than those who have turned against her'.

The afternoon effectively became Mrs Thatcher's personal resignation statement to the House, though delivered within the context of a formal reply to the Opposition's censure motion. As a result, she was able to spend some time defending her record, during which the Labour MP Dennis Skinner, with his usual brand of downbeat humour, decided to intervene. With tongue firmly in cheek given Margaret Thatcher's hatred of the idea of the single European currency, he suggested that she might now go off and become the head of the European Central Bank, presumably on the assumption that she would wreck it. 'What a good idea!' came the reply, as wave upon wave of laughter broke around the chamber. 'I hadn't thought of it,' she continued. 'But, if I were, there'd be no Central Bank accountable to no one, least of all to national parliaments.' She went on in the same vein, railing against the idea of the single currency at the top of her voice, for a couple more minutes, before declaring, 'I'm enjoying this. I'm enjoying this!' My comment on *News at Ten* that night: 'Some Tories would say that it is because she so often talked like that about Europe that she's got, ultimately, into so much trouble. But not even they would deny that, if that was her swan-song, it was quite a performance.'

*   *   *

For me personally, there was an astonishing sequel to all this. For all the fire and passion of many of her political utterances, Margaret Thatcher was not a woman who readily showed private emotion in public. There had been some brief glimpses of the softer side of her nature, but they were rare. One such moment had occurred, to be sure, after the birth of her first grandchild. A tip-off from a friend at Conservative Central Office to our newsdesk assistant at Westminster, Anne Lingley, meant that we had rushed a camera round to Downing Street. There we saw Mrs Thatcher, flushed with pride, emerge through the famous front door, not to declare some momentous matter of state, but to utter the words, 'We are a grandmother.'

We had seen her come close to tears in public when her son Mark had gone missing during a car rally across the Sahara Desert. When she left Number Ten for the very last time, six days after her resignation, on her way to Buckingham Palace to take her leave of the Queen, the whole country had seen her struggling to maintain her composure. Taking the few short steps to her car, her face had finally crumpled with grief. As the car made off, she could be seen, staring out, her eyes red-rimmed with tears. Such public displays of her feelings, however, had been extremely rare.

Six months after her resignation, Mrs Thatcher agreed to an exclusive interview with ITN, on the day when she announced that she would not be seeking re-election as an MP. This was the old Thatcher, with whom we were all familiar. During the course of the interview, she stated once again, and with her usual vigour, her total opposition to the idea of a single European currency. She also indicated that she expected to be in a position to carry on with her political life once she had been given a seat in the House of Lords. That particular piece of news emerged after I had asked her whether she would miss the House of Commons after so

With ITN's Foreign Editor, John Mahoney, at the 1976 Democratic Convention in New York. John's smile had been less broad when he discovered, on his arrival from London, that my right leg was heavily encased in plaster.

As ITN's Washington correspondent, I covered every kind of story. Here I had just filmed the ladies of Memphis, Tennessee who, despite their bible-belt upbringing, had taken up belly dancing.

I was only filmed once, to the best of my knowledge, in shorts. Here I was describing the RAF staging post on the Indian Ocean island of Gan during a 1972 Royal Tour – the pictures produced hoots of derisive laughter when viewed in London.

An interview in April 1975 with Prince Charles, conducted on the ice in the Canadian Arctic. Despite the unusual location, we discussed the possible abdication of the Queen.

Reporting from the Chinese capital, Beijing, in 1979. There was huge interest
in the so-called Democracy Wall, on which the authorities allowed, for a brief
period, the display of protest posters.

On location in Hong Kong, reporting on the difficult negotiations before Britain
handed the colony back to China in 1997.

My career as an ITN newscaster in the early 1980s was brief and unsuccessful. The tensed-up shoulders and the frightened look probably explain why.

An interview with President Mitterrand of France in October 1984, before his visit to London. The interpreter in the centre proved indispensable – the President did not speak English.

After an interview with the Foreign Secretary and former Chancellor of the Exchequer, Sir Geoffrey Howe in 1986. He had just acquired a new Yorkshire terrier called Summit, to replace an earlier one called Budget.

The tiny press cabin at the back of the RAF VC-10 regularly used by Mrs Thatcher during her many trips abroad. The conditions were not improved by RAF regulations that meant that we always flew facing backwards.

One of the strangest of Mrs Thatcher's many photo-opportunities during the 1979 general election – stroking a calf in a field near Ipswich as she conducted an impromptu news conference.

An early interview with the new Prime Minister John Major aboard a chartered jumbo jet. Such interviews cannot be shown at any length – the aircraft noise is simply too intrusive.

Before any Prime Ministerial interview, there is a great deal of fussing. Here, John Major gets a last minute briefing from his Press Secretary, Gus O'Donnell while ITN make-up assistant Joan Watson attends to me.

Interviewing Margaret Thatcher in November 1991, exactly a year after her departure from 10 Downing Street. Recalling those events was still painful for her and brought tears to her eyes.

Working conditions are not always ideal. Lack of desk space and noisy colleagues in our temporary offices forced me outside during one of the party political conferences in Blackpool.

Reporting the Maastricht summit in December 1991. It was bitterly cold and the communications broke down – contact with London during one broadcast depended on attaching my earpiece to the local telephone.

many years. She had, in typical fashion, replied that of course she would miss the Commons, but she went on to drop what she openly called 'more than a little hint' that she would like a seat in the Upper House.

However, exactly a year after her resignation, she agreed to a second exclusive interview, and here we saw a rather different side of her nature. Once again, the guard was to drop, to reveal her emotional side. One of Thatcher's Laws of Politics – 'the unexpected always happens' – was most assuredly about to come into play.

We met, to pre-record the interview, in the tiny but elegant townhouse close to the Houses of Parliament which her friend Lord McAlpine had lent her and where she had set up her office. I began by saying that she had never spoken in any detail about the precise events of the day, exactly a year before, on which she had resigned. I asked her to do so, beginning with what I suggested must have been a very difficult meeting of the Cabinet.

'Yes, of course it was,' she said. 'You don't take a decision like that without it being difficult, without heartbreak.' She went on to explain that it had, nonetheless, been the right decision, though I reminded her that she had actually broken down during that meeting around the Cabinet table. 'Yes,' she replied, 'but I carried on.' There was a long pause, as she appeared to bring it all back to mind. I broke the pause, reminding her that she had gone on to give a brave display in the House of Commons, which had included her exchange with Dennis Skinner. Her face broke into a smile. 'By that time, I was back, fighting fit.' There was another substantial pause. 'As you saw,' she added, leaning forward in her seat to emphasise the point.

The emotional strain of remembering that day seemed to have passed, but something made me take her back a step or two, to return to the precise moment when she had left

Downing Street that day to make her way across to the Commons. 'As you said,' I continued, 'the Cabinet was extremely difficult, and then you had to come out into Downing Street to face the cameras, in effect to face the world.' As I had started to utter those words, I noticed that her expression was changing once more and that her eyes had begun to fill with tears. While I was still speaking, she reached for a tissue to wipe those tears away. Something on such occasions, perhaps just long experience, comes to your assistance. I broke off to say, 'I see now . . . we notice that now, it's affecting you . . .'

She quickly regained control, though her eyes were still moist. 'Yes.' Then, after the briefest of pauses, she added, 'It's not affecting my voice now.' Then, in case anyone should think she had lost control, she said again, 'It's not affecting my voice.' She had recovered, though only just, I sensed. As though to explain why she had let her emotion show, she continued, 'You're thinking back to traumatic things. But I managed to get through them. I managed to get through the television, I managed to get through the Cabinet' – again, a pause, and then, with more heavy emphasis – 'because there was *so much to do*.'

We continued with the interview, but after a few minutes more the tape cassette ran out, and she knew it would take a minute or two to replace it with a new one. That was the moment when she quietly excused herself, to slip out for a moment to repair the damage to her make-up.

There were brief interviews later, notably when her two volumes of memoirs were published. There were her various speeches to report, both in the Lords and outside it, in which she clearly showed her disapproval of what she regarded as John Major's weakness and indecision on Europe. Nothing, though, was quite the equal of that emotional interview, one year on from her resignation. After so many years of reporting her activities, I had seen the Iron Lady with her defences down. She had shown that she was, after all, only human.

Those rare signs of human weakness, however, have done little to change the view that many people have formed of Margaret Thatcher. It is, indeed, almost impossible to be neutral about her. She evoked, and continues to evoke, black-and-white reactions. She is either a heroine or a hate-figure, which is why people who have never met her often want to compare their own perceptions of her with someone like myself who has. 'What was she really like?' they constantly ask. 'Did you get on with her?'

I admired her single-mindedness into setting about what she wanted to achieve for Britain. By 1979, James Callaghan's Labour Government had been ground down by the consequences of its failure to manage the economy properly, and the rise of union militancy which that helped to produce. It took Mrs Thatcher time to hit her stride, but the period from 1981 to 1986 were years of strong government, to which the country responded, particularly in 1983 when she was returned for a second term in office with an enormous majority.

I accept that, to many people, she was known as 'That Bloody Woman', and that she came across as an abrasive know-all or a bossy headmistress, or worse. On a personal level, she could certainly treat people very badly. At a joint press conference that she held with President Mitterrand of France after a summit meeting in London, I found myself standing next to a young woman from an American TV network. This young lady had plainly been told by her office in the United States to try and get a response from Mrs Thatcher on some foreign policy matter, unrelated to Anglo-French relations, and she tried to ask a question about that. 'Now just sit down, dear, and be quiet,' came the icy response. 'Everyone else has managed to stick to the rules except you.' It was a quite unnecessary public humiliation of a young journalist who was simply trying to do her job.

Over the years, I noticed that Mrs Thatcher would often react very badly to people she did not know, which led to accusations that she had her favourites. I believe it was more a case of her feeling that she needed to be sure about people, but once she had formed a positive view about someone she could be almost alarmingly friendly and helpful. On one occasion, when relations between Jordan and the Palestinians were in crisis, journalists were pursuing King Hussein across London, and he had refused all comment. I decided to try and interview him as he emerged from Ten Downing Street after a meeting there – another classic 'doorstep'. In those days, we were allowed to stand quite close to the front door, and as the King emerged and made a beeline for his car, Mrs Thatcher spotted me out of the corner of her eye. 'Oh, your Majesty,' she called out. 'Just one moment. I think Michael Brunson of ITN wants to speak to you. Could you just have a word with him?' The King did just that.

Towards the end of her time as Prime Minister, Margaret Thatcher lost her way. At Conservative Central Office in May 1987, on the night that she won her third term in office, she delivered the customary victory message. She spoke from a position halfway up the building's main staircase. Ranged below her were party workers, other supporters and a number of journalists, including myself. Her first remarks were addressed to those who had helped her win. She thanked them, and told them that they could celebrate and have the weekend off, but that she expected them back at work on Monday morning, since there was much to do. 'Now, we really must do something about the inner cities,' she suddenly, and unexpectedly, announced. It was a rare acknowledgement, I sensed, from a leader who had once declared, 'There is no such thing as society – only men and women and families', that the onward rush of Thatcherism was leaving too many people behind.

But she failed to follow through on the problem. Little was done which the less advantaged could perceive as helping them. Indeed, the poll tax and the recession of the late 1980s, the second during her term of office, only served to convince them that Mrs Thatcher's version of Conservatism meant that the rich simply got richer and the poor got poorer. In her last years in office, she seemed to lose her greatest asset – the ability to sense and to act on what the majority of ordinary people really wanted. She used to call it 'working with the grain of the people'; she no longer appeared to be doing so.

In her most confident years in Number Ten, 'working with the grain of the people' led her to truly radical action, like the sale of council houses to sitting tenants and the decision to face down Arthur Scargill and the miners. She was bitterly attacked, indeed reviled, for both courses of action. She was convinced, however, that she had public opinion with her. At the height of the miners' strike, a man was killed after a concrete beam had been thrown off a road bridge at his car. That morning she was in Paris for another meeting with President Mitterrand, and in the courtyard of the Elysée Palace I asked her about the incident. I suggested that, with such dreadful things happening, the time had come to seek a negotiated end to the dispute. Her eyes blazed and her gaze darkened. 'Mr Brunson,' she almost hissed at me, 'you never, ever, give way to violence. Never.' On that, as on so many other issues, she was utterly certain that she had judged the mood of the country correctly. No other politician or trade union leader or journalist was going to shake her from that belief. Such single-minded conviction is fine when you get things right. Margaret Thatcher's remarkable premiership showed how dangerous and disastrous it can be when you don't.

CHAPTER TEN

'What Would You Do, Michael?':
John Major and the Bastards

S oon after John Major became Chief Secretary to the
Treasury in 1987, we met for dinner in a rather pre-
tentious hotel near the House of Commons. Though
the food is nothing special, the establishment in question does
tend to adorn the table with an impressive array of cutlery and
a cluster of crystal wine glasses, doubtless to tempt its clientele
into ordering ever more extravagant meals. As we sat down,
John Major noticed me fiddling with the place setting. 'Oh,'
he exclaimed, 'I'm so glad that someone else is as baffled as I
am about which knife and fork to use!'

It was a trivial remark, but one which immediately struck
me as puzzling. At that time, I did not know him at all well,
which was the main reason why I had suggested that we
should get together for a meal. My automatic assumption was
that, as an MP and a Minister, he would be far more
accustomed to the formalities of the dinner table than I.
But no – here was the immediate indication of a plain,
straightforward man to whom formal behaviour of any kind
did not come easily, someone in whom a whole series of
contradictions seemed to be in almost continual conflict.

Faced with a momentous event, he had a famously deadpan

style. Opening his very first Cabinet meeting after his victory in the leadership election, he simply declared, 'Who would have thought it?' Three months later, in February 1991, the IRA tried to kill as many Ministers as possible by firing three mortar bombs from Whitehall towards the back of Number Ten. A meeting of the Gulf War Cabinet was in progress, which came to an abrupt halt as windows in the Cabinet Room were blown in by the blast from the only bomb that exploded, which had landed in the garden outside. After getting up off the floor, to which a private secretary had forced him for safety, John Major simply said, 'I think we'd better start again somewhere else.'

The attack took place during a heavy snowstorm, which resulted, incidentally, in the only broadcast I ever did while wearing a hat. We had quickly set up live commentary points as close to Downing Street as the police would allow, but a trial run showed that the snow was falling so fast that it was settling on my eyebrows and other parts of my face. A battered pork-pie hat, which I carried in my pocket for emergencies, was pressed into service. It may have looked odd, but not quite as odd as a talking snowman.

John Major could be extremely charming, particularly to those he met for the first time, and especially to women. On other occasions, however, he could display flashes of real anger, and not just in private. In February 1993, as Prime Minister, he was visiting Washington at a difficult time in Anglo-American relations, and had managed, somewhat against the odds, to have a successful first meeting with President Clinton. But during the visit some extremely poor employment figures, likely to damage economic confidence in Britain, had been published back home, and it was on those that I pressed him during an end-of-visit interview at which a number of other journalists were present.

As soon as we stopped recording, he began a blistering

tirade, accusing the British media in general, and myself in particular, of running down Britain and making the prospects for economic recovery more difficult. 'You talk about confidence,' he told me, 'but you spend half your time wrecking it by projecting the negative side of things all the time.' This, it was clear, was far more than another of those run-of-the-mill moans which all politicians have about the way they are reported. This was a Prime Minister who was just very, very angry and who did not care who knew it. Over the years, behind the closed doors of Number Ten, plenty of others were to experience the sharpness of his tongue, so much so that one member of his Cabinet once told him to his face, 'Prime Minister, I sometimes think that you don't know who your friends really are.'

Yet, just five months earlier, I had seen exactly the opposite side of his nature. For a time in 1992, while improvements were being made to the security of Number Ten in the wake of the IRA mortar attack, John Major was forced to work in the Old Admiralty building near the top of Whitehall. It was there that he had arranged to hold talks late in the evening with the Danish Prime Minister, Poul Schlouter, on European Community business, at a time when the crescendo of Euroscepticism among his own backbenchers was beginning to make an impact. Just a few hours earlier, he had been in Paris for a similar meeting with the French Prime Minister.

The temporary arrangements in the small courtyard of the Old Admiralty building meant that arrangements for the coverage of the Danish Premier's visit, which was taking place while *News at Ten* was on the air, were rather more chaotic than is normal. So, as a result, was my live broadcast from the scene, which involved, at one point, the need to step very smartly out of the way of Mr Schlouter's departing car. The somewhat nerve-racking broadcast over, I was preparing to leave when the Prime Minister's Deputy Press Secretary,

Jonathan Haslam, came over. Would I like to come in and have a word with him? Taken somewhat by surprise, I muttered that yes, I would indeed, wondering if something that I had just said was the reason for the summons.

Once inside, it was immediately clear that Major simply wanted to talk, despite the fact that he was clearly tired at the end of a very long day. Indeed, as our conversation began, one of his officials came in to enquire whether various members of the Private Office, who had already been to Paris and back with him that morning and were still on duty, could leave and catch up on some sleep. The answer was a surprisingly firm 'No'.

He and I sat side by side on a long sofa, and he came immediately to the point. 'What would you do, Michael, if you were in my position over the backbenchers and Europe?' Being asked so direct a question, coming on top of my initial surprise that this was all happening anyway, left me momentarily speechless. Eventually, I managed to suggest that he should make his own position on Europe and the single currency very clear, and then tell those backbenchers who had been expressing a contrary view that, as Leader of the party, he expected them to fall in behind it. 'That is exactly what I do,' he replied. 'And they all promise me to my face that they will support me. And then, the moment they're out of the room, they go and do exactly the opposite.'

This, I sensed, was a Prime Minister in despair, simply wanting someone to listen and to understand his position as he got things off his chest. Almost a year previously, during the negotiations over the Maastricht Treaty, he had negotiated an opt-out for Britain. That had meant that Britain would not be forced to join the single European currency, and that any future British membership would take place only when Parliament had decided that it was the right thing to do. On the day after he got back from the negotiations, Margaret

Thatcher was at an evening party and she was asked how he had done. 'Brilliantly,' was her reply.

Yet, by the time of our conversation, things had gone seriously wrong. A hundred of his own backbenchers had signed what became known as the 'Fresh Start' Parliamentary motion, making clear their opposition to any closer ties with Europe. In mid-September 1992, the Eurosceptics were hugely encouraged by the result of a referendum in France on the Maastricht Treaty, which the French people only approved by the narrowest of margins, 51 per cent in favour and 49 per cent against. On the Wednesday before that result, Britain had been forced to leave the Exchange Rate Mechanism. The fact that the Chancellor, Norman Lamont, had not resigned, and that the Prime Minister had not asked him to, created further controversy. Just one week after 'Black Wednesday' (which the Eurosceptics insisted on calling 'White Wednesday', so great was their relief at our leaving the ERM), the Heritage Secretary, David Mellor, was forced to resign. John Major and I had talked a week later.

He later described that autumn as 'the worst period by far' of his time in office. We now know that, during it, he repeatedly raised the possibility of resigning as Prime Minister with several of his colleagues, including at least one member of the Cabinet. At one point he actually drafted the text of a resignation broadcast. The pressure on him was enormous, and it showed.

Throughout his premiership, though, he was like the Grand Old Duke of York. When he was up, he was up, and when he was down, he was down. When he was in a good mood, he would show it, often physically, putting an arm around the shoulder of those close to him, giving the ladies a kiss, and using both his hands for a handshake. On one occasion, on a visit to ITN's headquarters building, he was enjoying a pre-lunch drink with a number of my colleagues. He spotted me and, noticing that I had lost a good deal of weight, gave me a playful punch in the stomach. 'Ah, the new slimline Brunson, I see!' he exclaimed.

But in his blackest hours, and there were many of those, he could become the very picture of misery, his gaze distant, his conversation snappy, his tone of voice angry, though he tried not to be deliberately discourteous. He was, however, a man who very noticeably wore his heart on his sleeve.

That helps to explain how the incident that became known as 'Bastardgate', in which I was deeply involved, came about. The phrase was used by some of the newspapers to describe John Major's off-camera outburst, immediately after I had completed an interview with him, against the leading Eurosceptics in his Cabinet. It was an extraordinary episode, which produced banner headlines, rumbled on for days and, for a short time, had one national newspaper offering a phone-in service to let people hear for themselves what had actually been said.

The context of it all is important. The battle with the Eurosceptics, which had already helped to bring the Prime Minister to the point of considering resignation in the autumn of 1992, had ground on, fuelled by endless debate in the Commons, as MPs fought over the Bill to ratify the Maastricht Treaty. A series of close votes had finally resulted in the high drama, on the night of Thursday, 22 July 1993, of the declaration of a tied result, 317–317, an event which was carried live on *News at Ten*. In accordance with the usual convention of the House of Commons, the tie was resolved by the casting vote of the Speaker in favour of the Government. It was, however, revealed the following day, after a more thorough check of the Commons' ludicrously antiquated voting system, that the Government had actually won by one vote anyway.

It was, incidentally, one of those occasions when *News at*

Ten had come into its own. I never believed that the happy and frequent coincidence of important Commons votes taking place at precisely the same time as ITN's flagship news bulletin was the chief reason for keeping it in its traditional place. Over the years, however, the timing frequently gave us the edge over the BBC, and that advantage was certainly one reason for not shifting the bulletin willy-nilly. On the night in question, we were also able to report that the Government had been defeated on a second 'take-note' vote, and to hear the Prime Minister forestall the obvious attempt by the Opposition to force an immediate vote of confidence by announcing one himself for the following day.

The next day, with the Commons sitting in the morning and early afternoon, as it does on Fridays, John Major won the confidence vote handsomely, and then, like Prime Ministers before and after him, decided to reinforce his victory by giving a series of television interviews. So the cameras were called in to Downing Street at around four o'clock on the afternoon of Friday, 23 July, so that interviews could be recorded, not just for the main television and radio news bulletins, but for *Channel Four News* and *Newsnight* too. In my case he agreed to two interviews – a short one that could be turned around quickly for use on ITN's early-evening news at 5.40 p.m., and, after everyone else had finished, a second, longer interview for *News at Ten*.

This is where the context is important for all that happened subsequently. He himself was on something of a personal high. He immediately saw that afternoon's confidence vote, and the winning margin of thirty-eight, as the end of a long and dark chapter, settling, for the time being at least, the question of whose view of Europe would prevail in the Conservative Parliamentary party – his or the Eurosceptics'.

I, however, was not alone among his questioners that day in suggesting to him that it had been a matter of some desperation that he had been forced to fire the 'Big Bertha' gun of a confidence vote, after the defeats and narrow victories of the previous months and days. At a moment of considerable personal satisfaction for him, here was a string of journalists, myself among them, trying, yet again, to belittle his achievement. He was 'up', and we were trying to do him down.

So, as he relaxed after the last interview – the one for *News at Ten* – the Prime Minister quickly cut through the small talk which I had begun about the forthcoming summer recess. He took off the small microphone which had been clipped to his tie for the interview, clearly signalling that he regarded anything that followed as a reasonably private conversation, though there were still a number of people in the room, including his Press Secretary, Gus O'Donnell, my producer from ITN, Sue Tinson, and various technicians from the BBC, who had provided the facilities on a 'pool' basis. He then said, 'What I don't understand, Michael, is why such a complete wimp like me keeps winning everything.'

It was a typical John Major remark, provocative, full of irony and made only half in jest. It was clearly intended to show his irritation at the spin I and others had put on what he regarded as an important political victory, and his annoyance at the way so many of his own backbenchers had been running him down for so long. My immediate reaction was to reassure him that he had made the point about his significant win quite clear in the interview, but, as the conversation continued, I responded to his point by saying, 'The trouble is that people are not *perceiving* you as winning.'

'Oh, I know. Why not?' he said. I thought I would pre-empt what I reckoned would be his own answer by replying, 'Because rotten sons of bitches like me, I suppose, don't get the message clear.'

In the spirit of that exchange, we both laughed, with John Major replying, 'No, no, no. I wasn't going to say that.' He did continue, though, by adding, 'Well, partly that, yes, because of S-H-one-Ts like you. Yes, that's perfectly right!'

The conversation might have ended there, but it did not. Once again, as had happened during our late-evening talk in Old Admiralty House, he seemed anxious to carry on the exchange. It was as though he wanted to talk to someone beyond his everyday circle of advisers, to get things off his chest, in order to underline his original point about the significant victory he had just won. The reason his message was being obscured, he said, was because those on his own side, who were opposed to Government policy, were using the same tactics as the Opposition and were making deliberate, personal attacks on him. That is how, as we talked on, the question of his style of leadership came up.

I mentioned the way he had dealt with another problem a month earlier. The Conservative MP and junior Northern Ireland Minister Michael Mates had eventually resigned over the issue of his relationship with the fugitive businessman Asil Nadir. The matter had begun trivially enough, with the revelation that, at the height of his difficulties, Mates had sent his constituent Nadir a watch inscribed with the words, 'Don't let the bastards get you down.' The matter had dragged on for several days, before Mates had been forced to quit.

I told John Major that, at the time, I had heard members of his own Cabinet asking why he hadn't sacked Mates on day one. 'Mates was a fly,' I said, with a swatting motion of my hand. 'You could have swatted him away.' That remark, incidentally, led to the delivery to my office a day or two later of a plastic fly-swatter from Michael Mates, with a none-too-complimentary message attached.

Responding, the Prime Minister said that, at the time, his Cabinet colleagues were certainly not telling *him* to take decisive action over Michael Mates, or David Mellor, or over the European issue generally, and that the whole conduct of

government business was made much more difficult by his
tiny majority. 'I could have done these clever and decisive
things that people wanted me to do, and I would have split the
Conservative Party into smithereens,' he continued, 'and you
would have said, "Aren't you a ham-fisted leader. You've
broken up the Conservative Party." ' It was a familiar argument. He had always maintained that holding the party
together was the number-one priority, and that such a priority
ruled out decisive showdowns, though two years later things
reached the point where he judged that only a showdown – his
shock resignation as party Leader to force a 'Who's the boss?'
contest – could resolve things.

Now, as we spoke inside Number Ten, in July 1993, I gently
suggested to him that a showdown with the three Eurosceptics
in his Cabinet was the only answer. I had in mind, though did
not name, Peter Lilley, Michael Portillo and John Redwood. A
full account of our conversation, published some days later in
the London *Evening Standard*, suggests that, at this point, both
of us knew we were in difficult territory. The *Standard* account
describes me as 'talking quietly to avoid being overheard, and
looking around the room.' I said: 'Three of them – perhaps we
had better not mention open names in this room – perhaps, if
you'd done certain things, the three of them would have come
along and said, "Prime Minister, we resign." So you say, "Fine,
you resign." '

John Major later wrote in his memoirs that he had no
particular Ministers in mind during our conversation, but at
this point, as the transcript confirms, he said to me, 'We all
know which three that is.' After a pause, he continued, 'Now
think that through. You are Prime Minister. You have got a
majority of eighteen. You have got a party still harking back
to a golden age that never was, but is now invented. And you
have three right-wing members of the Cabinet actually resigned. What happens in the Parliamentary party?'

'They create a lot of fuss,' I replied, 'but you could have probably got three damn good Ministers into the Cabinet to replace them.'

'Oh, I can bring other people into the Cabinet, that is right,' he said, 'but where do you think most of this poison has come from? It is coming from the dispossessed and the never-possessed. You and I can think of ex-Ministers who are going around causing all sorts of trouble. Would you like three more of the bastards out there?'

So there it was. The British Prime Minister had used the 'B-word' about three members of his own Cabinet. It was not, therefore, so very surprising that, when this became public knowledge, it caused an almighty stir. But the plain fact is that neither John Major nor I expected, as we spoke, that our conversation would remain anything but private. Neither of us knew, at the time, that every word we had spoken had been secretly recorded.

Over the years, I had had countless conversations with all kinds of people after the formalities of an interview had been completed. On all those occasions, a formal 'thank you' from me, and the relaxation of the crew, as they no longer operated their equipment, was the clear signal to the interviewee that what was being said 'on the record' had come to an end. According to the usual conventions, anything that was spoken subsequently was to be regarded either as 'off the record' or, with politicians, as being on Lobby terms – for use as background information, but not for quotation or attribution.

On this occasion, technology, and some questionable behaviour by the BBC, had betrayed us. Most of my interviews were conducted using an ITN video crew under my direction, with the interview being recorded in the camera, for later use. On this occasion, to avoid a large number of crews being brought into Downing Street, the BBC had been designated as the 'pool provider' of facilities for all the television broadcasters. It was therefore two BBC cameras that had produced the pictures of my questions and the Prime Minister's answers. It was a couple of BBC microphones that had picked up the sound. And it was the BBC's video recorders in a truck full of technical equipment, stationed on Horse Guards Parade, just the other side of the wall surrounding the Downing Street garden, which had recorded my interviews.

I do not know why the BBC technicians in that vehicle decided to continue the recording after my interview for *News at Ten* had come to an end. Was it just incompetence, or was it deliberate eavesdropping? Whatever the reason, a recording was made. Inside Downing Street itself, the extra lighting had been turned off, and the Prime Minister and I had both removed the small clip-on microphones from our ties and placed them on the table between us. But there was still sufficient light for the cameras to send out a signal as we talked on, and the microphones were still close enough to pick up some fairly poor-quality sound – all of which was recorded in the BBC outside-broadcast vehicle.

The first indication that something unusual had happened came at around seven o'clock that evening near our studio at Four Millbank, which is also home to the BBC's Westminster news operation. I bumped into one of their political correspondents, John Pienaar, who simply said to me, with a knowing grin, 'Great stuff in the interview, Mike.' The remark puzzled me, because, as far as I knew, everybody's interviews in Downing Street had contained broadly similar answers from John Major on the confidence vote.

During the course of the evening I began to sense that news about some interesting off-the-cuff remarks by the Prime Minister was beginning to spread among some of the political correspondents, but that my colleagues in the Lobby had no real details about what had been said. Driving home late that night, however, my concern grew, and I decided to alert the

Prime Minister's Press Secretary, Gus O'Donnell. I reached him on my mobile phone, and said that I thought he should be aware of what I sensed was going on. His initial reaction was relaxed. 'There wasn't anything in all of that which would cause a particular problem, was there, Mike?' I told him that, in my view, if the use of the word 'bastards' became public knowledge, there would indeed be problems.

And so it proved. That Sunday, two days after the interviews in Downing Street, the *Observer* newspaper published most of the details of what had happened. 'Major hits at Cabinet bastards' was their front-page headline. It was clear that their reporter, Paul Routledge, had been given a great deal of information about the BBC recording. In addition to reporting much of the actual conversation, he also gave details about the sound quality, the lighting and how, at one point, the camera that had been focused on me had been switched off. There was, incidentally, a delicious irony about Paul Routledge's position. After a difficult time at the *Observer*, he had actually decided to leave it by the time he wrote the story – the best scoop the paper had published for years.

Downing Street decided to try to hold the line. As other Sunday newspapers followed up the *Observer*'s exclusive in their later editions, a spokesperson at Number Ten was quoted as saying, 'We do not know if this conversation took place, and if it did, it would have been a private matter.' Since it was perfectly obvious that it *had* happened, I suggested to my editors at ITN that we should not attempt to deny its occurrence, but that we should stick rigidly to the line that it had been a private conversation. On Sunday afternoon, I did an interview at my home for our bulletins to that effect. During the following week, I busied myself with the campaign for the impending by-election at Christchurch in Hampshire, where the Tories suffered a crushing defeat later in the week.

But, before the by-election result finally diverted everyone's attention, the story rumbled on. By the Tuesday morning, the *Daily Mirror* had got hold of the bootleg recording. A lurid account subsequently appeared in the London *Evening Standard* describing how the *Mirror* had obtained the vital cassette. It had apparently involved a secret 2 a.m. rendezvous at a West London Underground station between a *Mirror* reporter and a code-named source wearing a pair of tan-coloured tights over his head, during which the tape had been handed over. Be that as it may, both the *Mirror* and the *Standard* published full transcripts. In addition, the *Mirror* published pictures of the Prime Minister and myself, superimposed on to television sets, taken from the video recording, and a telephone number on which their readers could hear what the paper described as 'the whole shocking tape'. The *Sun*, not to be outdone, said that it had discovered a second tape of another private conversation involving John Major, which its readers could also phone in to hear, but that was the last we heard of that.

In the end, did it all matter? At the time, opinions varied as to whether John Major had been damaged by the episode or not. Some commentators suggested that his robust language had shown that he was anything but the 'wimp' which he himself had suggested that people saw him as. Others felt that the Prime Minister was naive not to have realised that his unguarded comments would eventually become public knowledge.

As soon as the leak of the tape's contents to the papers occurred, ITN wrote to the BBC expressing its anger at what had happened. The Conservative Party Chairman, Sir Norman Fowler, also made his unhappiness plain. The BBC's Deputy Director-General, Bob Phillis, responded speedily to Sir Norman's complaint, saying that 'extensive enquiries over the last two days' had produced no evidence to support 'a most serious allegation about the BBC's role in this affair.'

Phillis said that a technician had played the tape back shortly after it had been recorded and had found the Prime Minister's remarks on it. The tape had been taken that evening into the personal possession of a BBC manager, and had subsequently been destroyed. 'We are absolutely confident', Phillis concluded, 'that this recording was neither copied nor played to any outsider.' It was an explanation of events which raised as many questions as it answered, but the basic fact remains that, had the improper recording not been made by the BBC in the first place, the whole episode would never have become as serious as it did.

For I believe that, in the end, it caused considerable damage. It helped to increase the bitterness and suspicion between the Prime Minister and the Eurosceptics, to the point where a group of them began to glory in their isolation. The right-wing Tory MP Teresa Gorman called her book about the fight over the Maastricht Treaty, published that autumn, *The Bastards*, inscribing my copy of it, incidentally, with the somewhat questionable dedication, 'To Michael who was my inspiration. Great title – thank you!' The term became an easy form of shorthand for those who wanted to attack the divisions in the Tory Party over Europe. As such, in his speech to the Labour Party conference that year, the Labour Leader John Smith specifically referred both to the 'bastards' and to the incident which had given rise to the word.

It had not been a particularly comfortable experience to be making the news, rather than reporting it, but six months later it happened again. Once more the background was the ever deepening split between John Major and his rebellious right wingers.

In mid-January 1994, reports appeared in two newspapers, the *Sun* and the *Daily Mail*, about what had taken place at a farewell dinner, and over the drinks which followed it, at Number Ten. The Prime Minister and Mrs Major had invited thirty guests, including myself, to bid farewell to his Press Secretary, Gus O'Donnell. Gus had been John Major's press spokesman during his time as Chancellor of the Exchequer, and had moved with him to Downing Street when he became Prime Minister. He was now returning to the Treasury to take up a high-powered job, unconnected with media relations.

The dinner was held on a Thursday evening. The following Saturday, the two newspapers in question reported that the Prime Minister had once more expressed his anger at the way right-wingers in the Cabinet and in the Conservative Party were treating him. They quoted him as saying, 'I'll f*****g crucify the right for what they have done and I'll have most of the party behind me if I do it.'

Neither the *Sun* nor the *Mail* had been represented at the dinner, but word quickly spread that I had been seen talking privately to the Prime Minister during the course of the evening. Other reports said that, on my return to the Commons, I had met and spoken to Simon Walters, who at that time was the political correspondent of the *Sun*. By the middle of the following week, a number of newspapers alleged that I was the source of the story, the *Daily Express*, for example, naming me as the 'innocent suspect'.

At the time, I refused to confirm or deny the reports, because I regarded the dinner and what took place at it as a private matter (I still do), but the pressure grew on me to break my silence. The Chairman of the Tory backbench Media Committee, the MP Michael Fabricant, wrote to me asking me to appear before them to explain what had really happened. I politely declined the invitation, since the Committee did not have the status of a Select Committee of the House of Commons, and I knew that I could not be compelled to attend. A cartoon by Jak in the *Evening Standard* showed me in the basement of Conservative Central Office, being stretched on a rack by Tory officials desperate to discover the truth.

The Prime Minister himself clearly suspected that I might have had some part in what appeared in the *Sun* and the *Mail*, though he never directly accused me of anything, on or off the record. After he had seen the first editions of the two newspapers on the Friday night, he spoke to me by telephone at my home shortly before midnight. I had, in fact, already gone to sleep, and I took the call in bed, having been brought sharply to my senses by hearing the voice of the Number Ten switchboard operator. The ladies who operate that switchboard have a justified reputation for finding anyone anywhere, awake or sleeping. I suspect that they are also fully aware of the impact they make when, having found the right person, they continue, as one of their number did that night, with the words, 'Would you hold on, please? The Prime Minister wishes to speak to you.' He himself, when he came on the line, set the terms for the conversation which, as he put it, 'I hope I can regard as private.' In essence, his message was that he had not said what the papers had claimed that he said, and that he hoped that I understood that.

Some days later, we exchanged letters, again on the understanding that the correspondence was private, though the burden of what was said was that the matter was to be regarded as closed. But not quite, however. Two years later, John Major spoke at another farewell gathering, this time for Christopher Meyer, who had succeeded Gus O'Donnell as his Press Secretary, at which I was also present. In his speech, John Major said that he had arranged the lunch for Christopher Meyer with some trepidation, after what had happened on the previous occasion. 'And if I ever discover who was responsible for that,' he said, 'I'll wring his neck.'

* * *

At the heart of both 'Bastardgate' and what inevitably became known as 'Dinnergate' were the same questions about John Major's leadership and, above all, about his personal authority as Prime Minister and Leader of his party. Could he have done more to assert that authority by taking a more firmly Eurosceptic line at a much earlier stage in his premiership and still have remained in office?

I believe that he could. There is no doubt that during his six and a half years in office he was forced, step by step, into revealing more and more of his private scepticism about Europe by the turn of events. Within four months of becoming Prime Minister, he had delivered a keynote speech that was strongly, though not uncritically, pro-European in tone. Six years later, it was a very different story. Things had reached the point where his Foreign Secretary, Malcolm Rifkind, could speak, without being rebuked by the Prime Minister, of Britain being 'hostile' to the idea of the single European currency. But in the intervening period he was twisted and torn this way and that as his party fought over the issue, without ever being sure exactly where their Leader himself stood on the matter.

At the start of his premiership, John Major had seemed to signal that he was ready to adopt a far more pro-European policy than that pursued by his predecessor, Margaret Thatcher. He said later that his 'heart of Europe' speech, delivered in the German capital, Bonn, in March 1991, was one of the most misrepresented speeches of recent times. Few speeches that he could recall, he said, had been so distorted by later interpreters. In it, however, he had declared, 'My aims for Britain and the Community can be simply stated. I want us to be where we belong, at the very heart of Europe, working with our partners in building the future.'

In truth, it had not been an uncritically pro-European speech. It had laid down, for example, Britain's deep reserva-

tions about European monetary union and the single currency, eight months before the signing of the Maastricht
Treaty. The speech, however, did seem to many to indicate
a clear change of policy by the new Prime Minister, and to
suggest that there would be a far more positive approach to
Europe during his administration than had been apparent
during the Thatcher years. At the very least, it showed that he
would attempt to steer a middle course on the issue. Speaking
in the House of Commons the very day after he had delivered
the Bonn speech, he said that there were only three possible
options on Europe – to leave, which was unthinkable; to stand
aside, which was untenable; or to be at the heart of the
Community, influencing events, which was the policy he
would adopt.

His problem was that a considerable number of his own
MPs, not to mention Conservative supporters up and down
the country, did not *want* him to adopt a middle course.
Those who were either strongly committed to or strongly
against closer ties with Europe regarded his doing so as a sign
of weakness. But there were, in addition, many Conservative
MPs who were prepared to accept the middle way but who
were angered by the fact that they did not know where the
Prime Minister himself really stood on the matter.

He himself would, on occasion, hint at what appeared to be
his own, personal scepticism. He told the Commons at one
point, for example, that he would take a great deal of
persuading that it would ever be right for Britain to join
the single currency. On another occasion, he said that he
would not like to have to be the Chancellor of the Exchequer
who told the House that British interest rates had gone up
because of a decision taken by the European Central Bank in
Frankfurt.

These, however, were only hints. Late in his premiership, he
reached the point of openly declaring his Eurosceptic position.

Even then, he still felt that, on EMU, the door should be left ajar. In April 1996, for example, five years after his 'heart of Europe' speech, he secured Cabinet approval for a manifesto commitment promising a referendum before Britain joined the single currency. It was, however, another nine months, with a general election imminent, before the full Cabinet adopted, in January 1997, a clearly more sceptical stand on Europe, leading to the remarks by the Foreign Secretary, Malcolm Rifkind, about Britain being 'hostile to the single currency'.

Several of those who served John Major as members of his Cabinet told me that he could not have adopted a tougher line on Europe earlier for fear of losing the fiercely pro-European Kenneth Clarke. Michael Heseltine, they said, was a different matter. He had, after all, acquired a reputation as a 'bolter' after storming out of Mrs Thatcher's Cabinet during the Westland affair, so doing it again would be seen as irresponsible. In any case, he had decided to back the Prime Minister through good times and bad. But Clarke, it was suggested, was in an altogether different class. After dismissing Norman Lamont as Chancellor in May 1993, the argument ran, John Major could not have survived the resignation of his successor. So Lady Thatcher had simply been wrong to take the lofty view which she expressed during an interview with me in 1995, that no Chancellor was worth preserving if it meant the surrender of your most deeply held principles.

Yet Kenneth Clarke told me personally in February 1993 that only one thing would force him to resign. Any declaration by John Major, he said, which categorically ruled out British membership of a single currency would have him heading straight for the Cabinet Room door. But the Prime Minister, he added, had made it perfectly clear that he would be uttering no such declaration. For the rest, Clarke said that he understood the political pressures on Major, and why that might require him to adopt an increasingly Eurosceptic tone. That, he told me, he could live with, provided the possibility of eventual membership was always left open – though, for his part, he would reserve the right to argue the case for British membership sooner rather than later.

In the event, for most of his time in Number Ten, John Major remained unshakeable in his belief that what mattered above all was holding the party together. Ever mindful of the damage the European issue had done in the last years of the Thatcher administration, he was convinced that he should do nothing which would shatter such fragile unity as had been achieved since then. Even with that situation to handle, however, I believe he could successfully have said at an early stage, 'You know my personal position. I am basically against the single currency, though we must wait and see,' just as Tony Blair was to argue much later, albeit with a huge majority behind him, that while he was basically *in favour* of the single currency, he too would wait and see. Had he taken such a stand, his position would still have been far removed from his predecessor's implacable opposition to the Euro.

But he did not take it, and, as a result, there was a constant whispering campaign against him, from the left, right and centre of the Parliamentary party, with MPs perpetually complaining about his lack of leadership. It was all deeply damaging. Day after day, you could scarcely spend any time in the Lobby outside the Commons chamber talking to Conservative MPs without hearing them openly criticising the Leader of their own party. Some *were* fiercely loyal – and not always the ones you might expect. Michael Heseltine, for example, was one who would not hear a word said against him in public or private, having decided from the start that the 'my leader, right or wrong' principle was the only one a Cabinet minister could honourably take. Nicholas Soames was another Minister who took the same view. But so many others would tell you, on strictly Lobby terms, of course, 'I just don't know where he stands – on anything.'

From the start, such disloyalty was deeply damaging, and John Major knew it, hence his reference in our 'Bastardgate' conversation to 'this poison'. But he never found a way to overcome it. His astonishing decision to resign as party Leader, and to force through what amounted to a vote of confidence, only stopped the whispering for a week or two. As a result, he led a Parliamentary party which was not just divided over Europe, but had lost confidence in his leadership. When the time came to fight the general election campaign of 1997, the country showed to a devastating degree that it too had lost confidence in him.

CHAPTER ELEVEN

Choosing a Leader:
Who Follows John Smith?

N o two political reputations grow in and around Westminster in quite the same way. For some, a great speech in the House of Commons from the backbenches may launch a political career in spectacular style. For others, it may be clear skill which is demonstrated within a party organisation like the Conservative Research Department, or during time as a young Parliamentary Private Secretary, acting as a Minister's eyes and ears on the backbenches, but with access to his department too.

As I began reporting events at Westminster in 1986, Tony Blair, although already a member of Neil Kinnock's front bench team, was not someone who immediately made an impact on a newly appointed political editor. He was, in fact, making rather more than routine progress in the ranks of the Shadow Cabinet. However, with all the excitements of the last years of the Thatcher Government to cover, it was some time before he came into my personal category of someone to watch, or, to put it in the more down-to-earth language of most political journalists, someone who needed to be taken out to lunch.

He had entered the House as MP for the seat of Sedgefield

in County Durham at the 1983 general election after two character-building experiences, of coming fourth out of a shortlist of five when he tried for a seat on Hackney Borough council in 1982, and of losing the Beaconsfield by-election that same year to the Conservative, Tim Smith. Nothing, perhaps, illustrates the unpredictable nature of politics quite as well as the fact that in 1994, three months after Tony Blair had been chosen as Leader of the Labour Party, I was reporting that Tim Smith had been forced to resign in disgrace in the 'Cash for Questions' scandal.

In November 1984, after less than eighteen months on the backbenches, Tony Blair was appointed the most junior member of the Opposition Treasury team, led by Roy Hattersley, and, after a respectable, though unsuccessful, first try in the 1987 Shadow Cabinet elections, he was made Shadow Trade and Industry Minister. After victory in the 1988 elections, promotions followed rapidly, as he took charge, successively, of the Shadow Energy and Employment portfolios; and after the 1992 general election the new Leader, John Smith, made him Shadow Home Secretary.

That was no mean record of achievement, but it says something about what it takes to break through into the public's, not to mention a political editor's, consciousness that my first 'getting to know you' lunch with Tony Blair did not take place until after his appointment as Shadow Home Secretary. The fact that it took so long may have been a lack of judgement on my part, but it also reflects the reality of the situation – that it is not until an Opposition MP is handed one of the really big Shadow jobs that people begin to sit up and take notice.

The lunch, incidentally, did not go well. I picked what, at the time, was thought of as a rather trendy Italian restaurant, the entrance to which was a mammoth concrete block next to New Scotland Yard. The main eating area was a large and noisy basement. The tables were too close together, and ours, I seem to remember, wobbled to and fro until a waiter jammed something under one of the legs to steady it.

Conversation was almost impossible, given the noise, and I do not recall if, as we discussed the way he was handling his Shadow portfolio, he rehearsed what became his trademark phrase about being 'tough on crime and tough on the causes of crime'. It would not be surprising, however, if he had. Some years previously he had, in effect, publicly endorsed what later became known as 'soundbite politics' by arguing that the best way of getting a message across was to be precise and to the point when making it. If it did not feature during our lunch, he certainly used the 'tough on crime' line often enough in the House of Commons. Its frequent repetition was an important part in helping to establish in the public's mind that, while Tony Blair was a young Labour moderniser, there was a marked streak of right-of-centre thinking in his political make-up.

On 12 May 1994, there came the sudden and tragic news for the Labour Party of the death of their Leader, John Smith. Coverage of that news and its aftermath resulted in another extraordinary time for me as a broadcaster. On the morning of his death, news of which began to emerge about three-quarters of an hour before the official announcement at half-past ten, ITV took the bold decision to mount another open-ended programme. It was a judgement that undoubtedly reflected the immediate public mood of shock and disbelief at what had happened. However, a decision to suspend all regular programmes on a national television network, and to replace them by continuous news coverage, a decision which was not, in the end, matched by the BBC, requires more than a simple assessment of public mood. In handing the network over to ITN, I like to think, the ITV bosses were fortified at

211

least in part by the knowledge that we had successfully handled a similar situation before, with our open-ended coverage of the resignation of Margaret Thatcher four years earlier.

The experience we had gained during that earlier broadcast proved invaluable. Our Westminster studio now became the centre of a crucial outside-broadcast operation, feeding pictures from the cameras there to ITN's main control room. I knew that, in the very different circumstances of this occasion, the prime requirement was simply to take things as they came.

Shortly after the news was confirmed, I went on air to pay my own personal tribute. I was Chairman of the Parliamentary Lobby Journalists that year, and, when I was asked to give my reaction to the news, I thought it was right, as Chairman, to begin by expressing sympathy, on behalf of all the political journalists at Westminster, to John Smith's family. One newspaper report said later that it looked as though I had been crying. That was not in fact true, but it did reflect the truly profound sense of shock and loss that everyone in and around the House of Commons was experiencing.

John Smith, after all, had about him a remarkable air of solidity, of being as steady as a rock, the sort of person you always imagined would be there. That was what the Labour Party liked about him, and one of the chief reasons why they had chosen him as Leader after Neil Kinnock had stepped down. Nonetheless, by May 1994, he had already suffered one serious heart attack, and, in retrospect, it was probably unwise of him to have returned gradually to exactly the same lifestyle he had maintained before that first illness. The fact remains, however, that he had, so much so that his wife Elizabeth had pleaded with another Labour MP, who was his neighbour in the Barbican apartment complex in the City of London, to keep a watchful eye on him, to try and make sure that he wasn't overdoing things, and that he got to bed at a reasonable hour.

That was more difficult than it sounds, for there was nothing that John Smith liked to do more than to enjoy a late-evening glass of wine or two with a political colleague or a journalist, chewing over the day's news, exchanging the latest gossip or simply talking about his own political vision. I speak from experience, having enjoyed a couple of such sessions myself in the Leader of the Opposition's quarters in the Commons. One such discussion seemed to me to give such a clear insight into the direction in which he wanted to take the Labour Party that we turned the substance of it into an interview on *News at Ten* two days later.

On the morning that John Smith died, and with our special programme under way, so many of his colleagues and friends at Westminster, from all the political parties, wanted to express their grief and their individual reflections on and memories of his life that they quite literally formed a queue in our Millbank office, and were happy to await their turn to go on air. Our technical resources were under very considerable strain, and we solved one problem by setting up a second camera outside on Abingdon Green so that we could cut from one tribute to another without too much of a jump. Those who were asked to make their tribute from our outside camera all readily agreed to do so.

It was an emotional broadcast to be involved in, but the occasion which brought me closest to tears in front of the camera was not that day, but John Smith's funeral in Edinburgh eight days later. Nothing could have reminded us with greater force of the strength of his Scottish roots than the service held that Friday morning in Cluny parish church in Morningside, just a short walk from his family home. I described it at the time as a service 'of plain dignity, as is the way of the Scottish church'. John Smith's friends and colleagues paid tribute to him. One of the closest of them, Donald Dewar, remembered especially his friend's political courage as he had fought for Scottish devolution, and then, remembering the other side of the man's nature, said that 'John could start a party in an empty room!' It was the music at that service, though, which brought the tears to my eyes. There was the emotion of the Scottish metric psalm, 'I to the hills will lift mine eyes', but above all there was the sound of a solo soprano who sang, with tears in her own eyes, the words of the Twenty-third Psalm in Gaelic. It was as though a piper's lament was being uttered by a human voice. Later that day, as I edited her singing into my reports, I had to listen to her haunting voice over and over again, and each time it produced the same spine-tingling reaction in me.

Even so solemn an occasion was not, however, without its lighter, almost farcical side. We had reached an agreement with a local householder, whose property faced the main door of the church, to build a small rostrum in his driveway from which any two-way interviews between myself and the presenters in London could be conducted. Ahead of our lunchtime programme, however, it became clear that things would be running a little late, and that some live commentary as the cortège left the church might well be required.

ITN is famed for travelling light, and on this occasion we were far from properly equipped for such an eventuality. Specifically, we had no television monitor on which I could see the pictures to which I would be expected to add a commentary. My producer, a canny Scot called John Curran, hit upon a solution. He asked the householder in whose driveway we were parked if he had a spare television set we could use, to allow me to see the pictures that London was actually transmitting on the live programme, to which I could instantly add my voice. An ancient black-and-white set, long since retired from regular use, was found in his garage and hauled on to our platform, and a quick visit to an electrical shop just around the corner produced enough cables of various kinds for the set to be hitched up to the house aerial and power supply. No one, I gather, had any idea, during the broadcast, of the precariously Heath Robinson style of television engineering on which it had depended. I like to think that John Smith, with his infectious sense of humour, would have had a wry chuckle about it all.

That was a day's broadcasting of which I was particularly proud, during which I believe I did the occasion justice. As it happens, it was the live, open-ended programme, transmitted eight days before the funeral, which later won a Royal Television Society award. The presentation took place at an event held the day before John Smith's widow took her seat in the House of Lords. ITN invited her and her daughter Sarah, then working for BBC Television and later for ITN, to the awards ceremony, and both attended it. In accepting the award on ITN's behalf, I expressed my sadness that it was such an unhappy occasion which had been the cause of the broadcast, which was now counterbalanced, in part, by our happiness at the elevation to the peerage of the new Lady Smith. As for the programme itself, there were, I added, some occasions when television, for all its preoccupation with pictures, simply had to fall back on words alone. On the day that John Smith died, words were all we had.

With his funeral over, it was time for those who might aspire to succeed John Smith to consider their positions. By this time, Tony Blair had made his mark. Both John Smith and Neil Kinnock had spotted his ability. In twelve years' service as an MP, he had spent just two of them as a backbencher. His had been an unusually swift rise to power, and that fact, combined with a steadily growing public profile, meant that, in the 1994 contest for the Leadership of the party, there was, in effect, no contest at all. The only question was whether

Gordon Brown would run against him, and, once the Shadow Chancellor decided not to, Blair's victory was certain.

All the potential candidates had agreed that the campaign proper should not begin until after polling day for the European elections on Thursday, 9 June. Before that, there had also been an agreement, which was only just adhered to, that there should be no overt campaigning or organising before John Smith's funeral. Now, with the completion of the European and five national by-elections, in all of which Labour did well, formal campaigning in the Labour leadership election could begin. On Friday, 10 June, John Prescott announced that he would run for both Leader and Deputy Leader, as the rules allowed him to do. He was clearly motivated by the sense that there should be some sort of respectable challenge for the job of Leader – Prescott is not the sort of person who likes to see anyone succeed on the basis of a shoe-in. His real sights, however, were on the Deputy Leadership, where he felt he could act as a brake on some of the wilder new thinking that was flying around, a guardian, in effect, of Old Labour's conscience. Margaret Beckett also ran for both offices, largely, it seemed, because she had done both jobs in her time – as John Smith's Deputy, and as Leader pro tem (the Labour Party constitution does not acknowledge an 'Acting Leader' as such) after his death. Tony Blair, so clearly the favourite by now to become Leader, waited for another day before announcing his candidacy. Unlike the other two, who made their announcements in London, he decided to do so outside London – in his Sedgefield constituency.

Any London-based political journalist who wants to understand part of what makes Tony Blair tick could do a lot worse than go to Sedgefield. The town itself, which gives the constituency its name, is a trim, almost picture-book little place complete with its own racecourse, not far from Darlington in the County Durham countryside. It comes as something of a surprise in itself if you have a preconception of that part of the world as an area scarred by the decline of the coal industry. The real surprise, however, comes when you reach Trimdon, which is the political heart of the constituency.

Trimdon is a rambling, split village, in which the first-time visitor can easily get lost. There are signposts to the little knots of housing and other buildings at Trimdon Station and Trimdon Colliery, a reminder of the times when there *was* a station and a colliery. The heart of the place, though, is Trimdon village proper, clustered around a large village green, with the church at one end of it and, almost at the other end, the local Labour Club.

To enter that club is to enter a working example of what New Labour means, because, as I discovered, everyone inside it will tell you so. Local officials combine their natural Geordie friendliness with an eagerness to explain how the building used to be the local working men's club, which fell on hard times as mining and other jobs in the area disappeared. They will also describe how they decided to take it over, and hit upon an entirely new way of running such a place, including some particularly innovative fund-raising. Out of those funds came not only the local party's subscription to the national party in London, and the running expenses of the local party and the club, but a number of sizeable weekly cash prizes too. Membership became, and remains, extremely popular. The moment you step into it, you sense that the place is quite unlike the ordinary, run-of-the-mill political clubs you encounter up and down the country. It has a buzz. Politics is not boring at Trimdon Labour Club.

Of course, it helps if your local MP is the Prime Minister, but those same officials will also, at the drop of a hat, explain that Tony Blair is only where he is because *they* had the good sense to choose the MP they wanted, rather than someone who simply emerged from the local party, or trade union, machine. In just the same way, they explain, they later chose to run their local branch and club in a different way too.

In the run-up to the 1983 general election, Sedgefield was the last constituency in the country to pick its Labour candidate. The seat itself was a new one; or rather it was a revival of an old one – the result of the redistribution of seats in County Durham. The sitting Labour MPs in the area had taken their time in choosing which of the rearranged local seats they wanted to go for. As a result, one month before polling in the general election, Sedgefield still did not have a Labour candidate.

To cut a long story short, Tony Blair heard about that situation, and at the very last minute decided to try and get himself on the shortlist for selection in Sedgefield. Fortunately for him, five local branch members in Trimdon took a shine to him, and decided to back him. Behind their decision, and that of other key figures in the constituency, ran a deep dislike of the hard-left politics of the other main contender, the former MP for Nuneaton Les Huckfield. In the end, the future Prime Minister made it on to a revised shortlist of contenders for the Labour nomination by just one vote, and two days later, after five rounds of voting at the full selection conference, he beat Huckfield by 73 votes to 46, to become the candidate only three weeks before polling day, eventually winning the seat, and his place at Westminster, by a little over 8,000 votes. As one of his biographers, John Rentoul, puts it, 'He had squeezed into Parliament, not at the last minute, but during extra time.'

So, in Trimdon Labour Club on that Saturday morning in May 1994, there was a sense of immense pride that Tony Blair was now about to make his bid to become, not just the Leader of the Labour Party, but, they hoped, leader of the country

too. Over a pint in the club bar, as I waited for the announcement, I was given a potted version of the story of how he had
become the local MP and of how they 'did things different' in
Trimdon and in Sedgefield, both in their local party set-up
and in trying to cope with the huge economic changes in the
area. What had happened in the constituency, the members
told me, would now happen in the whole of the country, once
Tony had won the election.

To the rest of us, that may have sounded like jumping the
gun, given that the occasion was about someone taking a first,
though clearly vital, step on the road to Number Ten, by
seeking to become Leader of the Labour Party. To those in
Trimdon Labour Club that morning, however, there was little
time for these tiresome preliminaries. We filmed two elderly
ladies, who between them had plainly clocked up years of
faithful party membership, arriving for the meeting. 'We're
here to watch Tony tell us that he's going to be Prime
Minister!' they told me in forthright tones. Inside the hall,
the burly, moustachioed man who led him on to the platform
was John Burton, one of the 'famous five' who had backed
him as the local candidate eleven years earlier. 'I'm sure it's
going to be an historic announcement,' he declared, and he
wasn't disappointed. Tony Blair's formal declaration that he
would, indeed, seek the Labour leadership soon had the
cheering audience on its feet. One woman caught Burton's
eye, and he gave her the floor. 'I just want to say that I know
you'll go all the way, Tony, and we're all right behind you,'
she said. That produced another round of cheering.

It would be some months before he announced the birth of
New Labour, but that was the idea that had already taken
shape in his mind. Outside the club, I interviewed him, and, as
usual, only a tiny clip of that interview eventually made it on
to the nation's television screens. Looking back, however, at
the unedited version of that interview now, it is possible to see

how many of the later building blocks of New Labour were already there.

I suggested to him, as many were to suggest later, that he was only offering a version of Thatcherism 'tinged with a bit of Blairism'. He strongly disagreed, and his answers, as he stood on Trimdon village green that morning, are worth quoting at some length, since they formed an early version of the message which eventually carried him to Number Ten. 'Mrs Thatcher,' he told me, 'said there is no such thing as society. The distinction between the two parties is that we *do* believe in a strong civic society, and that people can only have the chance to enhance their own opportunities and to succeed and to do well in life if they are backed up by the power of society, and for the good of each person within it. That is the distinctive Labour vision for Britain.'

Interestingly, I found, on reviewing the tape, that I was already asking him that day about Clause Four, that archaic, seventy-year-old formulation of Labour's aims and values, which talked about the need 'to secure for the workers by hand or by brain the full fruits of their labours . . . on the basis of the common ownership of the means of production, distribution and exchange'. Would he be changing that? The answer was cautious but was a clear indication that he would. 'The important thing for the Labour Party', Blair told me, 'is to set out its vision for Britain's future, *applying its traditional values to the modern world*'. The italics are mine, but those words, much used in the ensuing months, were a clear indication that Clause Four would eventually have to go. Ten months later the Labour Party voted to replace it.

Equally, that day, there were the signs of his belief that the way the Labour Party had modernised itself in his own constituency was something that could be repeated through-out the country. He talked about the way his local party had changed and reformed itself, to become a strong and active body, which represented the views and aspirations of the local community. 'Don't judge the success of a branch by the number of resolutions it passes,' he suggested. Soon he was making the direct connection between what had happened in a single party in County Durham and what might happen in national terms, talking of 'a vision of Britain that is a country of renewal and change, where a strong and active society backs up the efforts of individuals'.

The actual birth of New Labour was still some way off, but two of the chief ideas that informed it – the responsibility of every individual to make the best of his or her life, knowing that, when help to do so was needed, the state stood ready to provide it; and the way that a modernised Labour Party could be a successful Labour Party – were already clearly formed in Tony Blair's mind on the day he made his bid to lead his party.

The campaign for the Labour leadership was a relatively dull affair, largely because the outcome was such a foregone conclusion. We now know much about the stresses and strains in the Blair and Brown camps in the days before Tony Blair's Trimdon declaration. We also know much about Peter Mandelson's role at that time, which, ultimately, had a lot to do with his leaving the Government four years later. But once Brown had made his decision not to run for the leadership, the question of who would become the Leader was almost academic. Blair's supporters in Trimdon Labour Club were right. His announcement there had been a declaration for a far greater prize.

Given that a dull campaign was in prospect, ITN decided to try and liven things up a little by making a series of reports which might give an insight into what sort of people the three candidates really were, away from the familiar pictures of them making their speeches or at work in their offices. It was something we had done with some success, we felt, with the party leaders during general election campaigns.

Of the three candidates who eventually put their hats in the ring, John Prescott was the most willing to agree to the idea. Given his extrovert character, that was, perhaps, no surprise, but he also realised that most people had a picture of him as a rather difficult, argumentative member of the political awkward squad, and that anything that would soften the edges of his public image might actually be helpful. As I discussed the idea with him, he let slip that he had been taking what he called sailing lessons near his home in Hull. In the event, that turned out to be something of an exaggeration, but it emerged that he had been out for a day's sailing with the owner of a local sailing school, and had enjoyed it enough to want to repeat the experience. We arranged for a similar session one afternoon during the leadership campaign, and a highly successful occasion it turned out to be, despite the fact that the car which was bringing him back to Hull to join us, after a morning's campaigning elsewhere, had been involved in a crash on the way.

The weather was perfect – bright sunshine and a good breeze. John Prescott, once a steward on an ocean-going liner, seemed genuinely amused by the thought of his being seen on television at the helm of a private yacht, even though it wasn't actually his, and he wasn't doing much of the actual sailing. He certainly looked the part, though, as we sailed up the Humber estuary and back again, and his expansive mood led to some entertaining exchanges as I interviewed him at various times during the trip. Above all, he had been highly amused, he told us, by an encounter on a recent train journey, when a Home Counties military-type of chap, whom he automatically assumed to be a Conservative supporter, had come up to him and boomed, 'Prescott, I've been keeping a bit of an eye on you recently, and I must say I like the cut of yer jib!'

Compiling the profiles of the other two candidates proved much more difficult. Margaret Beckett has a very private side to her nature, and she and her husband Leo, who acts as her personal and political secretary, do not greatly enjoy any invasion of their personal space. In the end, they agreed to some filming at their home in Derby over Sunday lunchtime, and, frankly, we did not have much in the way of filming opportunities to exploit. A sequence, however, as they both went through the Sunday papers, expressing their opinions about some of the more colourful things that had been written about her, proved a good deal more successful than we had hoped. For the rest, we took endless pictures of them dead-heading their roses – though, to be fair to them, they are both keen gardeners and their large rose collection did make an exceptionally colourful show.

Of the three, Tony Blair proved the most reluctant to agree to any filming at all. Of course, he had a busy schedule of campaigning to keep to, and no doubt he felt that, with things going his way, another profile was something he did not need. His greatest worry, however, was exposing his children to any publicity, especially since it seemed likely that such filming as could be arranged would involve them and his wife Cherie. Eventually, he agreed, largely on the ground, I suspect, that it would have looked odd if we had run profiles of the other two candidates and not of him. We could have fifteen minutes or so to film him playing football with his children, we were told. My heart sank, knowing how such things can turn out to be so staged and unreal.

In the event, it went well, partly because it emerged that such occasions, in which the Blairs' two sons, Euan and Nicky, were joined by some of their friends for a kickabout in a little park behind their Islington home, were a reasonably regular event in the Blair family timetable. The boys soon seemed to forget the camera was there, and Dad wasn't too unhappy at showing off some of his ball-control skills either.

This was the first time I had met Mrs Blair, and, addressing me formally as 'Mr Brunson', she pointed out that I'd been appearing on ITN news bulletins since she was a child. Thankfully, we soon switched to Christian-name terms. Later, during a joint interview with her husband, once we'd got back to the family home, she became sufficiently relaxed to admit quite openly that she was indeed greatly looking forward to the prospect of life in Ten Downing Street, should it ever happen. Even as she was uttering the words, I could sense Tony Blair's considerable unease that his wife appeared to be mentally measuring up the curtains in the Prime Ministerial flat, before he had even been elected Leader of the Labour Party.

I begged for one last shot, inside their home, and with considerable reluctance they agreed. It turned out to be just what we wanted. Their son Euan, as well as being good at football, also turned out to be rather good at playing the piano, though all requests to Tony Blair himself to remind us of his prowess on the guitar fell on deaf ears. In the street outside, however, as we prepared to leave, he could no longer contain his anxieties about the whole operation, and especially about the interview with Cherie. He quietly suggested a deal – that we could use the pictures of Euan at the piano in return for not using Cherie's remarks about Number Ten. It's the sort of offer that, by instinct, journalists immediately find suspicious, and I had to weigh up the arguments for and against it in a matter of seconds. In the end, I did agree to it, judging in my own mind that what Cherie had said about Number Ten was innocuous stuff, even if her husband did not think so, for which it was not worth losing the sequence around the piano. Rightly or wrongly, such bargains are sometimes part of the trade, and sometimes, in my experience, you find yourself, however reluctantly, agreeing to them. It certainly showed one thing beyond all doubt – that, in his campaign for the leadership of his party, Tony Blair was not prepared to leave the smallest detail to chance.

CHAPTER TWELVE

In at the Birth:
The Rise of New Labour

.

D uring my time as ITN's correspondent in Washington, I once interviewed Walter Cronkite, the father figure of American television journalism and the main presenter of the CBS *Evening News*. I asked him whether it wasn't unfair that anyone standing as a candidate for the Presidency of the United States should be judged so much on his ability to perform well on television. We were talking during the 1976 Presidential election and it was an issue at the time. Governor Jimmy Carter, the Democratic challenger, was not all that good on television, but President Ford, who had taken over after Richard Nixon's resignation, was even worse.

Walter Cronkite gave me a look that combined a knowing approach to American politics with weariness that a young British reporter could ask such a question in the first place. 'Like it or not,' he told me, 'it's a simple fact of life. Any Presidential candidate who is a poor television performer suffers a huge disadvantage.' In Britain, the debate still continues as to how 'presidential' our own politics have become, but the issue of the part that television plays in the selection of our leaders is in far less doubt. As in the United States, so in the United Kingdom: a leader who does not handle television well suffers a big disadvantage.

Tony Blair has always realised the importance of television, and, by and large, he handles it well. Perhaps his appearances as a singer with his Oxford pop group helped him to develop the skill of getting up and performing in public. Even if they hadn't, there were soon plenty of advisers offering advice in that area, as he began his quest for the leadership of the Labour Party and, by implication, the position of Prime Minister, in the summer of 1994. At each stage of that quest, he used television to help him achieve his goals, and, as each stage was completed, he delivered major speeches, often backed up by a round of television interviews, to consolidate what he had achieved.

To the general public, the outcome of the Labour leadership election was certain. Within the Labour Party itself, there was a proper contest, to the extent that justified John Prescott's decision to run. The result, however, was decisive: 19 per cent of the combined vote of the party membership, the trade unions and Labour MPs, went to Margaret Beckett, 24 per cent to John Prescott and 57 per cent to Tony Blair. In the contest for Deputy Leader, John Prescott defeated Mrs Beckett by a thirteen-point margin.

The result was declared on the morning of 21 July, at a special meeting held in the auditorium of the Institute of Education, a large hall that formed part of the University buildings in the Bloomsbury area of London. It was a little off the beaten track of the usual venues for political gatherings. However, it was clear as our cameras recorded the arrival not just of Labour's good and great, but of rank-and-file members too, that the party was in a decidedly upbeat mood as it gathered for the occasion. Lots of hugs and kisses and other warm greetings suggested that such differences as had emerged between party members, and the candidates, during the contest had now been forgotten. All sections of the party were clearly excited by the prospect that they were about to endorse a new, young Leader who would finally, they believed, see off John Major and the Tory Government. There was still a sense, however, of the party not being quite sure of where that new, young Leader was ultimately going to take them. Many a true word is spoken in jest, and perhaps it was the Old Socialist in John Prescott that gave voice to that feeling. As the leadership formally passed into new hands, he raised a laugh when he declared that Tony Blair 'scares the life out of the Tories'. But he got an even bigger laugh when he jokingly added, 'And he scares the life out of me!'

The new Leader himself studiously avoided any show of triumphalism, well aware, despite Labour's commanding lead in the opinion polls, that the job of winning the next general election now rested firmly on his shoulders. 'I am ready to serve,' he declared, while immediately putting the party on notice that it had its responsibilities too. '*We* are ready to serve,' he quickly added. 'Let us make this a turning point. We are ready to change the course of our history, to make Britain a confident land of opportunity in a changing world.' That was the sort of language to be expected at such an occasion. The message, however, went several stages further, as he signalled to his party that it, too, had reached a turning point.

We now know that the phrase 'New Labour' was not truly forged until later, in the run-up to the 1994 party conference, where it was officially unveiled, embodied in the slogan 'New Labour, New Britain'. But, from the moment he had declared his candidacy in Trimdon, Tony Blair had been shaping a new policy blueprint for his party, and his speech now, accepting the leadership of the Labour Party, was an important restatement of the ideas that were driving his thinking.

I immediately sensed his emphasis on the need for change. It was not a speech that set out detailed policy, but there were plenty of pointers to future policy in it. There was an early reference to the requirement for 'a new language of social justice, of what is just and unjust, fair and unfair, right and wrong'. He went on to talk about putting people to work and about releasing the capital receipts from the sale of council houses. He discussed the need for reform of the House of Lords, the need for a crackdown on crime, and the problem of old-age pensioners having to pay VAT on their fuel bills.

There was a strong attack in the speech on the Tories, who had lost, he said, the nation's trust. 'But that does not mean', he continued, 'that we inherit that trust automatically. We have to work for it. We have to earn it. We must show, not just how *they* have failed, but how *we* can succeed.'

The reaction from the Conservative Party was airily dismissive, not least as voiced by the new, indeed the very new, Tory Party Chairman, Jeremy Hanley, who had just been handed the job in the latest of John Major's reshuffles. When I interviewed him shortly after the formalities of Tony Blair's election, Hanley declared that he had never known a contest before 'where a person is elected merely because of what he looks like'. Even allowing for the shadow-boxing that goes on at such times, it was far too lightweight a response, and it was not made all that weightier when Hanley demanded that Blair should explain how he was going to pay for 'the perfect world' he wanted to create.

Later that day, I talked to Tony Blair in the Shadow Cabinet room in the House of Commons, where I had often listened to Neil Kinnock and John Smith setting out their own strategies for overturning the Tories. I pressed him on the charge that he was being deliberately vague about the policies he would pursue, as the Tories were constantly claiming, a

230

charge which their Chairman, in his own fashion, had re-peated that day. He angrily dismissed that part of the Hanley attack, such as it was, which was based on an argument over tax. Almost shouting his reply, and using a phrase which would become very much part of his political vocabulary in the months and years ahead, he said he would 'take no lessons' from the other side. The Conservatives were a party which had not only raised taxes, but had imposed other financial burdens on the country through rising crime, social decay and high unemployment.

I turned to the clear warning about the need for a change of direction that he had given his party in his acceptance speech. I suggested to him that he was telling the membership that a whole new way of thinking was required, that, as I put it, 'it should drop all its bad habits, and that the days of simplistic, "put a fiver on the pension" politics were over'. He agreed, saying that the Tories had been running the country on dogma and prejudice, and that he 'did not want to come into power and swap one set of dogmas for another'. That was why, in his speech, he had been talking 'not about an old left or a new right. It's new left and new thinking.'

I freely confess that I was often in the slow lane when it came to spotting exactly where all this talk about Labour's new thinking would lead, but in that I believe I was not alone. Despite the fact that I had asked Tony Blair about Clause Four on the very day in June 1994 when he had declared for the leadership, his actual grasping of that particular nettle at the party conference in October that year came almost as much as a surprise to me as it did to most of the delegates in the hall in Blackpool.

In seventy-five years, no Leader of the Labour Party had succeeded in changing the hallowed words about rewarding the workers through the common ownership of production, though at least three of those Leaders had wanted to. Now, the party's new Leader had come to the conclusion that it would be the perfect test of whether Labour could, and would, accept the new thinking about which he had spoken on the day they had chosen him.

Both he and the party leadership knew they were walking on eggshells. Properly handled, it could lead to the rebirth of the party. Mishandled, it could split the party apart, and inflict permanent damage upon it. One of the campaign team, Philip Gould, has described how, in the weeks and days before the start of the conference, it became a matter of fierce argument and debate among the chosen few who knew it was on the cards. At one point, Gould claims, it led to him hiding in a wardrobe to avoid a damaging confrontation with other advisers, during a series of policy meetings being held in a hotel bedroom.

Such high feeling was one reason why Tony Blair felt he could not simply announce to the conference that he wanted Clause Four changed. However, in the hours just before the speech, word began to filter out, as it so often does, that something big was in the wind. There was talk of a 'surprise'. That was enough to make my colleague Elinor Goodman, the Political Editor of *Channel Four News*, follow a hunch, as she introduced the live broadcast on her channel of the Leader's speech. Her guest in the studio was the Labour MP Peter Hain. She asked him whether he believed an announcement about getting rid of Clause Four was coming. 'I don't think there's any chance of that,' was Hain's immediate reaction.

How wrong Hain was became clear some fifty minutes later. As the speech got under way, the text of it was, as usual, delivered to the ITN commentary box. That is an arrangement, worked out over the years, between the Labour Party and the broadcasters, which gives us an early chance to mark up in the text the sections which we expect to use later. It makes what is usually a long and complicated piece of editing that much easier. On this occasion, however, the practice only served to heighten the tension still further, because it was quite clear, as we skimmed through the text, searching for any bombshell announcement, that the end of the speech was not there in the text at all. There would indeed be a 'surprise'.

The missing three pages, released after the speech had finished, contained the announcement which, it was soon confirmed, was the definitive signal that Tony Blair and the leadership had decided to replace Clause Four. Even so, it was not put that bluntly in the speech itself. One of the reasons given for the change was that the party should 'say what we mean, and mean what we say'. However, when it came to the vital point, all that he actually said was this: 'It is time we had a clear, up-to-date statement of the objectives of our party. John Prescott and I will propose such a statement to the NEC.'

In the commentary box next to me, Elinor Goodman let out a whoop. 'I was right. It *is* Clause Four!' Yet such were the sensitivities of it all that Blair had not himself uttered the actual words 'Clause Four'. He had wanted, from the start, to put any change firmly in the context of the rewriting of the party's whole constitution. It did not take long, however, for the penny to drop among the delegates, and, immediately after the speech, the bars and hallways and corridors which surround the Blackpool conference hall were buzzing with arguments for and against the decision.

The traditionalists on the left of the party were aghast. I collared Tony Banks, always to be relied upon for speaking his mind in a pungent fashion. His reaction was, as usual, laced with ironic humour. 'There's nothing wrong with looking at the constitution,' he said, 'but dumping Clause Four is not something that is going to lead to peace and light and love in the Labour Party.' Dennis Skinner was far more blunt. 'The Tories must regard it as manna from heaven,' he told me, 'that the Labour Party, after concentrating for two years under John Smith on attacking the Tories day in and day out, is now going to start inspecting its own navel again.'

Listening to those remarks, however, was Mo Mowlam, and she immediately chipped in. 'I disagree completely with what Dennis was just saying,' she said. 'Forty-four per cent of eighteen-year-olds did not vote at the last election. What Tony was saying in his speech is that we have to use a language which is comprehensible to the general public, and particularly to young people.' The Labour MP Kim Howells joined in too. 'It's about us telling the nation the truth of what we believe in,' he said. 'If there are party members who can't stomach that, they shouldn't be in this party.'

Thus, within minutes of the speech ending, the party was splitting. It was what the leadership feared, and it moved quickly to counteract it. Along with several other broadcasters, I received an urgent message to come, with a crew, to the side of the conference platform. From there we were taken just behind the stage for an impromptu press conference with the Leader and, even more vitally, the Deputy Leader, John Prescott. Tony Blair, especially anxious to lower the temperature, still tried to avoid any direct references to Clause Four, concentrating instead on the revision of the whole constitution. 'This is not about dumping or ditching,' he said. 'It's about building and creating. It's about making it clear what we actually stand for as a political party.'

Beside him, John Prescott seemed ill at ease. He had been persuaded of the need to replace Clause Four some days earlier, but this man, whom I described in my report that evening as someone who had 'taken in Clause Four with his mother's milk', still did not find the prospect of abolishing it easy to handle. In a gnomic utterance, he fastened on to the

fact that Clause Four dealt with the issue of public ownership. If Clause Four was to die, he seemed to suggest, the
issue of public ownership that the clause dealt with would
not be killed with it. 'I know that I want to see public
ownership as an important strand of Labour Party thinking,'
he said, though noting that the conference had already been
rejecting demands for the nationalising or renationalising of
certain industries. It was support – qualified support, certainly, but support that was vital if the Clause Four battle
was to be won.

In my live two-way with Trevor McDonald that evening, I
talked about the decision being part of Tony Blair's 'new left'
agenda. Trevor had suggested to me that Tony Banks and
Dennis Skinner had been right in predicting that it would
simply open up a can of worms for the party. I replied that
those close to Blair were talking of the need to open up the
'dark corners' of what Labour stood for, to ensure that there
would be no ambiguity about the party's position.

Trevor also asked about the magnitude of the task, and of
the emotional attachment to Clause Four among ordinary
members. I was doing the two-way from the foyer of the
Imperial Hotel, surrounded by just such people, and I had
anticipated that we might need to talk in such terms. Not
being a Labour Party member myself, I borrowed a membership card from someone, which I now proceeded to show to
the camera, to make the point that such was the historic
importance of the old Clause Four to the party that every card
was inscribed with it. 'But these words', I added, 'are seventy-
six-years old, and the party leadership has decided that it's
time to get rid of this kind of old baggage.'

The party leadership, maybe, but by no means everyone in
the party. An instant campaign began, inside and outside the
conference, to 'Save Clause Four'. Petitions were printed;
signatures were sought for them. The campaign organisers

also secured an important tactical victory – the chance to debate and, hopefully, to vote on the matter on the floor of the conference two days later.

Before that, on the day immediately after the Clause Four announcement, there was the sort of poignant moment that often marks Labour Party conferences. The former Leader Neil Kinnock addressed the delegates, telling them, in a voice cracking with emotion, 'I will regret to my dying day that I failed to lead you to victory, the victory you deserve.' As the delegates roared their support, the cameras caught the Labour MP John Reid, who had been Neil Kinnock's Parliamentary Private Secretary, close to tears. But would the modernisation of the party, so notably started by Kinnock, be confirmed by a conference vote on the following day?

The first of the trademark 'bongs' on that evening's *News at Ten* provided the answer. Bong! 'Tony Blair shrugs off his defeat on Clause Four,' declared Julia Somerville, standing in for Trevor McDonald that evening, before she went on to announce that the conference had voted narrowly to keep the existing constitution of the Labour Party, including the old clause. I took up the story, suggesting that nothing could alter the fact that Blair had suffered an embarrassing defeat. The unions, with their block votes, had supported him; the constituency delegates, still at that time representing many of the militant voices in the party, had voted two to one against the change. As a result, the total conference vote to keep Clause Four had been extremely close – 50.9 per cent to 49.1 per cent. That, as much as any technicality about whether or not the vote put him under any obligation to act one way or another (which it did not), allowed Tony Blair to declare immediately that he would press on with his attempt to get it scrapped.

But plenty of passion had been unleashed during the debate. The proposer, a constituency delegate from Scotland, had quoted Labour's old anthem and told the conference not just to *sing* about keeping the Red Flag flying high. 'Let's *do* it,' he said, as he urged everyone to retain the words which, he believed, enshrined Labour's core socialist philosophy.

I was watching the debate from the special ITN booth, roughly built into one of the corners of the gallery. The construction was sufficiently minimal to allow me to see and hear some pro-Clause Four delegates who had crammed into a corner of the hall beside us. They cheered the opening speech arguing for the retention of Clause Four and other speeches like it that followed. They did not cheer people like Alan Johnson, then the leader of the Postal Workers Union and later a Labour MP. He told the conference that he wanted the election fought on 'policies, not on shibboleths', and that his members 'worried not a jot about words written by two middle-class Fabians in 1918'. That, and similar remarks by other modernisers, aroused the delegates next to our booth to real fury, their faces contorted with anger as they shouted 'Rubbish!' and 'Traitor!'

Those voices from the gallery underlined the problem that Blair faced. How could he move the party away from old-fashioned, emotional responses, in which those who shouted loudest could often win the day, to a point where it could make a cool-headed judgement about what was best for the party as a whole? One answer, he decided, was to put to use once again the one-member, one-vote machinery under which he had been elected as Leader. Through it, he would seek to obtain a clear mandate for the change, to be approved at a special conference in the spring. Ahead of such a conference, he would appeal directly, and in person, to as many individual members of the party as he and the rest of the leadership could reach. Thus was put in train another of the hallmark devices that New Labour created – the Road Show. This consisted of meetings up and down the country at which the Leader would come face to face with the party rank and file, to put a case directly to them, and to deal, equally directly, with their questions and anxieties.

I attended the first of the Clause Four Road Shows, in Gateshead, in early 1995. It was heavily stage-managed, with very little left to chance. The location was not far from Tony Blair's own constituency, and Tyneside was not exactly unknown to him, or he to Tyneside. Over the years, for example, his vocal support and, occasionally, support in person for Newcastle United Football Club had helped to make him a popular figure in the area. Gateshead itself was a powerful symbol of change and renewal. Despite the steady decline in heavy industry and the large areas of derelict landscape that had been left behind, one of the country's biggest and most successful shopping malls, the Metro Centre, had been established there. Indeed, the hall in which the Road Show was held was practically next door to it.

The careful planning meant that this first Road Show was, for the most part, held in front of a friendly audience. The atmosphere was overwhelmingly supportive and very similar, I felt, to that at Trimdon on the day Blair had declared for the leadership. At one stage on this occasion, a woman in the audience actually called out, 'God bless you, Tony.' That is exactly what the organisers had wanted, and it went very largely according to plan, despite the demonstrators outside with their posters talking of 'the battle for Labour's soul'. Inside, Tony Blair made his speech behind a small rostrum. At the end of it, in what became another hallmark of these occasions, he threw off his jacket and moved away from the rostrum to a chair at the front of the stage, so as to be closer to the audience for the question-and-answer session.

Such a 'meet the people' approach was not a particularly new idea. Out on the campaign trail, Paddy Ashdown never seemed happier than when he could throw off his anorak or suit jacket and talk to individual voters face to face. John Major had tried his version of the Road Show during the early stages of his 1992 general election campaign, taking over a school hall in his constituency and answering questions while perched on a bar stool in the middle of a set like a circus ring. For him, it hadn't worked. The way Central Office had set it up, and the way he handled it, had simply seemed wrong. Later Major came up with an impromptu replacement for the Tory Road Show idea. His famous soapbox turned out to be a brilliant success. It was right for him.

There were those in the Labour Party who had doubts about Tony Blair's man-of-the-people, jacket off approach too, but there was no question that he was extremely comfortable with it. More to the point, it came across that way on television. In other words, the Road Show worked for *him*, both on this first occasion in Gateshead and on the many occasions later when he used it to get a particular message across, even after he had become Prime Minister.

The prototype Road Show in Gateshead went well, though not all the questions were sympathetic. One member of the audience suggested, as had Dennis Skinner and Tony Banks at the party conference, that the whole Clause Four debate was a divisive distraction. Tony Blair replied that if, as Leader, he had believed that to be true he would not have started such a campaign, but that he was convinced that it was essential. Right on cue, there came just what the party leadership wanted – a round of applause.

Another questioner got up and began to describe himself, with heavy irony, as just a 'dope-headed socialist'. Every camera in the room, including ours, swivelled in his direction, like a pack of hunt supporters expecting a killing. The man was blunt, saying that he was suspicious that the new Leader was going to remove the 'historic socialist promise' of a better life for all. Tony Blair was equally forthright, replying that he did not think Clause Four *did* really hold out the prospect of inching towards socialism, and that the socialist promise, to him, was 'a strong, united, inclusive society in which everyone gets a chance to get on'. No killing there.

It was the Gateshead message – which was in truth no more than a reworking of the message already delivered in the Trimdon, Bloomsbury and Blackpool speeches – that was eventually fashioned into a new version of the party's constitution. The new Clause Four encapsulated that message. In language arguably rather less memorable than the original, it talked about 'a community in which power, wealth and opportunity are in the hands of the many, not the few'. In case anyone should be in any doubt about the authorship of the new clause, copies of Blair's handwritten draft were circulated ahead of the special conference that was to approve the change in April. We were told that the new Labour Leader, unhappy with a number of early versions, had written it as he returned from the Scottish Labour Party conference in early March, at which he had won a clear vote in favour of change.

The special conference to approve the change was held in the Methodist Central Hall in London on 29 April. By then it was certain that the new version would be accepted. Leaving his Islington home that morning, Tony Blair stopped for the cameras, to ram home the importance, for him, of what was about to take place. 'This is the change people said would never happen,' he said. 'It *is* going to happen, and it will mean the rebirth of the Labour Party.'

What followed at Central Hall that afternoon was another even more carefully orchestrated event, designed to reinforce the 'rebirth' message. As the conference began, an ITN camera caught Tony Blair's Press Secretary, Alastair Campbell, and his young assistant, Tim Allan, hopping about between the stage and the audience. Both were frantically waving their arms as they tried to ensure that everyone was in precisely the right place for the television spectacular that was to follow.

The whole day went according to the script. Everyone, for better or worse, played exactly the part that was expected of them. In the morning, I had waited outside Transport House a few streets away from Central Hall as a caucus of the Transport Workers Union reaffirmed its opposition to scrapping Clause Four. The T and G had reached that decision without balloting its members, as had another of the big unions, Unison. During the afternoon speeches, the T and G General Secretary, Bill Morris, said that his union accepted change, but not change at any price. 'So it is with a heavy heart, but a clear head, that we shall be voting against,' he told the conference.

The old and the new wings, battling it out for the soul of the party. It was just what the Blairites wanted, especially as they already knew they had won. One of those who took the floor to reject the T and G's position was a young moderniser. Two years on, he would spectacularly unseat Michael Portillo in his Enfield-Southgate constituency in the general election. At this point, it simply fell to Stephen Twigg to denounce the old attitudes that Bill Morris represented. 'Many of us in the party', he declared, 'would respect what we've just heard if it was based on a democratic ballot of the members of that trade union.'

Ironically, it was Michael Portillo who came, as the Tory spokesman, to our Millbank studio immediately after the special conference had approved the new Clause Four by 65 to 35 per cent. Portillo denounced the vote. 'All we've heard today', he said, 'is waffle, and it tells us nothing.' That was totally wrong, and I very much doubt whether, privately, he or the Tories believed it. The special conference, played out to perfection in front of the television cameras, had delivered an impressive boost to Tony Blair's authority as Leader. He had put that authority on the line by asking his party to change its whole way of thinking, and he had used every effort to persuade it to do so. They had responded by backing him.

Despite the victory, Blair was once again anxious to avoid triumphalism at the special conference. He knew that many in the party were supporting him only because they saw him as a winner. He had said as much in his speech at Blackpool the previous autumn, and so he now used his victory speech to try to rebut the suspicions in the party that he was really a Thatcherite Tory at heart. So, after a hesitant start, he faced the charge head-on, by acknowledging the thinking that lay behind the charge and then rejecting it. 'I wasn't born into the Labour Party,' he declared. 'I chose it. I'm proud to have been chosen its Leader, and it's the party I'll always live and die in.' The clear message: I am not now, and never will be, a Tory.

There was one lighter touch, though it was still related to the uneasiness in the party about how far and how fast their new Leader would take them down the modernisation road. There had been talk that he wanted to abandon the very name 'Labour Party' in favour of something that smacked more of social democracy. As I watched from the Central Hall gallery, I could certainly sense the frisson of anxiety that swept, albeit momentarily, among those below me as the delegates suddenly heard him saying, 'If I can turn briefly to the name of the party . . .' He paused, looking serious, and just long enough to let the anxiety grow a little more, before adding, 'It's staying as it is!'

Relief and laughter came in equal measure, as the joke worked, but only just. Judging that he may have pushed things just a little too far, he continued, 'You've got to admit I had you worried, didn't I?' Then he added, 'You know me. I don't spring surprises on you, do I?' The laughter that followed still had a twinge of nervousness in it. It was a party, then and for a long time later, which could never be quite sure that there wasn't another Clause Four-type surprise waiting for them just around the corner.

CHAPTER THIRTEEN

Exit Major, Enter Blair:
All Change at Number Ten

I t is hard to credit it now, but it was two full years after winning the Clause Four battle, which placed Tony Blair so firmly in charge of his party, before he won the general election and became Prime Minister. For him, it was doubtless a frustrating delay. For John Major, however, the same period was one of unremitting agony.

A great deal of my time had been spent on reporting the troubles of the Conservative Government and its Leader, even as I was chronicling the fortunes of the man who would eventually take over from him. Two weeks after Tony Blair had begun his campaign over Clause Four, the *Guardian* newspaper made the first allegations in the 'Cash for Questions' affair. Just over a month later, eight Tory rebels voted against the Government in a confidence vote. As a result, as the jargon puts it, they had the whip withdrawn from them – in other words, they were no longer regarded at Westminster as Conservative MPs. A ninth Tory, Sir Richard Body, later joined them, voluntarily. Collectively, the 'whipless ones', as they became known, caused the Government endless embarrassment until, in a major climbdown, the whip was restored to them five months later. In December 1994, the Government was defeated on the issue of VAT on domestic fuel, which it had committed itself to raising in two stages. Before the House was the Order to introduce the second stage of the increase, imposing the full 17.5 per cent rate. The Labour motion to block it was carried, with help from the other opposition parties and a number of Tory rebels, by eight votes.

Much later, when *News at Ten* was about to be killed off, *The Times* carried an editorial defending the programme and referring to what it called the 'personalities' it had produced. The leader writer described me thus: 'Michael Brunson, red-scarfed and over-coated against the chill, dashing across the road from the Commons on to College Green to broadcast, live, the outcome of some crucial 10pm division.' These were indeed the vintage years for late-night votes, the time when the scarf, the overcoat and its owner made almost nightly ap-pearances on *News at Ten*, as the Government's troubles mounted. As a result, and with the internal Tory squabbling over Europe raging on, Tony Blair's performances at Ques-tion Time grew ever bolder. Just four days before Clause Four was formally abolished, he wiped the floor with John Major at Question Time, saying that he knew exactly what marked the difference between himself and the Prime Minister. 'I lead my party. He follows his,' he declared.

As the year ground on, the Conservative Government's woes increased. The Tories lost 2,000 seats in the local elections in May 1995. That same month the Tory back-benches erupted in uproar over Lord Nolan's report on what to do about the sort of sleaze the 'Cash for Questions' scandal had revealed – Lord Nolan was proposing extra curbs on MPs. Major held a disastrous face-to-face meeting with his backbenchers over Europe, at which he was shouted at and heckled. There was open criticism of the Prime Minister by Lady Thatcher in a second volume of her memoirs dealing with her early life, a situation that she hardly remedied when I interviewed her about the book.

I asked her about the way in which the then Chancellor, Kenneth Clarke, was making no secret of his support for a single European currency. The woman who had seen off one of her own Chancellors, Nigel Lawson, replied with a thinly veiled suggestion that John Major should sack his. 'A Chancellor by definition doesn't last very long,' she told me. 'You don't surrender your currency and your responsibility and the City of London for a Chancellor – however good that Chancellor may be.'

There seemed to be no end to the Government's embarrassments, and I was shortly to be the delivery vehicle for yet another.

Leaks to the press are almost always carried out with a very specific purpose in mind. On very rare occasions, information is leaked by accident. Someone knows something and simply cannot keep his or her mouth shut. Equally rarely, leaks are the result of sheer devilment. Information is given to a journalist without there being any specific aim in mind, just for the hell of it. Most leaks, however, come about because the leaker wants to achieve something. That is why I was given access to the draft findings of a highly sensitive enquiry in June 1995.

Sir Richard Scott, an Appeal Court judge, had been appointed in November 1992 to investigate what became known as the 'Arms to Iraq' affair. During the Iran-Iraq War, sanctions had been imposed on both sides, and these included a prohibition, on the sales not just of arms but of other equipment, like machine tools, which might be put to military use by the Iraqi leader Saddam Hussein to bolster his war effort.

In 1992, four directors of a British engineering firm called Matrix Churchill had been charged with sanctions busting, and faced the possibility of going to prison if found guilty.

247

Their trial suddenly collapsed when Alan Clark, who had been a Trade Minister at the time, admitted that he had actually encouraged the four men in their efforts, because of the way he had applied the rules. There was outrage at the possibility that the Government might have knowingly been ready to let four innocent men go to jail. Furthermore, Ministers, it seemed, had at some stage secretly altered the guidelines on what could or could not be sold to Iraq, without telling Parliament.

By June 1995, after almost three years' work, there still seemed to be no end to the Scott enquiry. Sir Richard and his team believed in going into every last detail at very great length – his final report filled several books the size of large telephone directories. He had, however, got to the stage where he had started to send out to those people who had been individually investigated those sections of the draft report which specifically concerned them. There was, of course, much overlapping in all this, and, clearly, those who were advising such people also had access to the documents. As a result, one small section had already been leaked, which was sharply critical of William Waldegrave, a Foreign Office Minister at the time of the affair. Waldegrave's friends and associates were outraged, and it was one of them who was the source of the leak to me, two weeks later, of very large sections of the draft report. My source's aim was quite deliberate. He believed that by revealing, through me, Sir Richard's draft findings, several things would be made clear.

First, he hoped that people would accept that, following a ceasefire in the Gulf War, the guidelines on the export of such things as machine tools had been reinterpreted rather than radically changed. Second, he wanted to show that Waldegrave did not bear sole responsibility for what had happened, since a collective decision on the matter had been taken by him in consultation with two other members of the Government at that time, Alan Clark at the DTI and Lord Trefgarne at the Ministry of Defence. Third, he reckoned that Sir Richard's rather strange way of expressing himself would show that he had no understanding of the way Whitehall worked, and that his judgements on the process of government were, therefore, suspect. Fourth, there was the straightforward expectation that leaking the draft findings would so rock the boat and disrupt the long-drawn-out proceedings that the enquiry's final conclusions would appear confused and discredited.

The mechanics of the leak were worthy of a thriller. I had established with my informant that I would be able to see for myself some of the actual documents released by the Scott enquiry office, and not simply have to rely on his version of them. On that basis, a lunchtime rendezvous was set up some way from Westminster. There was no doubt that my source had begun to realise the enormity of what he was doing, as he led me, with evident nervousness, to a small, windowless room. 'You've got an hour to look through what I've got,' he said. 'You can't make copies, but you can take notes. By the way, have you had lunch?'

I replied that I had not, and a secretary was sent out for sandwiches and orange juice. As I skimmed through some 30 to 40 pages of the draft findings, while still managing a bite of sandwich here and a gulp of orange juice there, it did not take long to realise that what I was reading was explosive stuff.

I set about extracting the most vital material, and scribbled down as much as I could. Never have I regretted so much that I do not have shorthand, and that my handwriting, under pressure, becomes ever more illegible. My greatest fear was that I would not be able to read my notes once I got back to Westminster, and I deliberately made myself slow down and take more care as I transcribed what I was reading.

One of the best things about working for ITN is that it is a relatively small organisation. By comparison with the BBC, for example, there are very few chiefs to watch over the Indians. It therefore took just one short discussion with my Editor, Nigel Dacre, telling him of the circumstances under which the information had been passed to me, but not by whom, and outlining what that information was, before the decks were cleared for the story to lead that night's *News at Ten*. The resulting package, complete with the text of four sections of the draft report reproduced in the form of graphics, was rightly described by my journalistic colleagues as a bombshell, and created not only a massive and immediate impact but headlines and front-page stories for almost the whole of the following morning's papers, and a week of trouble.

Frankly, the immediate effect was not exactly what my source might have hoped for, despite the fact that my report stressed some of the points that he was anxious to bring to light. That was because nothing could diminish the impact of the judgement Sir Richard Scott had formed about the way the three Ministers had behaved. However much he qualified his main finding, both now and later, there was no doubting what his main finding was. Ministers *had* misled Parliament, and had done so deliberately. That much was abundantly clear from the first of the extracts from the draft report, which I now revealed. Sir Richard had found that there had indeed been a change in Government policy, and, as a result, he said, 'Parliament and the public were designedly led to believe that a different policy . . . was being applied than was, in fact, the case.'

But were the three Ministers actually guilty of the grave charge of misleading the House of Commons? Sir Richard suggested that they were. He had noted their contention that the guidelines had only been *interpreted* differently, rather than actually changed, but that position, he found, was 'incapable of being sustained by serious argument'. Answers given in the Commons and the Lords had not told Parliament of the true state of Government policy. 'This failure was deliberate,' Sir Richard declared, and was the result of an 'agreement by the three junior Ministers that no publicity should be given to the decision.'

Yet my source could take comfort in the way that Sir Richard Scott seemed to equivocate on one vital issue. Were the Ministers alone at fault? Had they, for example, seen all the intelligence reports on trade with Iraq that they should have done, and had they accidentally or deliberately over-looked such findings? Here, Sir Richard's somewhat curious style broke through. He raised the possibility of some doubt in this area, though he sought to dismiss it, as he passed judge-ment on the three Ministers' conduct. 'The reliance on the *possibility* of civilian use [of the machine tools] and the lack of *certainty* of an intended military use had become, in my opinion, equivalent to the use of the Nelsonian blind eye.' That got quoted everywhere.

The source of my story was never identified, despite a declaration by Sir Richard Scott that he would discover how the leak had occurred. He soon announced that no member of his enquiry team had been responsible. Sir Richard also said that the sections which I had seen had gone to only three people, which immediately suggested to most news-papers that one of the three Ministers who had been criticised was the source of the leak. That provoked a furious response from William Waldegrave, and an apology from Sir Richard for appearing to suggest that he might have been involved. The judge's letter to Waldegrave added, 'There are, of course, likely to have been a number of people, who may, quite properly, have been permitted, by each of the recipients in question, to have access to the extracts.'

The matter was raised in the House of Commons at Prime

251

Minister's Questions the day after my *News at Ten* report. John Major was pressed repeatedly by Tony Blair to say whether he would accept the findings of the Scott report if it contained in its final version what had now emerged from the draft version. In other words, would heads roll? John Major called the leak 'malicious' and said that it was intended to blacken Ministers' names before publication of the final report (which, as I have shown, it was not), but that he would not commit himself to any future course of action. Tony Blair said that any rejection of the final report would be seen as the 'final seal of contempt on a disintegrating Government'.

Of itself, the whole episode would have caused little damage, though it did have the effect, as my source had hoped, of blunting the impact of the final report when it was published ten months later. It was, nevertheless, damaging in the context of what Blair had described as a 'disintegrating Government'. It had, indeed, seemed for so long merely to be keeping its head above water, a situation that the Prime Minister now sought to change in dramatic fashion.

We now know that John Major had been considering a last-resort tactic of resigning and offering himself for re-election for some time before he actually did so, four days after my Scott leak. He had been thinking about much more than the leak during that time, but he was still angry about it. Asked for an interview on resignation day, he replied angrily, 'The way I feel about ITN at the moment, I don't feel like doing you any favours.' He did agree to a series of interviews, though, with all the broadcasters, after his announcement in what, by tradition, we call the Downing Street rose garden, though there are precious few roses in it. All the political journalists at Westminster were called in shortly after Prime Minister's Questions that Thursday afternoon.

It was an astonishing moment. John Major had kept his

secret well, and the possibility of his resigning was discussed
only as an outside chance among some of us as we sat outside
in the sunshine, perched on little gold chairs lined up in front
of a lectern, waiting for his arrival. His statement was brief
and to the point. He said that, while he had achieved much in
his five-year premiership, a 'small minority' in the Conservative Party had been opposing him, with the result that he faced
yet another formal challenge to his leadership later in the year.
'The Conservative Party', he announced, 'must make its
choice. I am no longer prepared to tolerate the present
situation. In short, it is time to put up or shut up. I have
nothing more to say this afternoon. Thank you very much.'
Whereupon he turned on his heel and left the garden.

I took him at his word about having nothing more to say,
especially since the ITN 5.40 p.m. news was only some twenty
minutes away. I had begun collecting my thoughts for my live
two-way from Downing Street, when my producer rushed up
with news that the Prime Minister might, after all, be doing
interviews. We squeezed one in, just minutes before the
bulletin. In it, the statement in the rose garden was underlined
– that things could not go on as they were, and that he needed
a decisive vote of confidence in his leadership to be able to
carry on.

The campaign began the following Monday. After a weekend of agonising, John Redwood decided to stand against
him. Norman Lamont, after dropping a sufficiently heavy
hint to allow me to report on the previous Friday's *News at
Ten* that he would run, decided not to. During the short,
sharp week of campaigning, every political correspondent
had his own private tally of the possible result. I decided to
arrange a 'pools panel' attempt at a prediction, which we
could broadcast. Over lunch with Peter Riddell of *The Times*
and Robert Hayward, a former Tory MP who had established
a good track record as an amateur psephologist, we came up

with a figure which, after a swift tally at the end of the gathering, was only four short of the actual result. I should have stayed with it. Back in my office, as I checked the list of Conservative members on which we had worked, I found that I had miscounted our findings, and, as a result, I upped the number supporting John Major by two. Our prediction was that John Major would get 224 votes, with those either voting for John Redwood or abstaining totalling 105.

Even so, we were not far out. The actual result was 218 to Major, with 109 either voting for Redwood or abstaining. It was safely over the 200-vote mark, which, by common consent, had become a benchmark figure though it was only three more than the 215-vote test which John Major had set himself. He revealed later that if he had not reached that figure, he had planned to resign.

Immediately the result was announced, the Conservatives launched a huge operation to bolster the Prime Minister's position. As is usual on these occasions, the stretch of open land between the Houses of Parliament and the broadcasters' headquarters at Millbank became a vast open-air studio. Abingdon Green was suddenly full of Ministers and other top Tories, darting from camera position to camera position. Every one of them was preaching the same message, that what had happened was a great personal triumph for John Major.

As Lord Cranborne, his campaign manager for the contest, admitted later, 'It was clear it was not going to be the most overwhelming of victories. So it was important that we got people out there to say that it was convincing.' As another member of the campaign team, Ian Lang, recalled, 'It had to be a line that was plausible, that they [the broadcasters] would be willing to accept. We got a big roll of ministers and trusties out on to College Green. It was bedlam, but it worked.'

I beg to differ. I, for one, did not accept then, nor do I

consider now, that John Major had won a terrific victory, when over a third of his MPs had failed to support him. The line that Ian Lang had asked his 'trusties' to spin was not, in my view, 'plausible', and, as the 5.40 news switched across to me, live, on the Green, I argued the toss with the Education Secretary, Gillian Shephard. She, like all the others sent out to face the television cameras, was sticking rigidly to the line that Major's margin of victory was greater than Tony Blair's had been against John Prescott in the Labour leadership election. That, frankly, was not comparing like with like. There was all the difference in the world between two candidates, starting from cold, contesting a vacant position, and a sitting Prime Minister and Conservative Leader finding that a third of his Parliamentary party had failed to support him.

One tabloid newspaper had a good deal of fun at my expense over the coverage that day. 'Well done, Mr Major!' the *Daily Star* snorted. 'That's more than you can say to ITN's political team. Michael Brunson was well dodgy. He should have seen that Mr Major was home and dry, yet he milked the moment for maximum drama.' For all the talk at the time, however, of boils being lanced and rot being stopped, events soon suggested once again that the Government was in terminal decline.

Two defections from the Conservative Party did not help. On the very eve of the 1995 Tory conference, the Tory MP Alan Howarth announced that he was joining the Labour Party, largely as a result of the hardline policies being pursued by the Home Secretary, Michael Howard. That most certainly did not stop Howard pressing forward with those policies during the conference. Indeed, so keen were sources within the party hierarchy to flag them up that I was able to lead *News at Ten* the night before his speech with the news that he would be announcing a tough new system of mandatory sentences for persistent offenders.

Four days after Christmas, another Tory MP, Emma Nicholson, defected – this time to the Liberal Democrats. This was a classic case of my being in the wrong place at the wrong time – in Norfolk, to be precise, taking a post-Christmas break. My opposite number at the BBC, Robin Oakley, was still in London, and it was to him that the Liberal Democrats gave the story, on the grounds, they said later, that his bulletin was at 9 p.m. Ours, in the chaos of the Christmas holiday schedules, was not until 11 p.m.

Panic broke out in North Norfolk, where my ITN bleeper went off just before the BBC bulletin warning me that Robin Oakley had the story. I watched his clear scoop, and set about trying to catch up. This involved, among other things, a hair-raising twenty-mile drive along dark, snow-packed and icy country roads to the local television station, while trying to have a serious political conversation on my mobile phone with the then Chairman of the Conservative Party, Brian Mawhinney.

A large, though sparsely attended street fair, which made access to the studio in Norwich difficult, was another hazard to be overcome. So was the fairly obvious fact that I was about to deliver a political commentary while not, unlike my opposite number, exactly at the centre of things at Westminster. I hoped that my superiors at ITN would be studiously vague about my precise whereabouts when crossing to me for the live two-way. 'Why not just say, "We're joined now by our Political Editor," and leave it at that?' I gently suggested to them. The introduction to me was indeed masterful in its imprecision. Unfortunately, what appeared on the screen was not. As I delivered my thoughts on Miss Nicholson's defection, a caption was flashed up beneath me which read, all too clearly, 'Live from Norwich'.

Nineteen-ninety-six seemed only to increase the catalogue of troubles for John Major and his Government. In February the IRA ended its ceasefire with a devastating bomb at Canary Wharf in London. The same month, another Tory MP, Peter Thurnham, resigned the Tory whip, cutting the Government's narrow majority still further. Soon, after the loss of another by-election at Staffordshire South East, that majority was reduced to just one. With the announcement in March 1996 of the possible link between mad cow disease, BSE, and its human equivalent, CJD, another serious crisis began, leading eventually to Britain withdrawing all co-operation with Europe. In the same month, there was the terrible shooting of schoolchildren in Dunblane, and, in June, another appalling IRA bomb in Manchester.

In the middle of all this, I had lunch with Michael Heseltine, who'd been made Deputy Prime Minister in the reshuffle which had followed John Major's re-election as Leader. Mr Heseltine was always the Dr Pangloss of the Tory Party – ever ready to see the best in everything, and never ready to admit the possibility of defeat. With the general election at most a year off, he confidently predicted, amid his party's sea of troubles, that the Conservatives would be re-elected with a sixty-seat majority. I expressed my utter incredulity. 'Well,' he said, 'you don't expect me to go around talking about defeat, do you?' I sensed from his answer that not even he believed in his heart of hearts that victory was possible.

As the countdown to the general election continued, so did the Tory Government's downward spiral. The row within the Conservative Party over Europe raged on. An autumn Budget which cut income tax by a penny, and promised extra money for schools and hospitals, and a decision by the Cabinet to take a markedly more sceptical line on Europe, failed to turn things around. The Prime Minister did not exactly help his own image by being caught by the cameras, including ITN's, wearing what appeared to be a remarkably silly tribal hat during a visit early in 1997 to the Khyber Pass, part of a tour of India, Pakistan and Bangladesh. Private jokes about 'Major up the Khyber' flew thick and fast among those of us who made up the accompanying press corps.

The loss in February of the Wirral South by-election, in a constituency which had been held by the Tories at the 1992 general election with a majority of just over 8,000, prompted another warning from Major about the extent of the danger he and his party faced. As Tory Leader, he was always devastatingly honest about such electoral setbacks, and, to the surprise of some of his campaign strategists, he would readily admit, far more so than previous Leaders had done, that things were actually as bad as they were.

So, as I interviewed him on the morning after Wirral South, he conceded that, with the general election a matter of weeks away, his party was facing the possibility of national defeat, and that everyone should wake up to the fact. We were sitting in the large conference room which forms part of the Chief Whip's quarters in Twelve Downing Street, which he often used for television interviews. There was no attempt to dismiss Wirral South as a freak result. Here was a Conservative Prime Minister telling me, 'If opinion doesn't change, then we are going to have a Labour government, and people will have to realise what a Labour government means.' It was clearly meant to shock his own Conservative supporters into action, but in the country as a whole it was seen as more negative campaigning – vote for us, the Tories, not because we are wonderful, but because the Opposition is worse.

As we now know, the British electorate did not respond to that appeal. The decision on 17 March 1997 to call the election struck most people, not as a leap into the unknown, but as a welcome chance to bring about a fresh start for the country, as Labour's overwhelming victory eventually confirmed. The idea of 'time for a change' which is present during most general election campaigns was felt far more keenly on this occasion. The perception of a government which was exhausted and which had run out of ideas while, at the same time, being torn apart by internal strife was simply too strong.

In addition, there was the perception of a government fatally infected by sleaze. Nothing else could explain the extraordinary events which unfolded in and around the contest for the seat at Tatton, in the Cheshire commuter belt near Manchester. The sitting MP was the Conservative Neil Hamilton, caught in the spider's web of the 'Cash for Questions' scandal, and insisting throughout that he had done nothing wrong. It was a sign of the times that, almost from nowhere, there was born the idea that he should be opposed, not by the usual array of opposition party candidates, but by a single 'White Knight' anti-sleaze contender, to increase the chances of him being soundly beaten.

Thus it was, with the agreement of the Labour and Liberal Democrat parties, that the former BBC war correspondent Martin Bell agreed to fight the Tatton seat as an Independent. Perhaps the fact that, throughout his courageous reporting of the conflict in Bosnia, he had conspicuously worn a white jacket had something to do with it – sartorially, at least, he fitted the White Knight role. In the end, it turned out to be far more than a matter of dress. As he had made clear when declaring his candidacy, he was driven on by local unease in Tatton, and by a sense of what he called 'a poison in the democratic system, which means that the system itself cannot operate'.

He had no illusions, though, about what he was letting himself in for. He admitted that there was a risk of simply making a fool of himself, and with, I suspect, just a touch of exaggeration said that he was finding the whole exercise more nerve-racking than braving 'Snipers' Alley' in Sarajevo. Neil Hamilton's wife Christine, ever the driving force in her husband's political life, called Martin Bell's decision to stand

'unbelievable cheek', adding that it showed he did not 'understand the mentality of Cheshire people'.

As so often during my broadcasting career, one of the pieces
of reporting which gave me the greatest satisfaction turned
largely on a measure of good luck. The plan had been for me
to cover most of the general election campaign in London.
Growing experience over the most recent campaigns had
taught us at ITN that the real meat of the day tended to
come from the morning round of news conferences in the
capital, and that was where, as Political Editor, I needed to be,
however much I may have wanted to get out and about on the
campaign trail away from London.

On this particular day, however, the ITN newsdesk had
spotted, rather late it must be admitted, that Neil Hamilton
was due to attend an evening selection meeting for formal
adoption as the Conservative candidate in Tatton. Given that
Martin Bell had, by now, also taken up residence in the
constituency, it was decided that I should go up and cover
the event, working with our correspondent Adrian Britton,
who was already keeping an eye on events there.

The last-minute decision provided me with a rare treat. The
only way to get to Tatton in good time was to use the ITN
helicopter as a taxi – an expensive, though in this case
practical, use of this particular company asset. It was a
gloriously bright morning, and the journey up across Middle
England, so often talked about in political circles, was a great
delight. We had a particularly good view, for example, of
some practice laps under way at the Silverstone racetrack near
Northampton. Touchdown at Manchester airport, and a
short ride by conventional taxi to the constituency, meant
that I was in position, just outside the Conservative Party
headquarters in Knutsford, in time for a quick two-way for
the lunchtime bulletin at 12.30. I had immediately picked up
talk of a possible head-to-head confrontation between Ham-

ilton and Bell that afternoon, with Hamilton threatening to turn up at a press conference Bell had called, and I mentioned this in my remarks to London.

We had been alerted to the fact that Martin Bell's press conference would have to be held out of doors, on a patch of open ground called Knutsford Heath. His campaign head-quarters was, at that time, a tiny basement room in a small guesthouse where he had taken up residence, and the room, it was explained, would be quite unable to accommodate the considerable number of journalists expected to be present. With Neil Hamilton likely to try and disrupt things, there was every chance of a classic confrontation.

Adrian Britton had a brilliant idea. Why didn't we pool the output from all the cameras that might be prepared to work with us in order to achieve the best possible coverage? My producer for the day, Candida Watson, sought out Channel Four News and Granada Television, who readily agreed to the plan. As a result, we decided that one camera would stick like a limpet to Martin Bell, another would do the same with Neil Hamilton, and Granada's camera would 'hang loose' for wide shots and other eventualities.

The plan worked splendidly, especially since the BBC did not seem to have monitored my lunchtime broadcast hinting at what might happen. Our rivals were therefore unprepared for what was to unfold. The cameras, working in our com-bined operation, picked up Neil Hamilton as his car stopped close to the appointed location. They also captured Martin Bell from the moment that he emerged in his white suit from his guesthouse. The third camera had long shots of them both as they made their way to the open ground.

The opening of my commentary ran thus: 'This was like some strange medieval pitched battle, each side moving for-ward through the trees, with an accompanying army of cameras and microphones. Mr Hamilton, the Defending

Member, who'd come, he said, as a "potential constituent", to challenge Martin Bell, the White Knight, emerging from his small hotel headquarters, to hold his open-air press conference, of which Mr Hamilton had got wind. They came together to fight it out, on Knutsford Heath.'

What I later described as 'the strangest of political debates' then unfolded. It began with a handshake, duly recorded by our cameras, in close-up. Everyone had formed a tight circle around the two men. Our cameras were right in the middle of the circle – those from the other broadcasting organisations were not. Hamilton demanded to know whether Bell, by standing as an 'anti-corruption candidate', was thereby accusing him of corruption. Bell said he did not want to make things personal. 'I don't want to talk about you at all,' he said. 'I want you to run on your record. The issue of trust is important.'

Mrs Hamilton dived in. In a tone of voice that contained all the loathing of Martin Bell that she could summon up, she demanded, 'Do you accept that a man is innocent unless proved guilty?' Quietly Martin Bell replied, 'Yes, of course I do.' Christine Hamilton snapped back, 'Do you accept that my husband is innocent?' In case Bell hadn't quite got that, she repeated the question. Seeing the trap she had opened up for him, he replied, 'I'm not going to go on facing an ambush here.' In answer to her direct point, he said he did not know whether Neil Hamilton was guilty or not. 'So', Hamilton chipped in, 'you are prepared to give me the benefit of the doubt?' 'Absolutely, absolutely,' was Bell's reply.

That seemed to be a major point scored by the Hamiltons, as the argument raged on and on. The fact wasn't lost on Colonel Bob Stewart, a former commander in Bosnia, who'd struck up a friendship with Martin Bell while they were both there, and who had now come to do what he could to help the Bell campaign. In the way we had organised things, the

Granada television team and their correspondent Mark Lyons seemed to have drawn the short straw. They were not in the middle of the circle surrounding the combatants, but had stuck to the agreement to hang back a little. Now, however, they were in exactly the right position to capture a magical moment. Colonel Stewart, even more of a political novice than Martin Bell, strode away from the mêlée in disgust. 'Silly, isn't it?' he said, as he marched towards the Granada camera. 'Do you really think so?' Mark Lyons prompted him. With some feeling, Bob Stewart simply said, 'Yeah!'

From my vantage point inside the circle, I did not know of Colonel Stewart's departure until I saw the pictures later, and, with the argument between Bell and Hamilton going round and round, I attempted to draw things to a close. Hadn't Bell accused Hamilton, if not of corruption, at least of a poor standard of public behaviour? He agreed he had, but said the matter was now 'between Mr Hamilton and the electors'. To Hamilton, I suggested that he bore at least some guilt, because he had accepted benefits which he had failed to declare in the proper way. 'So did Tony Blair. So did John Prescott,' Hamilton replied, referring to rather minor infringements of the rules involving the two Labour leaders which had come to light.

Finally, the two of them had had enough. 'I don't want to hijack the whole press conference,' Hamilton declared. 'Well, you haven't done badly,' Bell shot back. That, indeed, was the truth of it. Between them, the Hamiltons had succeeded in wrecking the event, something that no doubt accounted for the satisfied smiles on their faces as, hand in hand, they left the field of battle.

The confrontation over, the hardest part of my day was about to begin. My video editor and I now had a great deal of material from three different cameras to pull together into an organised whole. First, though, we had to discover how much time we would be given on ITN's early-evening news bulletin, which lasted in total for a little over fifteen minutes, for the package we would now put together.

I called the Editor of the programme, Phil Moger. Phil is someone who wears his South London origins like a badge of honour; his editorial judgements, and his ways of expressing them, always have the needs of what we rather patronisingly call the 'ordinary viewer' at heart. He was also given to the most wonderful Malapropisms. Trying to explain to me once that he wanted a short series of snapshot-style observations included in one of my reports, he told me, 'Mike, what I really want is a little series of vinaigrettes.'

On this occasion, Phil had already sensed from the Press Association news agency reports coming into the ITN newsroom that something reasonably extraordinary had happened in Knutsford between Martin Bell and Neil Hamilton, so, as usual, he came straight to the point. 'Now then, Mike,' he said. 'Just how good is all this?' I was equally blunt in my reply. 'Phil, you are going to love every second of it, I promise you,' I said, before giving him a brief rundown on what had happened. There was a slight pause, as the man in charge of a fairly short bulletin, who regularly regarded a correspondent's report that lasted for a minute and a half as being on the long side, considered his options. 'All right, Mike. If it's that good, four minutes.' I decided to push my luck. 'Phil,' I replied, 'I think it's worth quite a bit more than that, I really do.' 'All right, Mike,' came the reply. 'Four and a half minutes!'

It was the most complicated four-and-a-half-minute edit I ever embarked on. Fortunately, I was working with one of the very best of ITN's videotape editors, Bill Frost, who, once he senses what the correspondent with whom he is working wants to achieve editorially, is a genius at making it happen technically.

While our three cameras had captured everything that had happened, we did not have the sort of smooth, continuous output that can be achieved by a normal outside-broadcast operation, where a director makes sure that everything fits together as the event itself unfolds. Here we had cameras that had been operated, without direction, by individual cameramen. Of necessity, camera angles, colour balance and sound quality were all different, and needed correcting and matching, to the extent that the facilities in our small editing van could handle such demands. While, for most of the time, each camera had caught Neil and Christine Hamilton or Martin Bell in a clear shot as they spoke any of the words which we particularly wanted to use, that was not always the case, and sometimes the sound from one of the cameras had to be matched up with pictures from another. In addition, you cannot simply put a succession of soundbites together without paying particular attention to suitable words and pictures in between to make sense of it all.

In the end we had the report ready, and I was immensely proud of what a remarkable team effort we had managed to produce that day, an operation which continued with further coverage, for *News at Ten*, of the meeting at which Neil Hamilton was confirmed as the Tory candidate. Perhaps the greatest compliment came from Phil Moger, back at ITN headquarters, after my initial report had provided him with the lead story of his bulletin. 'You were dead right, old son,' he told me after the 5.40 news. 'I *did* love every single second of it!'

By comparison, the rest of the campaign seemed flat and lifeless. Overall, this was the most tedious of the five general elections in which I have been involved. There were several reasons for this. First, it lasted much longer than usual – six weeks instead of the usual three and a half, because John

Major, way behind in the polls, believed a long campaign would give him a better chance of explaining his policies and getting his message across.

That, however, was the second problem. Most of the issues raised had already been argued over, again and again, during the five long years since the last election, and, in some cases, for much longer than that. Europe, for example, which the statisticians told us later was the top subject in the broadcast coverage during the 1997 campaign, had been the issue which had dominated British politics for years, and which had overshadowed the entire six and a half years of John Major's premiership. The third problem was the simplest. The result of the election was already a foregone conclusion – it was very clear from the start that Tony Blair was going to win it.

The early-morning press conferences became a real slog, especially since it had become fashionable in news bulletins to demonstrate what was known at ITN as 'RI' – Reporter Involvement. Our Editors wanted the active participation of their on-screen correspondents in the day's events to be seen on the screen. This was meant to engage the attention of the viewers by showing that the familiar pre-election faces, the regular reporters on the bulletins, had truly been involved in the gathering, or even the creation, of the campaign news, rather than simply voicing over a collection of soundbites.

It led to a ridiculous battle between myself, Robin Oakley and John Sergeant of the BBC, and Adam Boulton of Sky News, to try and be called first at each of the parties' presentations. It was bad enough in any case that so much of the questioning was restricted to the broadcasters. It became much worse as, despite our shouted entreaties, the Party Chairmen seemed to settle into the habit of always picking the BBC first, ITN second and Sky third each morning, especially at the Conservative event. It reached the ludicrous stage where, at one of the Labour press conferences,

Gordon Brown, following the pattern that had emerged, called on me to ask a question when I wasn't even in the room. I had insisted on getting out of London to go and listen to some ordinary voters, and to try and gauge what was happening in a vital clutch of marginal seats in the East Midlands.

Towards the end of the campaign, I let my frustration at the tedium of the morning press conferences in London get the better of me. At the Conservative gathering, I was, unusually, called first by the Tory Chairman, Brian Mawhinney. 'I'm glad to see that, at last, I've broken the BBC's monopoly on the first question,' I began, unwisely. A chorus of 'Oooh, listen to him,' ran around the room from my fellow journalists.

One issue in particular caught my attention because of what it said about Labour's campaigning methods. Just before the election had been called, the Tories had released details of how they would tackle the problem of pensions, and particularly the way that people often failed to make sufficient pension provision for themselves, thus leaving them dependent on the state old-age pension, which, in many cases, then had to be topped up by additional state benefits.

The Tory plan, called Basic Pension Plus, envisaged the creation of a market-based pension for everyone, backed by state guarantees, a scheme which would eventually replace the present old-age pension. It would be introduced very gradually, over some fifty years, as young people entered the world of work for the first time, though everyone who had currently started to pay National Insurance contributions towards the present pension would stay on that scheme. It was an innovative, if complicated, attempt to deal with the problem that, as the population lived longer, the state's pension bill was going up and up.

Towards the end of the election campaign, Labour deliberately raised the temperature by attacking the Tory plan. They simply painted it as an attempt by the Tories to privatise the old-age pension, though the truth was far more involved than that. Talk of privatising the pension, Labour knew, would raise anti-Conservative fears, especially among older voters. They coupled this with a number of other broad-brush assertions, claiming, for example, that the Tories would put VAT on food if re-elected. The Conservatives got extremely angry. They accused Labour of lying, and denounced their campaigning as scurrilous. At Labour's morning press conference, Tony Blair first defended his allegation about VAT on food by saying that the Tories had broken election promises on VAT in the past, so they were bound to do so again.

I had a day-long, public set-to with Blair on the pensions issue. At his morning press conference, I pointed to a panel behind him, listing Labour's predictions of the results of another term of Conservative Government. It baldly stated, 'State pension abolished'. I pointed out that the Tories had categorically denied that claim, saying that there would always be a pension guaranteed by the state, though delivered in a different way, and that the present pension would be continued for those already in it. Had not John Major got a point when he talked about Labour's 'scurrilous' campaigning?

Tony Blair replied that the Tories' new idea was based on making everyone, ultimately, take out a private pension. Despite their denials, he thought that they would have to switch older people out of the present system and into the new one far earlier than they had planned and that, buried in the small print, there was provision for so doing, in order to finance the huge start-up costs of the new scheme.

I immediately challenged his use of words, pointing out to him that he had said, 'why I *think* they will have to do it'. I suggested to him that, while he was expressing an *opinion* of how things might turn out, he was going to the country on the issue, presenting his prediction as *fact*, by using the three simple words, 'State pension abolished'. It was clear to me that he could have used some phrase like 'State pension at risk' or 'under threat', but, no, he had settled on the word 'abolished'. Blair replied that he was inviting people to look at the small print, and to ask themselves whether the Tories could fund their scheme without bringing older people into it. Labour was 'perfectly entitled to warn people as to what the Tories' pension proposals mean'. But to state it all as certainty, as fact? That had surely been going too far.

The Conservatives certainly thought so. They called a second press conference in the afternoon to refute Labour's morning claims. In front of a video backdrop of an image of Tony Blair constantly changing colour, chameleon-style, headed with the words, 'You can't believe a word of what he says', Health Secretary Stephen Dorrell said of the Labour Leader, 'The tougher the questioning, the more he panics, and the more he panics, the more he lies. Bare-faced, despicable lies.'

It so happened that, on that evening, Tony Blair was scheduled to do a live interview with me on *News at Ten*. He flatly denied, again, that he had been caught lying, as the Tories had charged, and in answer to my suggestion that he was merely expressing a view, but not the facts, about what might happen under a Tory government, he repeated that state pensions for young people would be replaced by private pensions. I produced the original Tory proposals, which I had taken the precaution of having with me, and read out the Prime Minister's words at the time they had been put forward. 'Let me make clear', John Major had written, 'that the state will continue to guarantee that everyone will continue to receive at least their basic state pension, uprated for inflation.'

'Are you saying that that's a lie?' I asked. 'They are saying the *private* pension will meet the basic state pension,' Tony Blair replied, 'but the basic state pension *is* to go.' We continued to argue the toss, not just about pensions, but about his claim that VAT would go on food, which produced the standard answer about the Tories always breaking their promises. I waved the Tory manifesto at him, which I had also taken the precaution of having with me, and asked him if he regarded the whole thing as a pack of lies. He wouldn't go that far, but said that he wasn't going to let the Tories get away with making proposals that were not rigorously scrutinised.

I believe that interview was typical of the work of all the broadcasters in their attitude to the 1997 election, as they dealt with all the parties and their promises. No one could accuse us this time, as they had during previous elections, of simply being obsessed with photo-opportunities, and of not thrashing out some of the issues.

A week before polling day, in a similar live interview with John Major, I went round the course with him one last time. He was not giving up without a fight, even though he had, by now, privately accepted that he was not going to win. The interview took place, once again, in the conference room at Twelve Downing Street, where, exactly eight weeks previously, he had issued his public warning about of the possibility of a Labour government. Now, at my prompting, he repeated that claim, saying that 'self-evidently there could be a Labour government seven days from now', as he urged people to wake up to the realisation of what that would mean. There was no prediction of a Conservative victory, only the assertion that things were changing in the Conservatives' favour, and that 'on the doorstep, it feels very similar to 1992', when, of course, John Major had snatched a narrow victory.

ITN's Editor-in-Chief, Richard Tait, had asked to be present with me at the interview, perhaps because this would almost certainly be the last time that we would both be speaking to John Major as Prime Minister. Once again, after we had finished the live broadcast, he seemed anxious simply to chat. I had noticed, over the years, that he had kept up the practice, despite the grief it had once caused him in the 'Bastardgate' affair. Ever since, though, he had made very certain that, after interviews were finished, the microphones were turned off. Now, talking to Richard and myself for some fifteen minutes or so after the live broadcast had ended, he insisted that things were nowhere near as black as everyone was trying to paint them. The Conservatives' private polling, and the general feel which Central Office was getting, he said, suggested that things were going much better than expected, especially in Scotland.

When, six days later, three Scottish Cabinet Ministers lost their seats, and when the Conservatives were left without a single MP in Scotland, I reflected on that conversation. Had John Major simply been whistling in the wind, trying to convince himself that the inevitable was not going to happen? Or had Central Office's reading of the true situation in Scotland been way off beam? Perhaps they knew the awful extent of what was to come, but simply hadn't dared tell him? The truth was, almost certainly, much more mundane. I believe that he simply did not want to allow two journalists, even at this late stage, the satisfaction of being able to report that he had given up, or that there was a whiff of catastrophe already permeating Downing Street. Like Michael Heseltine before him, why should he go around talking up defeat?

Such a defeat, however, was certainly the assumption upon which ITN had based all its preparations for its huge election-night operation. Cautious souls to the last, all our rehearsals had begun with the suggestion that, on the night, our exit poll would be predicting a Labour majority of around sixty to

271

seventy seats, the sort of margin of victory which even Tony Blair, privately, was assuming.

In the event, of course, things turned out very differently. On election night itself, our real exit poll, conducted for us by MORI, led us to begin eight hours of broadcasting with the prediction of a Labour majority of 159, just twenty short of the eventual result. Even so, as I made my first contribution to the night's broadcast, I still, in my heart of hearts, did not really believe it. The swing of votes required for such a result was so immense that I felt I had to enter some sort of caveat about how wrong the polls had been last time. My comments intensely annoyed Bob Worcester, the MORI chairman, as he later made abundantly clear to me.

The fact that I was commenting at all was the result of a decision by ITN, at the request of the ITV companies, that our election-night programme should be distinctively different from that provided by our main rivals, the BBC. We knew that the BBC would hurl all their very considerable technical resources into their normal, massive operation, centred on a very large, and very busy-looking, election-night studio. Presenters, experts, politicians and of course, Peter Snow, his arms waving in front of his complicated graphics like sails on a crazy windmill, would all be there. ITV decided that it wanted a far more 'user-friendly' programme, an aim with which I totally agreed, though I still doubt whether it warranted a rather cringe-making claim in our programme's introduction that ours would be the 'friendliest service'.

To that end, it was decided that I should join Jonathan Dimbleby as co-presenter. He would keep things moving along as the main 'anchor', bringing in all the usual elements, above all the declarations in the key constituencies. I would be at his side to add, in conversation with him, my comments and reactions as events unfolded. A small panel of number-crunching experts backed up both our efforts. They were only called up and shown speaking directly to the cameras as required, speaking from a sort of 'boffins' area', which, during the rest of the programme, was only half seen behind us through a gauzy backdrop.

The studio was, in fact, the long, thin atrium at ITN's headquarters, and its shape determined two other important elements. One side of the atrium became a video wall, on which Alastair Stewart kept a tally of marginal seats that would give us a clear indication of the way things were going. We had severe problems with the video wall in the early rehearsals, with most of us arguing that the prototype looked like the old destination board at Waterloo station, a vast and rightly famous contraption of wooden shutters and levers which used to record the arrival and departure of London commuter trains. Our final version, thankfully, looked a little more sophisticated.

At the opposite end of the atrium to the presenters' desk was a studio audience made up of members of the general public, with Sue Lawley there to question them. They were drawn from the people who had formed part of the ITV 500, our own version of a focus group, and whose opinions we had tracked throughout the campaign. I thought that their presence added a great deal to the programme, not least because we heard their spontaneous reactions as events unfolded. There was a great round of applause from most of them, for example, when we finally declared an outright Labour victory.

I was delighted to be playing a full part in the programme. There were no commercial breaks, and I was told that I had to be ready to interject with a comment or observation at any time. The prospect of eight hours without going to the toilet had, therefore, required a certain amount of dietary pre-planning. Curiously, though I had been Political Editor since 1986, my part in the two previous election-night programmes had been minimal. Now, Jonathan Dimbleby and I had struck up an excellent working partnership during the many hours of rehearsal. As a result, the very different style of ITV's coverage, coupled with, yet again, a much faster results service than that provided by the BBC, received plenty of critical approval, even though, as usual, most people watched the BBC.

The night itself passed in something of a blur. It was certainly the shortest eight hours of my career. It seemed to flash by, from the first indications of a Labour landslide through to confirmation of the complete trouncing of the Tories – the true impact of that brought home by Michael Portillo's crestfallen face as he lost in Enfield. In a very short time, it seemed, we were reporting Labour's dawn victory rally, held outside the Festival Hall on the South Bank in London.

That rally, for me, provided us with one of the most telling sequences of the whole programme. As usual, the Labour Party team which stages all their public events had done an astonishingly professional job. As Tony Blair stepped on to the stage at around five o'clock in the morning, the giant electronic graphic behind him, which had been displaying the familiar campaign slogan 'New Labour – New Britain', changed to 'New Labour – New Government'. As we watched in the ITN studio, the outside-broadcast director switched to a wider shot of the whole event, showing the morning sky just beginning to brighten. It was, literally and politically, a new dawn.

Alastair Campbell told me much later that he was overwhelmed at that rally by an immense sense of anti-climax. His temper was not improved by the fact that, after flying down with Tony Blair from his County Durham constituency and landing at Stansted Airport for the journey into London, their driver had actually got them quite seriously lost for several minutes in the streets around the Festival Hall. In addition, as both men were getting themselves, and their various bits and pieces, out of the car, the driver ran over Campbell's foot, which, in the ensuing hours, became extremely swollen and turned a deep shade of purple. Campbell's sense of anticlimax, though, came from the fact that years and years of planning and fighting to get rid of the Tories had suddenly come to an end with Labour's landslide victory. Uppermost in his mind was the realisation that Tony Blair and his team could afford precious little time for celebration, and that an immediate and even more difficult task now faced them as the victors – how to deliver in government what had been promised in opposition.

The bits you don't normally see: the wires, the microphone, the notebook between my legs and the carefully marked square on the grass were all kept out of the TV shot. Unfortunately the logo on the umbrella was not – the television company TVS had gone out of business six months earlier.

Another one-off: appearing in a hat on the day in February 1991 when the IRA
fired mortar bombs at Downing Street. The hat provided some protection during
a heavy snowfall that day.

Interviews can happen anywhere – and often do. The setting in September 1994
was the British High Commissioner's garden in Cape Town at the end of John
Major's visit to South Africa.

29 July 1993 – and
a seemingly routine
interview with the Prime
Minister. Minutes later
we began what we
thought was a private
conversation but John
Major's reference to the
three 'bastards' in his
cabinet became headline
news. His words had
been secretly recorded
and leaked out two days
later.

Receiving the Royal
Television Society's News
Event award in 1994 for
ITN's coverage of the
death of the Labour
Leader, John Smith.

The peaceful surroundings in Cyprus during the Commonwealth Conference in October 1993 belie the terrible news back home. I was asking John Major to react to the Shankill Road bomb in Belfast.

John Major announcing his surprise resignation as Conservative Party leader in June 1995. I am in the front row, suddenly summoned with the rest of my Lobby colleagues to the Downing Street garden.

Earnest discussion during preparations for ITV's general election results programme in May 1997. We began a full year early which is why the background refers to 'Election 96'.

With Tony Blair after a live television interview during the 1997 general election. Despite the smiles, we had just exchanged sharp words over pensions.

Yet another press release and yet another news conference – covering Labour's 1997 general election campaign. Beside me, my ITN colleague Hugh Pym seems equally bored.

July 1997: I take a tumble during Jonathan Aitken's chaotic walkabout. Meeting at his perjury trial two years later, he said he hoped that I was 'more steady on my feet.'

You're never alone when you work in television – here with ITN's crew at the Birmingham world leaders' summit in 1998.

Margaret Thatcher berates me in March 1999 over the demise of *News at Ten*, at the party to launch its replacement, the *ITV Evening News*.

CHAPTER FOURTEEN

'We Shall Govern as New Labour': Life with the Spin-doctors

T he new Government got off to a cracking start. The exuberance of election night took a long time to evaporate in Downing Street and in the new Ministers' offices in Whitehall, however much the private thoughts of the Prime Minister and his aides were already being tempered by the enormity of the task ahead.

Publicly, the scenes of the Government's first day in office provided the television correspondents with a precious resource, not normally available to us during the ordinary run of political reporting. The day was full of good pictures. John Major's departure from Downing Street was dignified. 'When the curtain falls, it is time to get off the stage,' he said, addressing the great bank of cameras and microphones set up outside the front door. He then climbed into the Prime Ministerial Jaguar for the last time, on his way to his farewell audience with the Queen at Buckingham Palace.

Bad luck, however, dogged him to the last. Halfway up Whitehall, the police directed his car around the wrong side of a traffic bollard. A simple, straightforward journey, one that he had made hundreds of times before as he attended his weekly audiences with Her Majesty, was disrupted as the

Jaguar crawled to a halt in the traffic into which it had been misdirected. The embarrassment of the whole incident was made worse by the fact that an airborne camera in the ITN helicopter, which was tracking the outgoing Prime Minister's final trip to the Palace, had faithfully recorded it all. Even on his very last day in office, things had gone wrong. No wonder that it was a sombre-faced ex-Prime Minister we saw later at the Oval taking his usual refuge from the pressures of politics by watching a cricket match.

By contrast with the problems of John Major's departure from Downing Street, Tony Blair's arrival at Number Ten was carefully planned and flawlessly executed. Another Jaguar from the official fleet had picked up the Blairs. It now drew up in Whitehall, just outside the entrance to Downing Street, where they got out, and walked through the gates and up the street to the resounding and constant cheers of the large, specially invited crowd. It was a classic Labour photo-opportunity. The faces of the delighted crowd, as Tony and Cherie grasped their outstretched hands, were the perfect images to underline the message that the new Government represented a fresh start, and that the hopes and expectations of it among ordinary people were high. I did not need to make that point in my commentary and reporting later. The pictures, as the Labour spin-doctors knew they would, said it all.

The cascade of new policy announcements began almost immediately. Four days after the Blairs' walk up Downing Street, Gordon Brown, confirmed as Chancellor of the Exchequer, marched into the great pillared conference room of the Treasury. There he took up his position behind a lectern with the Treasury seal emblazoned on its front (another new touch), and announced that the Bank of England was to be given its independence, specifically in the setting of interest rates. Three days later, Tony Blair announced that, in future, he would be answering questions in the Commons only once a week for half an hour, rather than twice a week for fifteen minutes. At the first of those Question Times, he announced a complete ban on landmines.

Within a month of taking office, the Government also announced a ban on the private ownership and use of hand-guns, the scrapping of the nursery-voucher scheme, a Defence Review and an enquiry into Gulf War Syndrome. It was also announced that, in future, Cherie Blair would be hosting tea parties for various charities, especially those that involved children, in the garden of Number Ten.

That last announcement, made in mid-afternoon, particularly caught my eye. I am not really sure why, since it was hardly the most earth-shattering of the new decisions, but I immediately saw it as an opportunity to do a live two-way into the 5.40 p.m. news from the Downing Street garden. It would be a good test of the new way of doings things if, not just Alastair Campbell, but the officials who run Number Ten, agreed to something which we had never done before. Within ten minutes of my asking permission for the broadcast, it had all been agreed. I was much criticised for doing it. The Tories were angry, since, as they rightly pointed out, John Major's wife Norma had quietly hosted similar parties without making a great fuss about it. Some of my colleagues at Westminster, and the television critics, said it was a case of my dancing far too easily to New Labour's tune, despite the fact that doing the spot from the garden was my idea, not theirs.

It was another example of making the most of the opportunities that presented themselves under the new all-change, anything's possible, People's Britain agenda which the new Government, and particularly the Prime Minister's Press Secretary wanted to promote. I was not entirely alone among political journalists in giving the Blair Government, in its early days, an easy ride. Were we, therefore, from the very first day of that new Government, being 'spun'? Of course we were, just as we had been during the years of Labour's revival in opposition and during the successful election campaign itself. Simply to say so, however, raises all the questions about the use of 'spin' and 'spin-doctors'.

The term 'spin-doctor' derives from the terminology of one of America's national sports, baseball. First came the use of the word 'spin', as applied to the movement of the ball. Next, the word 'spin-doctor', to refer to the coach who corrected a player's technique. By the mid-1980s the word had crossed over into the world of American political campaigning, to describe someone whose job was to embellish a straightforward piece of news with the particular spin required by this or that political camp. From the start, therefore, the term had a pejorative ring about it, implying a process that is not quite proper – the attempt to make a piece of news seem more important or relevant than it really is. In addition, a baseball player is not supposed to resist the advice of the spin-doctor who corrects his technique. Transferring the terminology to the world of political journalism is often meant to imply that those on the receiving end of spin are either unable or unwilling to resist the pressures brought to bear on them by political media managers.

Discussing the issue, however, in such broad terms does not, in my view, get us very far. In the autumn of 1996, with the election imminent, an edition of the BBC programme *Panorama*, to which I was invited to contribute, devoted fifty minutes to exploring the issue of relations between politicians and political journalists. Those responsible for the programme had also started, I felt, with the preconception that there was something wholly immoral or wrong about the relationship between the Labour Party and the press. The programme did uncover some particular instances where undue pressure had been brought to bear, but, by general consent, it failed to make the case that the whole relationship was a poisoned, rotten business. I found it revealing that I was given almost the last word in the programme. 'The idea', I said, 'that political journalists simply wait around with their notebooks open, ready to take down the outpourings of the spin-doctors at dictation speed, is preposterous. Nor, if that is what really happened, would the public stand for it.'

Spin-doctors are, after all, hired hands, employed to get across a message for those who hire them, be they governments, political parties, commercial enterprises, pressure groups or private individuals. They are not a particular phenomenon of the 1980s or 1990s, nor were they invented by Peter Mandelson or Alastair Campbell. They used, however, to be called press or public relations officers. There were some fearsome early practitioners of the craft. In my days as Diplomatic Editor, I could almost guarantee that, on any occasion when I reported on developments in the Middle East, the press officer from the Israeli Embassy in London would be on the phone, either making an official complaint or offering his 'spin' on events.

Mrs Thatcher's Press Secretary, Bernard Ingham, was a spin-doctor. He strongly and repeatedly disputes the fact, on the ground that he never sought to suggest that things were other than they really were. Bernard's observations, however, on events and, indeed, on various Ministers and ex-Ministers were frequently 'spin' of the purest kind, and were protected by the arrangements governing the reporting of them at the time. His briefings, well peppered with his 'bunkum and balderdash' catchphrase, as he lambasted us for our shortcomings, could be attributed only to 'Government' sources. Neither his actual words nor the fact that he was the source of them could be quoted. Two newspapers, the *Guardian* and the *Independent*, found those rules so unacceptable that they stopped attending the Ingham briefings. They returned only when John Major's press secretaries took a rather less combative view of relations with political journalists, and after it was agreed that what was said at their briefings could be attributed to 'Downing Street' rather than 'Government' sources.

It is, however, the Labour spin-doctors and their practices that have come under particular scrutiny. What made the Mandelson–Campbell approach during Labour's years in opposition and government different, and began all the talk about spin-doctoring in the first place, was the extent of it, and the single-mindedness – some might even say the ruthlessness – with which it was carried out. From the very moment that I was appointed ITN's Political Editor in 1986, I was one of the targets of Peter Mandelson's attentions. He was, by then, well into his job as Labour's Director of Campaigns and Communications, and had established one clear rule for himself. Like the assiduous press officers of the Israeli Embassy whom I had encountered during my previous position, he never let an inaccuracy go uncorrected, or what he regarded as an unfair or misinformed comment go unchallenged. In that, of course, he was only doing what any efficient press officer should do. His operation, though, went much further.

From the start, Mandelson was determined to try and set the agenda for the reporting of the Labour Party in the British media, to ensure, if he could, that the coverage went according to *his* game plan rather than anyone else's. He would go to great lengths in pursuit of his goal. I had a furious row with him at one Labour Party conference, for example, simply because ITN had secretly filmed the building of the platform the day before the conference opened, thereby revealing, before he wanted it revealed, the slogan for the week.

Alastair Campbell became Tony Blair's Press Secretary in September 1994, two months after the leadership election, and eighteen months before Labour's election victory. He knew all about Peter Mandelson's methods of operation, since he had himself been a political editor and commentator, first on the *Daily Mirror* and later on the short-lived *Today* newspaper. Campbell had, therefore, been on the receiving end of Mandelson's observations, though his clear, indeed openly declared, support for the Labour Party presumably meant that he enjoyed a rather less confrontational relationship with him than the rest of us.

As Blair's Press Secretary, Alastair Campbell soon served notice that he would be no less devoted than Peter Mandelson in seeking to set the agenda. That became clear in the weeks and months following his appointment, and was certainly confirmed during the 1995 Labour Party conference. Competing for media attention that week were two big stories – the O. J. Simpson murder trial in the United States and events at the conference. On the Tuesday of conference week, Campbell contacted both the BBC and ITN. He suggested that, instead of leading our bulletins with the impending verdict in the trial of O. J. Simpson, we should give the top slot to Blair's speech. 'While, of course,' he wrote in his letter, 'news judgements must be made in the light of other stories on any particular day, and while I fully understand there is much interest in the verdict, I would implore you not to lose sight both of the news value and of the importance to the country of Mr Blair's speech.'

To our astonishment, the BBC seemed to agree that the Campbell view of things was the correct one, and, at 6 p.m. and 9 p.m., they gave the Blair speech the top slot in their bulletin. The head of BBC news was later quoted as saying, 'There is always a debate about news priorities, but to suggest that the running order of BBC news programmes was influenced under pressure is defamatory.' ITN simply ignored Campbell's request, and, in an extended edition of the 5.40

p.m. news, made the imminent verdict in America the top story, ahead of the Blair speech. The Simpson verdict was also the top story on *News at Ten*.

The whole incident was an entirely typical example of the Alastair Campbell way of doing things. He was part of an extremely pro-active Opposition, and, from the start, he approached government in the same way. He made no secret of his view that the handling of the media was, and is, an essential part of achieving the Government's programme, by trying to ensure that its message and record of achievement are put across on its own terms. That is why journalists must have a better than arm's-length relationship with any Government's spin-doctors. They have a job to do – getting the message across. We have a job to do – not just reporting what that Government is doing or plans to do, but asking whether it is doing it or is right to be thinking of doing it, and whether it is being honest about the claims it makes on either score.

There is no question that Alastair Campbell has run the most effective, and efficient, communications operation of any recent government. Most major policy announcements, for example, are handled like a military exercise, and he himself talks of his strategic skills. First, there will be one or two stories, outlining the plan in general terms, carefully placed in one or more newspapers, often simply to fly a kite, to test the water, to see how the ideas are likely to be received. Then, on the day itself, there will be an interview on the BBC Radio Four *Today* programme, in which the responsible Minister will reveal a little more of the detail, while constantly protesting that he cannot say anything until he makes a statement in the Commons. That, of course, alerts everyone in and around Westminster, especially the political journalists.

Specially held back for the Commons statement will be some final detail – the actual amount of money to be spent, for example, or the number of people to be involved. That is intended to keep the Speaker sweet, though she herself has increasingly voiced her annoyance at the way things are handled. Television's role in the Campbell game plan is to be the medium that records the formal unveiling of the policy, and finally presents the whole package to a large mass audience.

Specific operations like policy launches are backed up by the daily briefings for political journalists at Westminster. Under a further refinement of the rules, Campbell decided that, for the first time, such briefings should be on the record, and attributable to 'the Prime Minister's Official Spokesman'. Further, more detailed briefing is usually available for those who ask for it.

Most of the time, though by no means always, the Labour Government's handling of the media has stayed within the bounds of how an exceedingly pro-active public relations operation might be expected to operate. The temperature certainly went down with the departure of Charlie Whelan, Gordon Brown's exceedingly talkative spin-doctor. Even that event, however, produced another classic example of how Campbell works.

Whelan was widely suspected of being the source of the information which eventually came to light about Peter Mandelson's large loan from his fellow Minister, Geoffrey Robinson. Just before Christmas 1998, revelation of the loan, which had enabled Mandelson to buy a smart house in Notting Hill in West London, led to his resignation. Whelan repeatedly denied that he had been the source of the story. This was, however, one controversy too far in which he appeared to have been involved, and, within days, he had resigned as well.

On the day in question, ITN decided to lead its early-evening news bulletin with Charlie Whelan's decision to quit, rather than with what Alastair Campbell regarded as a far more important event – the first day of trading in the new currency of the EU, the Euro. Immediately after the bulletin, a fax arrived from the Prime Minister's Press Secretary at ITN headquarters, complaining that the media's obsession with press officers 'is completely at odds with any objective assessment of what really matters to your viewers'. The fax also referred to the famous light-hearted item that traditionally ended *News at Ten*, and suggested that, later that evening, it should begin with the words, 'And finally, has the media gone mad?' It was vintage Campbell, trying it on again. ITN politely reminded him, once again, that the order of stories in bulletins was our business, not his.

The incident was also a classic example of another weapon in the Campbell armoury – the not-so-subtle use of sarcastic humour. Unlike Peter Mandelson, who could be exceedingly abrasive, he would often cloak his criticisms by using a jokey approach, by which he hoped to soften the delivery, though not the substance, of what he was saying. More than once, he came on the phone, after watching an ITN bulletin, to ask me with ironic laughter in his voice, 'Now what was that load of old rubbish you had at the top of your news?' He would then go on to complain, in the same style, about the content of a particular report, or that such and such an item about the Government or the Labour Party should or should not have been the lead item. My regular reaction was to listen to his representations about content and to argue the points through with him. I never did accept his right, or any other press officer's right, to dictate the position in a bulletin at which a story should be placed, and I always told them so. Where his interests clashed with mine, however, Alastair Campbell never ceased to make his case.

Sometimes, his rebuttals of some of my colleagues' wilder imaginings were genuinely funny. After the *Financial Times*, no less, ran a story that the cares of office had caused Tony Blair to go bald, he authorised the issue of a press release, under an official Labour Party heading, showing 'before' and 'after' pictures of the Prime Minister. They were the same photograph, and both showed Tony Blair with plenty of hair. The ability to see the funny side of life redeemed the relentless way in which the Number Ten Press Office operated. There was no better example than the saga of Humphrey the Cat.

Humphrey was a large black-and-white tomcat who had arrived at the Prime Minister's official residence, during the Major years, as a stray. As we whiled away the long hours, waiting for yet another interview or statement outside Number Ten, we would often spot him, padding along Downing Street, usually on his way to or from St James's Park near by. Not long after the Blairs took up residence, rumours began to circulate that the Prime Minister's wife was less than enamoured of this extra addition to the household, and that she had arranged for him to be quietly disposed of. The Tory MP Alan Clark even went so far as to raise the matter in the House of Commons. From there, it was but a short step to the matter being raised with the Prime Minister's Press Secretary at his morning briefing.

Not surprisingly, Alastair Campbell seemed less than well informed on the matter, and gave what were regarded as less than satisfactory answers. As we left the room, I approached him and with mock seriousness told him, 'You do realise, don't you, that you are going to have to produce this cat?' Rolling his eyes heavenwards, he replied, 'I know, I know!' He was as good as his word. His assistant, Hilary Coffman, was assigned to the case and told to devote her entire energies to the matter. It turned out that Humphrey's health, and in particular his control of his bladder, had meant that life in Number Ten was no longer a practical option. He had, therefore, started a new life in South London, at the home of a member of staff in the Cabinet Office, which adjoins Number Ten, on the strict understanding that there would be no publicity about the matter.

Now, however, publicity was exactly what was required to establish Humphrey's well-being, not to mention his continued existence. A top-secret operation was, therefore, set in train. I was given the address of his new home, after a promise that the only person to whom I would divulge the information was our Westminster cameraman, Mike Turner. He duly set off for South London to take some pictures of Humphrey on a pool basis, which meant that all the television companies would have access to them. Back came the pictures, showing Humphrey in apparently fine form and much tantalised by his new owner's pet goldfish. All this I reported, in a slightly less than serious tone, on the early-evening news. On *News at Ten*, we reported the fact that we had shown the pictures to Bob Jordan, the recently retired doorman at Number Ten. Publicly, Bob told us what a joy it was to see Humphrey looking so well. Privately, he confessed that he'd been quite relieved to see the back of him.

On occasion, however, the humorous approach backfires. Shortly before Tony Blair was due to visit Washington at the height of the Monica Lewinsky scandal, John Sergeant of the BBC asked the same question of Alastair Campbell at two of his morning briefings in a row. On both occasions, the questions were, quite legitimately, designed to try and discover whether an important visit would be affected by all the controversy surrounding the President. On both occasions, Campbell said that the visit would not be affected, and then delivered himself of a tongue-in-cheek tirade against what he called the overmanned and bureaucratic BBC. It had become, he suggested, a body which apparently had nothing better to do than to send out one of its senior correspondents day after day to ask the same ridiculous questions.

This strange *pas de deux* was played out for the third and last occasion in Washington itself, as the visit got under way. Among those present at the briefing on this occasion were all the journalists who were travelling with the Prime Minister, including John Sergeant, Peter Riddell of *The Times*, who does not regularly attend the briefings in London, and myself. Peter Riddell was not in on the running joke, if joke it was, and he had therefore not previously heard the tirade against the BBC, which was now repeated. He therefore wrote it up, and it was reported on the front page of the next day's *Times*, headlined as a serious attack by the Government on the BBC. The new rules, which meant that everything Alastair Campbell said was on the record, had entitled Peter Riddell to do exactly that. Nor was he wrong to do so since, behind the jokey humour, some of the Government's true thoughts about the BBC, especially Alastair Campbell's, were in fact being revealed.

Sometimes, however, no humour whatsoever was involved. Six months after the election, I broke the story on *News at Ten* that the Government had changed its mind on the question of sponsorship of Formula One motor racing. Ministers were ready, I reported, to agree to a European Union directive which would give Formula One far more time to phase out the sponsorship of the sport by the tobacco companies, on which it was heavily dependent. Almost immediately, it was revealed that Bernie Ecclestone, one of the most important people in the world of Formula One, had given a million pounds to the Labour Party. To put it very bluntly, it looked as though the Government, which prided itself on its squeaky-clean record, had been bribed.

The allegations against the Government reached a crescendo on 7 November 1997, the day which had been set for a summit meeting with the French. This had been billed as the 'Cool Britannia' summit, to be held almost at the top of

Canary Wharf, the skyscraper that dominates the redeveloped Docklands area of London. The relevant floor had been decked out with examples of the best in modern British design, and both the furnishings, and the location, were supposed not only to impress the French, but also to reinforce the Government's 'New Labour, New Britain' message in the UK too.

Now a major scandal was threatening to wreck the whole thing. Alastair Campbell told me later that his instinct had been to accept the fact that the media would ignore the summit in the light of the increasing revelations. He therefore wanted to get a full explanation of the entire Formula One episode out, on the record, that very day. Others, particularly Gordon Brown and Peter Mandelson, had argued that nothing should take the shine off the summit, and that the Government should simply, for the moment, try to hold the line. It was that delaying course of action that was followed.

It was a disastrous mistake. The story grew and grew. Three days later, the Labour Party was forced to announce that it would be handing the million pounds back to Bernie Ecclestone. Two days later, the Government announced a full review of all party funding. Four further days later, Tony Blair, in a desperate attempt at damage limitation, agreed to an hour-long interview with John Humphrys on the BBC's Sunday-lunchtime television programme *On the Record*. Most of the interview was taken up by the Prime Minister's explanation of what had gone on, during which he apologised for the way in which the whole affair had been handled. It was the new Government's first humiliation, in which the press had played a major role. It had shown that 'spin' was no substitute for the truth.

Five months later, there was a similar confrontation, after James Blitz, the *Financial Times* correspondent in Rome and a former Political Correspondent at Westminster, reported that Tony Blair had lobbied the then Italian Prime Minister Romano Prodi on behalf of Rupert Murdoch. Campbell at first tried to kill the story, by simply refusing to say anything at all about the contents of what he said was a private conversation. When that failed, he turned his fire on the newspaper that had led the way in reporting the story. He denounced the Political Editor of the *Financial Times*, Robert Peston, and the paper's Political Correspondent, Liam Halligan. Halligan had been especially persistent with his questioning at the Number Ten briefings. The *FT*'s reporting, Campbell said, had been a 'complete joke', a 'non-story' and 'crap'. Throughout, he relied on the narrow technicalities of the affair – on who, for example, had first called whom – in denying that Tony Blair had intervened on Murdoch's behalf, or that anything improper had taken place. At one stage, he challenged any of the political journalists at Westminster to say that he'd been lying. He hadn't, but he had been extremely selective in his use of words.

A few weeks later, Liam Halligan, who had continued to display his terrier-like tendencies in his dealings with the Number Ten Press Secretary, got his own revenge. He was attending one final Campbell briefing, before moving on to a new job as the Economics Correspondent of *Channel Four News*. 'When are you leaving the *FT*?' Campbell asked him at the morning briefing in Downing Street. 'Today,' Halligan replied. 'Good riddance!' said Campbell, half-seriously. A few minutes later, as the briefing ended, Halligan very deliberately and very publicly went up to him and gave him a big kiss on the cheek. 'Goodbye, Alastair,' he said, before adding with heavy irony, 'I shall miss you.'

What, then, does all the talk about spin and spin-doctors tell us? First, that the issue has only achieved such recent prominence because of the nature and extent of the Labour

Government's media-handling operation. Second, that there have been instances when, taking their cue from their master, some of Alastair Campbell's acolytes have put totally unacceptable pressure on young reporters. Third, that by and large political journalists in and around Westminster have not been suborned by it all, even if, in the early stages of the new Government, its agenda was accepted too readily and uncritically. Fourth, that the Blair Government, and many of those who work for it, take criticism very badly. They do like to get their own way, and, given that the Government's gigantic majority has weakened the checks upon it in Parliament, the role of the press has become more important, not less, in holding it to account.

I am not saying that all is well, and that there is no cause for concern. Some Government and Labour Party spin-doctors have clearly been engaged in some distinctly murky activity. Glenda Jackson, for example, reacted with total fury when a story appeared in a couple of newspapers that suggested that she was ready to drop out of the race for Mayor of London. It was untrue, and was obviously intended to try to force her into giving up and backing Number Ten's favoured candidate, Frank Dobson, as two other candidates had already done. Such up-front briefing against a particular individual does not usually come my way – those practising it do not see television news bulletins as the place for such stories. A quiet word to a newspaper correspondent here or a gossip columnist there is the way these things are handled. It has always gone on, but it does not sit especially well with the idea of a Labour Government that wants to clean up politics.

There have been occasions, however, when accusations about the Government's control-freak tendencies and the supposedly improper behaviour of its spin-doctors have, in my view, been unfair. One example is the way that Campbell and his team were accused of taking over at Buckingham

Palace at the time of the death and the funeral of Princess Diana.

This was an extraordinary time in the public life of the United Kingdom. As many others noted at the time, Britain and, to a considerable degree, the rest of the world behaved during that week as it had never behaved before. On the evening before the funeral, I walked up the Mall from Admiralty Arch towards the Palace. It was a truly astonishing sight. Those already in position for the next day had set up thousands of individual shrines. Each consisted of flowers, lighted candles and usually a picture of Diana. As the darkness increased, the warm scent of the candles and the flickering lights were the first sign, confirmed the following day, that the whole of the area around Westminster Abbey, Buckingham Palace and Whitehall was being converted into a huge open-air cathedral.

It had all begun with the news of Diana's death a week earlier. By chance, I had decided to pick up the reins after my summer break by going to Darlington, where Tony Blair was speaking at one of his regular Road Show presentations. I was staying in a hotel near the town, and I was woken, as was everyone else on ITN's staff, by an 'all-stations' alert on my message pager at around 5 a.m. My first reaction was disbelief. Political journalists hear more false rumours, I suspect, than most of their colleagues, but a check on the hotel's television set confirmed the worst. Since Darlington is close to the Prime Minister's constituency of Sedgefield, I headed there as quickly as possible.

Tony Blair's constituency home is almost next door to a short row of terraced houses. As a small group of us gathered outside, waiting for a decision as to how and where he would make his first statement, we could see many of the occupants of the houses already listening and watching inside. Their shock was as great as ours, yet one of their concerns was for *our* welfare. Did we want tea or coffee? A bacon butty, perhaps? In one house, over just such a cup of coffee, I watched the unfolding events, as my colleagues in London were describing them, with the occupants of the house on their television.

The Prime Minister, we soon learnt, had been woken as soon as the first report of the car crash in Paris had come through, at around one o'clock in the morning, and he could not bring himself to go back to bed. Instead, he began to prepare for any and every eventuality, both with those of his advisers who were with him in the constituency and, by phone, with people like Alastair Campbell and others who were not. The result, by mid-morning, was his tribute outside the church in Trimdon village in his constituency.

That was when Tony Blair first spoke of the 'People's Princess'. Some later criticised him, and his Press Secretary, for the use of that phrase. It was felt to have mixed politics and the Government's agenda for a 'People's Britain' with a moment of national grief. On that bleak morning, however, it was a phrase that genuinely summed up for many people what Diana had meant to them. It was intended to make a simple point. She had become a member of the royal family, but she had continued to identify herself with so many of the concerns of ordinary people, not least through the disappointments of her own life and the charity work that she had undertaken.

The events of the following week showed that the use of the 'People's Princess' phrase had been fully justified. It was, above all, the people of Britain who decided how Diana would be mourned. Their own outpouring of grief began immediately, but, as Buckingham Palace and Number Ten began to work together on the details, it was what the public wanted that ultimately decided how events should be ordered.

Once more, there was plenty of criticism, both at the time

and for several weeks afterwards, of the way in which the Prime Minister and his aides appeared to be dictating to the Royal Family. In fact, a working relationship between the Palace and Number Ten had begun within hours of Princess Diana's death, and the first suggestion that there should be such co-operation, particularly over the handling of the press, came not from the Government, but from the Palace.

The two sides first had to finalise the arrangements for the return of Diana's body from Paris on Sunday 31 August. Both sides agreed that it would be fitting for the Prime Minister, as well as Prince Charles, to be at Northolt RAF station, to the west of London, where the plane carrying the coffin was to land. As a result, Tony Blair met the Earl of Airlie, the Lord Chamberlain and the Head of the Royal Household, at the airfield. The two men discussed the days ahead, and it was the Lord Chamberlain who asked the Prime Minister for assistance, and suggested that the Palace Press Office and the Number Ten Press Office should work closely together. Tony Blair agreed, and a meeting between the two teams was quickly set up for early the following morning.

However, as Alastair Campbell drove into the Palace forecourt with his colleagues for the meeting, he was spotted by one of the many photographers waiting at the gates – the photographer in question was working for the *Daily Mirror* where Campbell had once worked, and immediately identified him. News therefore emerged of Number Ten's involvement, as the first of the regular meetings between the two sides began. However, while sources at the Palace told me later that they were grateful for the help that they received, they also stressed the fact that, in all the discussions that took place prior to the funeral, each side had worked towards collective decisions. Some of the help Number Ten could offer was on the simple question of logistics – one of the Number Ten team, Hilary Coffman, had been deeply involved, for example, in the arrangements for John Smith's funeral. But Campbell, in particular, was also able to offer a forthright second opinion when it came, for example, to judging the public mood over whether or not normal royal protocol should be broken to allow the Union Flag to fly at half-mast over Buckingham Palace. There was, however, one problem. As the discussions continued, and despite the caution of those at Number Ten who were involved, the first word of what had been decided – that the Queen would broadcast to the nation, for example – still emerged most frequently through the Lobby journalists. This tended to reinforce the idea that Campbell was running things.

As to the funeral itself, it was clear on the day that the right judgements had eventually been made. I began my day's broadcasting by joining the commentary team at Canada Gate, diagonally across from Buckingham Palace, at the end of Constitution Hill. The length of the funeral procession had been extended to allow more people to pay their respects by lining the route. Then, just as the cortège began to approach the Palace, we suddenly noticed movement in the forecourt. That was the first indication that the Queen, and most of the other female members of the Royal Family, would not be going on ahead to Westminster Abbey as expected. Instead, they came, on foot, each of them dressed in black, across the Palace courtyard to the corner gate, to stand there as a mark of respect as the procession passed directly in front of them. As much as the later sight of the young princes walking behind their mother's coffin, it was one of the most telling images to fill the world's television screens that day.

I then moved to Whitehall, to a commentary point alongside the Cenotaph. This meant crossing St James's Park, just as the service in the Abbey was beginning. I wanted to hear it, and I had with me a small pocket radio, on which I tried to listen to what was happening as I made my way across the park. The radio, I soon discovered, was entirely unnecessary. The service was being relayed to the crowds in the park on loudspeakers, and in their tens of thousands people were joining in all around me.

As I paused to cross Whitehall, just as one of the readings was in progress, one man in the crowd recognised me. I was already somewhat overcome by the emotion of it all. 'My God,' he said, 'you look absolutely shattered. Would you like some coffee?' I thanked him and politely declined his offer, but it was astonishing to discover yet again, as I had found near Tony Blair's home in County Durham, that Diana's spirit of compassion, the concern for others, seemed to be so much in evidence that day. I saw it again when an older man in the crowd, openly crying during the service, noticed a young girl sitting on the wall just behind with tears streaming down her face too, and gently offered her a paper tissue to dry her eyes.

Much was later made of the fact that the applause in the Abbey at the end of Earl Spencer's address began outside the building and was taken up inside it. At the spot where I was standing in Whitehall, public support for his words had begun long before he finished. Despite the fact that it was not easy to hear the public address system, the crowds around me hung on every word, and their first clapping came as he openly attacked the way that Diana had been, as he put it, hounded by the media. When it came to the two-minute silence at the end, a mobile telephone belonging to a young man close to us began to ring. He turned it off as quickly as he could. The crowd around him had made it very clear that they wanted nothing to disrupt their private, silent moment of grieving for Diana.

In the years since her death, it has become fashionable to dismiss that grieving as a silly rush of blood to the national head. Such views are usually coupled with remarks about

Diana's slender achievements in life and the problems she caused the Royal Family. I think that displays a terrible cynicism. The public's instinctive reaction at the time was born of two things – natural shock at the death of any young mother, and the widespread view that her husband, Prince Charles, had treated her appallingly. At the end of her life, she was most certainly not the shy young innocent who had married him in 1981, but her death seemed too cruel to many of us to let pass without a genuine and public expression of sorrow.

In and around government, however, the onward rush of events soon replaced the grieving. Within days, Scotland had voted decisively to establish its own Parliament. The Welsh voted far less decisively for a Welsh Assembly. Within weeks, Gordon Brown had declared that there was 'no constitutional bar' to the United Kingdom joining the European single currency. His statement was a clear indication that the Government was, in principle, in favour of joining. The overriding condition which would decide whether Britain did so or not, he declared, would be the simple test of whether or not it was in the country's best economic interest to do so. The statement had the effect of making the other main parties set out their position in forceful terms. The Conservatives, under their new Leader, William Hague, decided that they would effectively rule out joining for the next ten years. The Liberal Democrats repeated their demands that the Government should say when, not if, it was joining.

The problems of Northern Ireland demanded hour upon hour of Tony Blair's time, as they had of John Major's. A new 'framework document' in January 1998 proved to be the building block on which the Good Friday Agreement was finally constructed in Belfast in the spring. ITN's coverage of Northern Ireland affairs was chiefly the responsibility of our correspondent in Belfast, John Irvine. My own involvement was restricted to those occasions when the matter came clearly to the top of the Prime Minister's agenda. I was, therefore, in Belfast when Tony Blair flew there in early April 1998 to take personal charge of the negotiations.

He had talked on his arrival about feeling the hand of history on his shoulder. It has to be recorded that the cold hand of the Belfast climate did little to help the press as they settled down to watch history being made. For three days and nights the talking ground on. Only the most basic facilities were provided for us, as we waited outside the grimly utilitarian Castle Buildings, a late and ugly addition to the complex of Parliamentary buildings at Stormont where the negotiations were taking place. Every kind of weather descended upon us, sunshine and showers, driving rain, snow and hail. Throughout, a biting wind kept temperatures around the freezing mark.

Gradually, a tented village grew up around the two or three temporary structures the authorities had seen fit to provide. The local hardware stores were no doubt puzzled as to why, in early April, given the freezing conditions outside, there was such a sudden surge in their sales of gazebo-style dining tents, designed for eating out on warm summer evenings. The television cameramen had discovered that these structures, despite their flimsy nature, provided at least some protection for their equipment, even though nothing could prevent the ground all around them turning into an ankle-deep quagmire of mud.

On the final night before the agreement was reached, conditions were so bad that everybody huddled, refugee style, in the temporary cabin that served as a briefing room. At least it had heaters in it, even though seating was at something of a premium. Everyone snatched such moments of sleep as they could, many curled up on the floor. There were frequent false

alarms, as rumours of a possible deal filtered through to us. I
decided that sleep was impossible, and kept myself awake by
listening to classical music throughout the night on a tiny
personal radio, grateful that two radio stations now provide
such a service around the clock throughout the United Kingdom.

Eventually, late on Good Friday afternoon, agreement was
reached, and even then the weather did its worst. Tony Blair
and the Irish Prime Minister Bertie Ahern were forced to
dodge the showers as they delivered their statements just
outside Castle Buildings. Nothing, though, could diminish
the feeling that a document and an agreement of genuinely
historic proportions had been hammered out. John Irvine, an
Ulsterman himself, could not hide his emotion during a live
two-way shortly after the deal had been done. 'This', he said,
'is the most momentous political event to have happened since
the setting up of Northern Ireland in 1921.' My own comments on *News at Ten* that night focused more on the hard
road ahead, especially for David Trimble and the task he
faced, as I put it, 'in selling a new kind of Unionism', based on
real partnership with the other parties in Northern Ireland.
With hindsight, I was right to sense how difficult that road
was to be.

A little over a year later, and with progress on implement-
ing the Good Friday agreement stalled over the issue of the
decommissioning of terrorist weapons, we all returned to
Stormont. As another long vigil began, the media village
was reconstructed. This time the facilities were a little better,
and the weather, mercifully, was a little, though not much,
warmer. The Northern Ireland Office provided a larger
marquee. There were some catering facilities of a rudimentary
kind. Until the sandwiches arrived at six o'clock each evening,
coffee, tea and tins of biscuits were all that was provided.
Much journalistic effort that week was sustained on a diet of

custard creams and chocolate digestives. Outside, instead of the emergency gazebos of the previous year, most of the broadcasters erected sturdier structures. They were put to full use as the week dragged on.

All week, our reactions went from high optimism to deep pessimism and back again. After a session that lasted until 4.30 a.m. in the middle of the week, I was reporting by early evening on the Thursday that the talks were close to collapse. By midnight, hopes were raised again by a new document from Sinn Fein which indicated that the IRA could well agree to a timetable for the handing over of its weapons, once it was admitted to government. Tony Blair talked of a 'seismic shift'. The Unionists remained sceptical – or worse. It was enough, however, for the Government to produce another 'blueprint' on the way things could, and indeed would, proceed. It set out the timetable for the weapons hand-over, as well as triggering the procedure for picking the Ministers in the new devolved Assembly. In an interview with me before he left Belfast at the end of the long week of negotiations, the Prime Minister pleaded with all sides to accept the deal. At the end of the interview, just before the customary 'thank you', something made me say, 'We pray God that it all works.' With heavy emphasis, Tony Blair responded, 'So do I.'

But severe difficulties remained, and they surfaced in the Commons the following week, as the Government tried to rush emergency legislation through to implement its proposals. Frantic last-minute efforts at fine-tuning the timetable, designed to try and resolve Unionist demands for certainty over the decommissioning issue, were made while the Bill was still going through the Commons, notably after some suggestions put forward in a speech by the former Prime Minister, John Major. I began checking out the likely reaction to such proposals, and reported on the ITN *Nightly News* at 11 p.m. that they might produce a solution.

Shortly before midnight, the Opposition spokesman on Northern Ireland, Andrew MacKay, rose to speak in the Commons as the Bill moved to its final stage, the Third Reading. 'I am at least heartened to learn', he told the House, 'that, on the ITN news at eleven o'clock tonight, the Political Editor Mr Michael Brunson – presumably with the help of spin-doctors from Downing Street – said that the Government will take into account what my Right Honourable and Honourable friends have said. Whether that is true, I do not know. I hope that is accurate.'

It was accurate, but ultimately to no avail. The Ulster Unionists rejected the package, and the proceedings at Stormont to appoint the Ministers turned into a grim farce. The Ulster Unionist Leader, David Trimble, refused to nominate anyone from his party, thereby collapsing the whole procedure. After so many hours of waiting and reporting, both in Belfast and in London, I felt both angry and depressed. I could fully understand how much more frustrated all those people in both the Conservative and Labour Governments who had laboured so long and so hard for a settlement were feeling. Agreement, as Tony Blair had told me in an interview many months before, had always been agonisingly close, especially at the end of the second round of Belfast talks. The hope must be that, with so much positive work done, enough can be salvaged from it all to construct a permanent settlement for Ulster.

While Northern Ireland remained at or near the top of the Government's agenda, Ministers were also deeply involved in a great deal of other change and reform. Events over which it had little control also demanded its attention, and mine. There was a huge review of public spending. There was the reordering of the NHS, and the large-scale alteration of the provision of pensions and welfare benefits. There were problems ranging from the resignation of the Welsh Secretary, Ron Davies, to the extradition of General Pinochet and the difficulties of House of Lords reform. There were also the military campaigns in Bosnia, Kosovo and Iraq. All of that meant that there was much to report upon. Unusually, I also had a chance during this time to stop simply being a reporter of events and to become actively involved in one of the Government's major concerns – educational reform.

It is always difficult for a political journalist, whose work demands a high degree of impartiality, to become either directly or indirectly associated with any part of a government's programme. I thought long and hard, and so did my employers, before I agreed to become part of a group which was asked to advise the Government on the question of teaching citizenship and democracy in English and Welsh schools.

I was reassured in my eventual decision to join the group by the fact that it was made up of a genuine cross-section of people. Some had been active politically, but most had not. The former Conservative Education Secretary Lord Baker had, for example, agreed to be a member. So had people like Judge Stephen Tumim, the former Inspector of Prisons. Teachers and academics, and representatives of the voluntary sector, were also members. I was asked to join them because of my connections with an organisation called the Citizenship Foundation, which had for several years organised an annual Youth Parliament competition. This involved the submission by schools of videotapes showing the mock parliaments they had organised, of which I had been one of the judges. I was a strong supporter of the competition, because it was such an innovative way of teaching children about the workings of Parliamentary democracy, as well as encouraging them to develop the skill of forming and expressing judgements about contemporary events. I felt that the work of the Advisory

Group I was now asked to join could help to further those aims.

Our brief was to recommend to the Education Secretary, David Blunkett, whether or not we felt that education for citizenship and the teaching of democracy should, for the first time, form part of the national curriculum, which was itself under full-scale review. We quickly decided that it should, and caused a good deal of controversy when we also recommended that 5 per cent of curriculum time in schools should be devoted to such teaching.

Our discussions on the matter were extremely lively. The group was led by Professor Bernard Crick, who had for many years been a passionate advocate of more public involvement in the nation's political life, first set out in his book *In Defence of Politics*. Bernard was a great talker, and eventually a secret system of signals among the rest of us would help us to decide that the time had come for a well-placed interruption or intervention designed to stem the flow. Kenneth Baker constantly argued that our recommendations would be achievable only if the school day was extended, and that we needed to say so. In the end, we hammered out a form of words on the matter to which he and the rest of us could all subscribe. A formidable lady called Elizabeth Hoodless, the Chief Executive of Community Service Volunteers, which promotes voluntary work of all kinds and for all ages, repeatedly pressed upon us the benefits of such work in promoting citizenship among the young. One member of the group, a teacher who was deeply disillusioned with the national curriculum in general and our deliberations in particular, went public with his criticisms. He had to be asked to resign.

I found that my own contributions, apart from whatever general observations I could offer, often centred on questions of how our report should be drafted. It was vital that, in dealing with what many politicians, teachers and the general public might see as an attempt to introduce political indoctrination into schools, we should state the reasons for our recommendations, and the means of achieving them, with the utmost clarity.

I was asked, for example, to be part of a small sub-committee charged with setting out some guidelines on the teaching of controversial issues. The Chairman of the sub-committee, Dr Alex Porter, a former lecturer in education at London University, had written a first draft on the matter, which made many valuable points. The problem, which struck me and Marianne Talbot, a moral philosopher from Oxford, who was another sub-committee member, was that the shape of it all needed drastic revision. We proceeded to make more and more suggestions about the order of things, which Marianne, armed with a large felt-tipped pen, wrote up on the large pages of a blank flip-chart, which happened to be in the room where we were meeting. It soon looked as though the room was being redecorated, as more and more sheets of white paper, covered with a great deal of blue writing, were distributed all around it. In the end, Alex was presented with what looked like a roll of wallpaper to take away and work on, from which he somehow managed to produce an even better report.

The Speaker of the House of Commons, Betty Boothroyd, gave us strong support. Her personal representative, Sir Donald Limon, a former Clerk of the House of Commons, had attended most of our meetings. I suggested to the Advisory Group that the Speaker might wish to contribute a foreword to our final report. Sir Donald arranged for her to do so, and she used it to mount a vigorous case for citizenship education, the lack of which, she said, 'has been a blot on the landscape of public life for too long, with unfortunate consequences for the future of our democratic processes'.

Throughout, the Education Secretary, David Blunkett, remained utterly determined to see citizenship education included in the national curriculum, backed by statutory authority. At one stage, he addressed a Road Show on the Advisory Group's report, arranged for teachers and others in Sheffield, the city that includes his own Parliamentary constituency. He set out in a short address why he was so anxious to see citizenship taught in schools. 'I do not think it is right', he said, 'that our children should simply become voyeurs and bystanders while other people determine the future shape of their lives. Citizenship education will help to ensure that they do not.'

It was not an easy battle for David Blunkett to win. Plenty of strong and vociferous voices were raised against the idea, as I saw for myself. At a later stage of the operation, in which I was also involved, the proposals were considered as part of the overall review of the national curriculum by a body called the Qualifications and Curriculum Authority. At these meetings, the Chief Inspector of Schools, Chris Woodhead, made his opposition to the whole idea of formal education for citizenship very plain. He took the view that the finest preparation for adult life was to ensure that all our children were fully literate and numerate, and he wanted nothing to do with any plan which might make the achievement of that aim any more difficult. Teachers' representatives also made clear their continuing concerns over what they saw as yet more direction from central Government as to what they should teach, and how they should teach it. Where, they asked, will we find the extra time to teach an extra subject?

Those were real concerns that David Blunkett had to address, not least as he put his case to the Prime Minister, whose approval was required for the drafting of the necessary legislation. In my view, the answers probably lie in the realisation that much of what is already taught in many schools, under the heading of personal, social and moral education, will form a large part of the teaching of citizenship. A more innovative approach to the timetable in individual schools would also help. A legal requirement, however, is the only way to ensure that the subject is taught to proper standards in all secondary schools. For me personally it was a satisfying experience to see something which I had helped to shape reach the stage where it will now be put into practice as part of the education system of this country, since the Government announced that it was accepting most of the Advisory Group's recommendations. Parliamentary democracy is a precious thing, and it is surely worth encouraging anything that helps to strengthen and preserve it.

CHAPTER FIFTEEN

How We Won and How We Lost: The Battle for News at Ten

My career in broadcast journalism has had one unusual aspect. I have always been identified, in the public's mind at least, with one programme – *News at Ten*. For over thirty years, I appeared on it with great regularity, until it was taken off the air in March 1999.

Most journalists change jobs frequently, a trend which has increased in recent years. Now, it seems, new owners, managers or editors take charge of one or other of our national newspapers almost every week. In broadcasting, change has been less volatile, and in the case of the BBC its unique position certainly rules out change of ownership; but, even within the BBC, internal reorganisation has left its mark over the years on many journalistic careers. Commercial television has not been without its upheavals either. Those upheavals, however, tended to occur as the independent companies' franchises came up for review, or, as happened during the disgraceful events of 1991, when that review became an auction. Those changes, too, have led to many regional journalists moving from one employer to another.

In my case, with the exception of four years at the BBC, my time as a journalist has been spent with a single employer, which has itself enjoyed remarkable stability as a news provider. ITN's position has certainly not gone unchallenged over the years, but, despite all the changes within commercial television, it has been the sole provider of news on ITV for the whole of ITV's history, since the BBC's monopoly of television broadcasting was first broken in 1955.

However, it was not just a question of having worked for one company with a remarkable track record. My career had also been intertwined with a single programme. *News at Ten* was launched in July 1967. I joined ITN and began to work on it fourteen months later, in September 1968. While I was expected to contribute to all ITN's bulletins, there was no doubting where the company's maximum effort, and that of its senior reporters, went. As a young recruit, I watched and was impressed, in those early weeks, as my more experienced colleagues sent in their reports to the programme from the length and breadth of Britain, and from the world's hot-spots.

My own turn to contribute came rapidly. Just a month after joining, I was sent to Gibraltar as the back-up reporter, working with one of ITN's political staff, Bill Norris, on the coverage of the talks aboard HMS *Fearless* between Harold Wilson and the Rhodesian leader, Ian Smith. At one stage, I took it upon myself to hire an ageing Dakota aircraft, known locally as the 'Yogi Bear', to fly some film, and myself, across the Straits of Gibraltar to Tangier airport, so that our coverage could reach London, shipped aboard a connecting flight, as soon as possible. Chartering the plane for the round trip cost me the not inconsiderable sum, in 1968, of £70, but it spoke volumes to me about the effort that went into producing *News at Ten* that nobody ever queried my decision to spend the money. It was also an example of the exhilarating be-there-first, get-up-and-go atmosphere that surrounded the programme during its entire history. It frequently set the pace, and the standards, for television news in

Britain. It won a host of awards. With delicious, and perhaps deliberate, irony, the Royal Television Society honoured it as Programme of the Year in May 1999, two months after it had been killed off.

Time and time again, we would see innovations, everything from the employment of two presenters to the much greater use of live contributions from its correspondents and reporters, being copied by our main rivals, the BBC, with whom there was strong, but healthy, competition. As the BBC correspondent Fergal Keane wrote in a generous tribute as the arguments over *News at Ten* raged on, the first question he and his colleagues would ask, on arriving at any location, was a simple one: 'Is ITN here?' If the answer was yes, and it usually was, Keane and his colleagues would know that ITN's main effort would be directed towards its flagship bulletin, *News at Ten*.

The programme had far more ups than downs, and the downs were usually the reason for one of the several face-lifts that the programme underwent. It received, during its lifetime, much critical praise. Yet it was a programme which, over the years, many ITV chiefs had yearned to kill off. The birth of ITN itself in 1955 had shown how difficult relations with the programme companies which had come together to form the ITV network were likely to be. As Marshall Stewart, my former colleague on *South East News* at the BBC and now a leading media consultant, points out, 'No one should ever forget that Independent Television is, and always was, commercial television. The bottom line is the companies' balance sheets and share prices. None of them has ever gone bankrupt.'

From the start, there were suggestions from the companies that too much space was being given to news bulletins – eventually the Independent Broadcasting Authority put its foot down and insisted on twenty minutes of news a day. In an

311

uncanny foreshadowing of things to come, the companies managed to have one of the bulletins, scheduled for 10 p.m., put back until 10.45 p.m. There was even argument about whether ITN needed to go to all the expense of including so much film. Eventually, the Chairman of the IBA declared that 'the news should not consist of a featureless recitation, but be told or shown to the viewers in such a way as to be enlightening'. He helpfully added that the bulletins 'must be allowed whatever length and position in the programme schedules are necessary to let them do this democratic job'.

The launch of *News at Ten* in 1967 was also the cause of heated debate within ITV. Eventually, the companies agreed to a cautious, twelve-week trial period. The programme was an immediate success, soon laying legitimate claim to the half-hour slot at 10 p.m. each weekday evening that it commanded throughout its life. As a result, *News at Ten* became as much a fixture in the viewing habits of millions of Britons as *Coronation Street* at 7.30 p.m. Yet the programme companies continued a love–hate relationship with it throughout its life. They happily basked in the public praise for its successes, and enjoyed the huge revenue they derived from the much-sought-after advertising break halfway through it. Yet the ITV bosses constantly argued that its transmission time made late-evening scheduling a nightmare.

The chief problem was the 9 p.m. 'watershed'. The broadcasting authorities had long decreed that television programmes containing material which was not suitable for viewing by children could only be shown after nine o'clock in the evening. The result, the companies claimed, was that many of the films and serious dramas that they wanted to screen could be transmitted only by inserting a long break for *News at Ten* in the middle of them. That, they suggested, cut down both the size of the available audience for such films and dramas and the resulting advertising revenue.

The first serious attempt to get rid of *News at Ten*, based on those arguments, was made in the summer of 1993. News leaked from a supposedly secret meeting of the heads of the ITV companies that they would be making a formal application to the Independent Television Commission (ITC), the body charged with the policing of the ITV franchises, to be allowed to make the change. This was despite the fact that eight of the sixteen companies which had submitted their schedules during the bidding for new franchises two years earlier had said that they wanted to keep the 10 p.m. news slot.

ITN immediately decided to fight any attempt to kill off *News at Ten*. Life, however, was not quite that simple. The ITN board, which had on it a number of representatives of the very companies that wanted to make the change, had recently appointed a new chief executive, David Gordon. Immediately after the news had leaked of the companies' intentions, he decided that ITN would actively oppose any application by the companies to shift *News at Ten*, despite the fact that picking a fight with so many of ITN's paymasters was an extremely high-risk strategy.

At that time, the chairmanship of the ITN board rotated among the chairmen of the ITV companies. By mid-1993, with the future of *News at Ten* in doubt, that method of choosing the chairman of ITN had produced a difficult situation. The position had gone to Michael Green, who was also the Chairman of Carlton Television. Carlton, the new holder of the London weekday franchise, was known as one of the companies that was keen to see *News at Ten* moved, and Carlton's Chairman was known as a man for whom the financial health of any company he ran was of paramount importance. His favourite question was always said to be: 'Why do we need to do this?'

As Chairman of both Carlton and ITN, Michael Green was

now faced with a difficult conflict of loyalties. As a result, he very properly adopted a neutral public stance as the battle for the programme got under way. In private, however, it was rather more obvious where his sympathies lay. At one point, he asked to meet a number of senior figures from the management and staff of ITN to discuss the possible change with us. I was among the group of people invited to the meeting, which Green began with brisk efficiency and a subtle variation on his own favourite question. 'Right,' he said, 'why not just state your case? Why should this change *not* be made?'

He listened as we rehearsed the familiar arguments, making only the briefest of comments, until we came to the companies' proposal for a late news at 11 p.m. On our side, we said that we believed that many people started to go to bed at around 10.30 p.m., after *News at Ten*, and that a bulletin at 11 p.m. would command only a tiny audience. 'I simply do not accept', Green retorted with some vigour, 'that millions of people in this country are tucked up in bed by eleven o'clock at night. I think that's an absurd argument.'

Absurd or not, it was clear that the argument over people's viewing habits was going to be a crucial part of the campaign. Equally vital, however, was the mobilisation of support among leading politicians. Indeed, at the meeting with Michael Green, I had told him that my initial soundings suggested that the politicians would be particularly hostile to the change. At that stage, ITN had not formally begun to lobby them, but that was a course on which we now embarked.

In overall charge of the lobbying operation was Dame Sue Tinson, once a producer of *News at Ten*, who had become an associate editor at ITN. She had always had particularly close links with people in the upper reaches of the Conservative Party, and she told me that she felt sure that the Prime Minister, John Major, would be prepared to support the retention of the programme. She asked me to approach the then Leader of the Labour Party, John Smith, to see if he would do the same.

I decided to make my first approach in that direction through David Hill, Labour's Chief Press Officer, who was in effect John Smith's Press Secretary. David's immediate reaction was extremely positive, as he told me that he was certain that John Smith would be prepared to go public on the issue. Indeed, he asked me for some guidance on the main arguments for keeping the programme, which I gave him.

I had, in fact, already gone public on the matter myself, during a conversation with Valerie Grove of *The Times*. Every week she conducted an interview for the paper which was then given feature-length treatment, and, hearing of the developments over *News at Ten*, she had asked to talk to me. I used the interview with her to set out some of the main arguments for keeping the programme where it was. Chief among them was the fact that so much can happen in British politics late into the evening. In the weeks before the *Times* interview, I had been able to broadcast two exclusive stories, both of which had developed after ITN's early bulletin at 5.40 p.m.

The first, indeed, was the direct result of something I had said on that early bulletin on a Tuesday evening at the end of May. I had suggested that the reshuffle of John Major's Cabinet, about which there was a great deal of speculation, was not imminent. A Minister, having heard my remarks, had got in touch with me during the course of the evening. 'I strongly advise you to change that story,' he told me. 'The reshuffle will happen by the weekend.' And it did.

Two weeks later, I had struck lucky with another developing story. There had been much talk about a formal challenge to John Major's leadership, despite the reshuffle. Behind the scenes, Mrs Thatcher was rumoured to have been quietly encouraging such talk. I decided to ask her directly whether there was any truth in the rumours that she wanted Major to go, and managed to reach her by telephone at her London home at around 9.15 p.m. Her answer was forthright. 'There can be no question of a leadership challenge at the moment. Any such challenge would be ill judged and ill timed.' At that stage, a public declaration of support by Mrs Thatcher was an important political development, to which we were able to give due prominence on *News at Ten*, and which was widely reported in the morning papers.

Talking to Valerie Grove of *The Times* about *News at Ten*, I described both those stories as 'classic cases of how politics in Britain never comes to the boil until about 8 p.m. All you can do before that is to tell the story so far.' By their very nature, neither report was ready for broadcasting on ITN's bulletin at 5.40 p.m. That served to underline the chief point that I wanted to get across about *News at Ten* during the *Times* interview – that the programme's unique timing enabled us to give as full a picture of the day's events as it was possible for an on-the-day news bulletin to give. I also believed then, and still believe, that with the BBC's main bulletin being broadcast at 9 p.m., the extra hour gave *News at Ten* a real competitive advantage. In addition, I certainly did not want to leave the provision of news during what most people regarded as their main evening viewing entirely open to the BBC. As I also told *The Times*, 'Television is the prime source of news for the majority of the population, and I don't want to leave the hours of 7 to 10.30 p.m. open to the competition. Selfish – but that's how it sits with me.'

In the autumn, I set out those same arguments for the Labour Leader, John Smith, through David Hill. I imagined it might be some time before David would be able to focus the Labour Leader's attention on the matter, but I was wrong. Within a matter of a day or so, John Smith had written to the Chairman of the Independent Television Commission, Sir

George Russell. 'Were this plan to go ahead,' he told Sir George, 'it would be a major blow to the coverage of news and current affairs on British television. At the moment, *News at Ten* provides first-rate news coverage at a time when Independent Television viewers are able to watch it. Were it to be moved to 6.30, many viewers . . . would be left without any access to a serious news bulletin at any time during the day.' Whether my colleagues at ITN who worked on the lunchtime and early-evening news programmes appreciated the suggestion that their bulletins were not 'serious', I do not recall. I did realise that we could hardly have had a more forthright defence of *News at Ten* than that set out in John Smith's letter.

News of the letter emerged in one of the Sunday papers, and that seemed to have the effect of prompting action by the Prime Minister. I knew that Sue Tinson would be approaching him in the same way as I had contacted John Smith, though my own view was that John Major might be wary of getting involved. It was, after all, something he could safely have left to the Minister in charge of broadcasting, the Heritage Secretary Peter Brooke.

In the event, and to everyone's considerable surprise, John Major wrote to Sir George Russell at the ITC in terms which were, if anything, even stronger than those used by Smith. 'I am concerned', he wrote, 'that one of the strengths of the Independent Television network may be seriously impaired, if the main evening news is not a central part of the schedule.' The Prime Minister's letter continued, 'It is important that Channel Three continues to provide high quality news services, and competes effectively with the services provided by the BBC throughout the peak evening hours.' We most certainly could not have wished for more. The letter had highlighted one of the arguments which we had always reckoned would play best with the politicians – the fear of

317

allowing the BBC a monopoly of news programmes during peak viewing times on the two channels, BBC 1 and ITV (Channel Three), which most people watched.

Nor did we accept the argument that a half-hour bulletin at 6.30 p.m. on ITV would be a satisfactory replacement, despite the fact that it seemed likely that such a programme would satisfy all the various rules and regulations. The 1990 Broadcasting Act called for 'news programmes of high quality dealing with national and international matters . . . at peak viewing times'. The Independent Television Commission defined the evening 'peak viewing time' as running from 6 p.m. to 10.30 p.m., though it later confused things by seeming to suggest that there should be both an early-evening news *and* a later thirty-minute news programme within that period of time.

It was generally accepted, however, that there was no strong case for suggesting that a half-hour bulletin at 6.30 p.m. was formally out of order. ITN did feel strongly, however, that the ITC's definition of peak viewing time, and particularly the inclusion within it of the period from 6 to 7 p.m., did not square with the actual viewing habits of the nation. We argued that many people, especially in the southeast of England, did not arrive home until well after 6 p.m., and therefore did not settle down to watch television until much later in the evening. In our view, while transmitting ITN's main bulletin between 6.30 and 7 p.m. may have satisfied the formal requirement for a full news bulletin in peak viewing time, it did not do so in practice.

The Prime Minister's personal intervention, added to all the other representations that had been made, particularly by the Labour MPs Gerald Kaufman and Peter Mandelson, had an enormous impact on the public debate, though Sir George Russell at the ITC said later that his mind was already made up before the politicians' interventions. He reached a speedy

318

decision that, with the new franchises having been awarded so recently, he would not allow *News at Ten* to be moved for several years, and wrote to the ITV company chairmen to tell them so. As a result, no formal application to change the schedules was even submitted by the ITV companies on this occasion.

We had, incidentally, always had high hopes of Sir George. He had already proved himself to be a very tough, 'hands-on' head of the Commission. In addition, while we knew that he would have to take an impartial decision on the *News at Ten* question, it was certainly not a disadvantage to us that, prior to his ITC appointment, he had been the Chairman of ITN. His swift action also had one important spin-off for ITN. Had it lost *News at Ten* in 1993, it is conceivable that the company simply would not have survived the competitive pressures that were beginning to surround it. In the event, it had five years to build up its corporate strength before the next attack on its flagship programme.

Sir George Russell's decision, however, left one person exceedingly unhappy. The current Chairman of ITN, Michael Green, had privately hoped that the decision would go against us, since Carlton, the programme company of which he was also Chairman, was in favour of the change. What really rankled with Green, however, was that David Gordon, the Chief Executive whom he had so recently helped to appoint, had quietly orchestrated such a successful campaign to save the programme. The relationship between the two men never survived such a huge early shock. Two years later, David Gordon resigned as ITN's Chief Executive.

A good many of the other company chiefs were equally angry at the decision Sir George Russell and the ITC reached in 1993, but they knew that they would have to back off and abide by it. Part of the problem was that the whole organisation of ITV was something of a shambles. One insider described it, at that time, as 'like a pantomime horse with fifteen legs'. It was, therefore, inevitable that, when ITV finally got its act together, another attempt to get rid of *News at Ten* would be made. Five years later, it happened.

The second battle over *News at Ten* began at the beginning of 1998. In the intervening years, ITV had shaped up. It had established a 'Network Centre', with two powerful figures running it. The Chief Executive was Richard Eyre, who, as a former advertising executive and Managing Director at Capital Radio, knew all about the successful operation of commercial broadcasting. He resigned, suddenly and surprisingly, in late 1999. The Director of Programmes was David Liddiment, whose twenty-three-year career in television, at Granada and the BBC, had included responsibility for *Coronation Street* and the commissioning of such highly successful programmes as *Cracker* and *Men Behaving Badly*. In addition, Steve Anderson, who had once worked briefly at ITN, had become ITV's Director of News and Current Affairs. Much of his career had been spent working on such current affairs programmes as *World in Action* and *Newsnight*. In 1995, he had become the BBC's Head of Consumer Programmes, responsible for *Watchdog*.

It was clear that these three men, who now brought to the ITV Network Centre such a wide experience of popular programming, would hold no particular brief for preserving *News at Ten*, or its traditional place in the schedules, but it went further than that. All three were passionately in favour of shifting the programme. Their main argument was that, in its regular slot, *News at Ten* was doing serious damage to ITV's overall ratings. Those ratings had been slipping for some time, and, as a result, ITV was under considerable pressure from its advertisers. Faced with that situation, Richard Eyre, the Chief Executive, had made a public promise to get ITV's audience share back above 40 per cent. Time and time again, he and his colleagues at the Network Centre quoted the statistic that ITV lost 27 per cent of its audience when the news came on at ten o'clock. Some viewers, they said, simply switched off; many others found alternative programmes, like *Have I Got News for You?*, on other channels, the result of more aggressive programming at 10 p.m. by BBC2 and Channel Four.

My own view was always to express surprise that *only* 27 per cent of the ITV audience failed to continue watching. News has never been able to command the very highest viewing figures, but for just under three-quarters of the ITV audience to stay with us on a regular basis for *News at Ten* was, I believe, a remarkable achievement. The ITV bosses however, disagreed. In their view, if ITV was to increase its audience share, major rescheduling was required, especially after the 9 p.m. watershed. That, in the Eyre–Liddiment scheme of things, meant shifting the news. In other words, killing off *News at Ten*.

Over the five years since the previous battle, the whole atmosphere within television broadcasting in Britain had also changed. It had all become far more competitive, as Mrs Thatcher's Broadcasting Act of 1990 had intended it should. It is hard, incidentally, to over-emphasise the effect that Act had on commercial television in Britain. In the short term, it resulted in the shameful and muddled franchise auction of 1991. For the first time, the applicant companies were required, not only to give details of the nature and quality of the programmes they would transmit, but also how much they were prepared to pay for the right to do so.

A combination of the amount the companies were prepared to bid and the quality thresholds imposed by the ITC produced a bizarre series of changes. One of the leading existing contractors, Central Television, which held the lucrative

franchise covering the East, West and South Midlands, realised that it was unlikely to face any serious opposition, and
won back its contract on a bid of just £2,000. It had actually
considered bidding just a thousand pounds, and decided to
increase it, not as a result of any fears over the seemliness of
such a ludicrously low figure, but through anxiety that they
might not have covered any hidden fees that they might be
expected to pay. Carlton Television, on the other hand,
mounting what ultimately turned out to be a successful
attempt to retain its franchise in London, put in a bid of
almost £44 *million*. Even Mrs Thatcher was eventually forced
to admit the absurdity of the way the auction turned out.
When the process resulted in the morning programme con-
tractor TV-am losing its franchise, she wrote to its Chairman,
Bruce Gyngell, whom she had always regarded as the very
model of a television mogul. 'You of all people,' she told him
in a handwritten note, 'have done so much for the whole of
television. I am painfully aware that *I* was responsible for the
legislation.'

In the longer term, the Act greatly helped to increase the
impact, in later years, of Richard Murdoch's BSkyB, the
result of the merger in November 1990 between Sky and
its early rival, BSB. It also meant that those who ran the
nation's commercial television stations were unlikely to take
kindly to the idea of non-commercial strictures being placed
upon them, when it came, for example, to the matter of
deciding the future of *News at Ten*. For the most part, the
companies had been forced to defend or obtain their franchises by observing a strictly commercial criterion, namely
the payment of large sums of money to the Government,
either through the size of their initial bids or through what is
called the PQR, the percentage of qualifying revenue. The
PQR means, for example, that while Central was successful
with its £2,000 franchise bid, it still pays the Government

something in the order of £20 million a year in extra, special payments.

In addition, ITN itself had become a different kind of company. It had been specifically required by the 1990 Act to turn itself from a subscription service, paid for by the ITV companies, into a profit-making organisation, selling its services to its various customers, including ITV. As a result, its ethos had changed from being an outfit that simply fulfilled ITV's public service broadcasting requirements to a much more aggressive company, fighting for business in an increasingly competitive market. There had already been suggestions, for example, that ITN could be replaced as ITV's news provider by another company – Sky itself, perhaps, or the international news agency Reuters, which had entered the television news business in a big way. All of that meant that the new battle over *News at Ten* would be entirely different from the old one.

Stewart Purvis, who had risen through the ranks of ITN to become its Chief Executive after David Gordon's departure, took a distinctly pragmatic view of things. As someone who had once produced the nightly editions of *News at Ten*, he had more than just a sentimental attachment to the programme. On the other hand, in the new commercial climate which the 1990 Broadcasting Act had ushered in, there was no absolute guarantee that ITN would forever remain the provider of the news to ITV. He himself was now in charge of a rapidly expanding and increasingly profitable company. He was convinced that providing ITV with the sort of flagship news programme that it wanted, when it wanted it and at a price it was prepared to pay, would be the only way in the long run to strengthen ITN's position. There had already been quite a struggle over the budget for the programmes, including *News at Ten*, which ITN was providing for ITV.

Stewart Purvis decided, therefore, that this 'purchaser–

provider' relationship required far more detachment than the thin veneer of neutrality which ITN had adopted at the time of the previous battle over *News at Ten*. This time, he decided, ITN had to be seen to be making no effort of any kind to influence the outcome. Dame Sue Tinson, for example, was expressly told, this time round, not to lobby the politicians for support.

In addition, it was clear that there were those within ITN who had grown tired of the old format. The Editor responsible for ITN's bulletins on ITV, Nigel Dacre, was properly cautious about taking sides. Nevertheless, he spoke with clear enthusiasm to all of us on his staff about the exciting opportunities which not just one, but two new programmes – a main news at 6.30 p.m. and a shorter, late-evening bulletin at 11 p.m. – would offer. Later it was suggested that this had all been part of a deliberate strategy for maintaining staff morale – that if *News at Ten* were lost there would still be rewarding and demanding work for those who had worked on the programme to do. However, it was very clear to me that the prospect of playing with a new train set was exciting a good many people at ITN's London headquarters in Gray's Inn Road, well ahead of any official pronouncement by the Independent Television Commission. I think it is a matter of great regret that ITN as a whole did not put up far more of a fight to keep *News at Ten* within a revamped ITV schedule.

A certain amount of licence, however, was given to one or two of us who wanted to carry on the fight. I decided to use it. In April 1998, I was invited by a group called the European Media Forum to deliver their annual lecture. The Forum describes itself as an independent, cross-party think-tank devoted to policy issues affecting communications. Its links to ITN, however, had always been strong. Its Director, the Conservative MP Damian Green, had once been a reporter on

Channel Four News, which ITN also produces, and ITN was the sponsor of the annual lecture that I had been asked to give.

My main subject was the question of the Labour Government's relationship with the press, in other words the whole business of spin-doctors. However, with the future of *News at Ten* beginning to come to the boil again, I decided to make my personal position clear. I set out what I described as the Government's highly pro-active approach to the business of governing in general and to its relations with the media in particular. 'That', I said, 'is one reason why I am personally so opposed to any suggestion that *News at Ten* should be shifted to the outer edges of ITV's evening schedule.' I continued, 'I do not at any time, and particularly at a time of so much political activity, wish to see the BBC have a monopoly of news reporting on the two main channels for most of the traditional evening viewing.'

Stewart Purvis and the rest of ITN's senior management knew what I was going to say and raised no objection, provided I made it clear that I was expressing a personal view. As a result, as events unfolded, people knew where one of ITN's most senior correspondents stood, despite the company's officially neutral position, and my name was, as a result, frequently cited alongside others who were against the change. Stewart's decision over the lecture also allowed me, I felt, a continuing personal right to do what I could, behind the scenes, to try and save the programme. I was in regular contact, for example, with Sir David Nicholas, ITN's former Editor, who had, once again, emerged as a champion of the status quo. On this occasion, as on the last, his devotion to *News at Ten*, and what it stood for, was absolute. After the battle for it was eventually lost, he was invited to the launch party for the new programme which replaced it. Even on that occasion Sir David told the assembled guests, 'I cannot find it in my heart to admire the decision to end *News at Ten*.'

Some months before that decision, Sir David had reminded me of the effect of John Major's intervention during the previous battle, and wondered aloud if Tony Blair would act in the same way this time. I said I would find out, and began to make some discreet enquiries among my contacts at Number Ten. I was pleasantly surprised at the positive feedback that I received. At one stage, it seemed likely that a carefully placed enquiry during Prime Minister's Questions would allow Blair to make a very public declaration of support for the programme. Unfortunately, news of the plan leaked out through some injudicious gossiping by one of my ITN colleagues, and, as a result, things did not happen that way.

Nevertheless, in early September 1998, with the Independent Television Commission having announced that it would be ruling on the matter in the near future, Blair did make his views known. At a Downing Street briefing, his official spokesman said, 'The Prime Minister supports *News at Ten* staying where it is, because it has got a deserved reputation for reporting often complex political, international and other issues in a very digestible and even-handed way.' We were also told that he felt 'that it would be regrettable if this move led to any marginalisation of TV news, or any further move down market in the media more generally'.

The Prime Minister, however, did not contact the Independent Television Commission directly, as Major and Smith had done in 1993. Nor did the Conservative Leader, William Hague, despite his view that *News at Ten* should not be moved. Among the political leaders, only the Leader of the Liberal Democrats, Paddy Ashdown, wrote directly to the Commission this time, with a strongly worded letter expressing what he called his 'gravest reservations' about the plan. He suggested that moving the programme would send a signal that ITV was abdicating its responsibilities to cover Parliament properly, and that a short bulletin at 11 p.m. would be an insufficient substitute. 'If it sinks its flagship news,' he concluded, 'ITV would be acting against the public interest, and would also do great damage to its own reputation as a defender of high broadcasting standards.' Clearly such a forceful communication had benefited from the briefing Paddy Ashdown had received from his recently appointed Communications Director, David Walter, who just happened to be a former ITN political correspondent.

My part in all this had been limited to behind-the-scenes activity, though my name was constantly cropping up in the reporting of the issue. As a result, ITV's Director of Programmes, David Liddiment, and the Head of News and Current Affairs, Steve Anderson, suggested a meeting. I expected that this might be some kind of private warning to back off entirely, but that turned out not to be the case. Over a lengthy drink at Westminster, both Liddiment and Anderson set out, in some detail, the familiar arguments for the change. I stuck to my view that news bulletins at 6.30 and 11 p.m. would be no substitute for *News at Ten*, which was ideally placed in the schedules to provide the public with a full picture of the day's events. 'As a competitive journalist,' I told them, 'that is where I want ITV's main news. After the BBC's, and before the country goes to bed.' At the end of the meeting, we simply agreed to differ.

In addition to the politicians' contributions, it was noticeable this time around that the public debate was far more extensive. Thousands of words in newspaper and magazine articles were devoted to the subject, with the balance firmly in favour of keeping the programme It was clear, however, that the two Murdoch-owned newspapers, *The Times* and the *Sun*, did not share that view. In an editorial, *The Times* took issue with those politicians who wanted *News at Ten* saved. 'Rather than treating ITV with suspicion,' *The Times* said, 'politicians should help the commercial broadcaster to adapt, so it can woo the new digital generation.' Rupert Murdoch's BSkyB is, of course, a leading player in that 'new digital generation'. The *Sun* lived up to its reputation of producing pithy, public-bar-style comment in an editorial on the morning before the last *News at Ten*. 'Bong! It's goodbye to *News at Ten* tonight. Bong! Do we care? Not a bit.'

By then, after months of public debate, the Independent Television Commission had ruled that the changes ITV wanted to make could go ahead. The Commission's role this time had been a curious one. On the face of it, it had taken far greater efforts than in 1993 to discover what the public's mind on the matter was. As a result of the large-scale consultation exercise it had mounted, it received over 2,000 submissions, many from ordinary members of the public, and most of them against the change. It even commissioned its own opinion poll, which, again, showed clear support for keeping things as they were.

Yet it ultimately became apparent that public opinion was not the overriding factor in the Commission's decision. It ruled, in mid-November 1998, after a seven-to-three vote by the Commissioners, that the schedules could be changed, and that, as a result, *News at Ten* could go. It was confirmed that the deciding factor had been its view that commercial television should be just that – truly commercial. The ITC had seen it as no part of its 'light-touch regulation' to intervene in a commercial operation. As Sir Robin Biggam, the businessman who chaired the Commission, put it, 'In a multi-channel age, direct intervention by a regulator to dictate the precise scheduling of a programme, even an institution such as *News at Ten*, looks increasingly inappropriate.'

I believe that huge question marks remain about the role which the Independent Television Commission played in the whole affair, and whether more than a simple desire not to interfere in a commercial decision came into play. I am very clear in my own mind, however, that the ITC failed in what should have been one of its foremost regulatory duties – that of protecting the interests of ordinary viewers, who, when asked, made it quite plain that they did not want news bulletins pushed to the outer edges of the ITV evening schedule. Even before the ITV Network Centre's formal application, the ITC had quietly let it be known that they would be happy to consider a well-argued case for shifting *News at Ten*. Richard Eyre and David Liddiment met Sarah Thane, the Director of Programmes at the ITC, before submitting their application to do so. In an interview with the *Guardian* after the decision was announced, Sarah Thane said, 'It would be silly if they hadn't come to me to ask . . . where I thought they would need to address potential ITC concerns.' That really does sound like the examiner letting the candidate have a look at the examination paper in advance.

Sarah Thane's long career at the ITC meant that she had also been part of the organisation when Sir George Russell had ruled so swiftly against any change in 1993. In her *Guardian* interview, her lingering resentment, and that of the ITV companies, at the way that the 1993 decision had been taken is clear. 'The bruises are still very fresh', she told the *Guardian's* reporter, 'on the skin of some of the ITV executives from last time, when the idea [of abolishing *News at Ten*] was bounced on so fast.' It is at least open to question whether an official of the regulatory body, the ITC, should see it as part of her duty to sympathise with the hurt feelings of the heads of those companies the ITC is charged with regulating. It also suggests that those who were advising the Commissioners regarded it as part of their duty to promote the cause of what they saw as a potentially more successful ITV network, under its new administrators Richard Eyre and David Liddiment. The small matter of why the ITC decided to ignore the overwhelming public reaction against the changes, which its own research had confirmed, was dealt with by Sarah Thane in an article in the magazine *Broadcast*. 'While our audience research showed a majority in favour of retaining *News at Ten*,' she wrote, 'we found that the more viewers learned about what would replace it, the more supportive of ITV's proposals they became.'

Once the ITC's verdict had been announced, ITN's Chief Executive, Stewart Purvis, issued a statement declaring that the company was glad a clear decision had been reached after a long period of uncertainty. 'Since it was first broadcast in 1967,' his statement went on, '*News at Ten* has been the most important news programme in Britain. We are naturally sad that it will be coming to an end.' My own thoughts that day went beyond mere sadness. I was genuinely perplexed that the 'most important news programme in Britain', this admitted jewel in the crown of ITN and ITV, was being abolished, with no clear certainty that the successor programmes would ever achieve the same, unique reputation. Gerald Kaufman, the Chairman of the Commons Heritage Committee, who had fought so long and hard to save the programme, did not, as usual, mince his words. 'This decision,' he said, 'is a milestone in the dumbing down of Britain.'

Eventually, it was decided that the new ITV schedules would come into force at the beginning of March 1999. It was one of the ironies of the situation that, in the last four months of its life, *News at Ten* secured some of its best audience figures ever, regularly getting around a million more viewers than the BBC's *Nine O'Clock News*. During that time, I had managed to keep up our tally of exclusive stories with a report that the controversial beef-on-the-bone ban was to stay. There were a number of stories, like the resignation of Peter Mandelson, which developed strongly in time for *News at Ten*.

We also had a truly memorable edition of the programme

on the night, in December 1998, when Britain joined the United States in launching another round of air attacks on Iraq. The timing of that announcement simply served to highlight, in my view, why a mid-to-late-evening, full-length news bulletin in Britain was so important. The announcement in Washington was scheduled, as are so many American pronouncements, for around 5 p.m. – 10 p.m. London time – though, on this occasion, the start of the military operation itself was clearly the overriding factor. I had picked up enough information during the course of the evening to be certain that an announcement from Downing Street about the launching of cruise-missile attacks would be made during *News at Ten*, and I had alerted the editor of the programme accordingly.

We were, therefore, ready for the eventuality of a live statement in Downing Street by the Prime Minister. Shortly before we went on air, I was given firm background guidance that there would be just such a statement, though I was asked not to say so categorically in advance of it happening, for fear of compromising the military operation. It was therefore a question of using my live commentary, delivered from outside Number Ten, to hold the fort, and to give an indication of what Tony Blair was likely to say, until the Prime Minister stepped out into the street to say it.

Fortunately, there was enough activity going on all around me to give increasingly heavy indications of what I knew was about to take place. I was able to refer to the setting up of the necessary lectern and microphones, and to the appearance in the street of Alastair Campbell, his official spokesman, as evidence that the Prime Minister would be speaking very shortly indeed. I also had confirmation from Campbell, off camera, just before the Prime Minister's arrival, that the raids had in fact begun. Shortly before 10.15 p.m., Tony Blair began his detailed explanation of what was taking place and why. *News at Ten* carried it live, and in full.

The BBC were all over the place that night. They broadcast only a short newsflash about the announcement, apparently because no one senior enough within the BBC could be found to authorise anything else. Of course, ITN had been fortunate with the timing of it all, but it seemed to me that this was one last example of the sort of operation at which *News at Ten* had excelled over the years.

The last edition of the programme went out on Friday, 5 March 1999. We all tried not to be too maudlin over it all, but I felt that it was a moment to let my guard drop just a little. During the course of a live two-way with Trevor McDonald about the Budget, due to be delivered the following week, he asked me to share my thoughts about what would be in it, 'as we've done so many times over the years'. It was all beginning to sound like a re-enactment of that famous scene in Anthony Trollope's novel *Barchester Towers* between Warden Harding and the Bishop of Barchester. The two old men recall their many conversations together, and the Bishop tells Septimus Harding that he was the only friend he could ever really talk to, especially as he was so good at poking the fire in his study back into life.

It also occurred to me that I had, in fact, only covered a mere dozen or so Budgets, but never mind. I confessed to Trevor that there was 'a certain moisture in my eye too' as I set about making my points. It also went through my mind that Trevor and I would be doing exactly the same thing on the new *ITV Evening News* within a matter of a day or two, albeit at the earlier time of 6.30, and I said so. Later, at the end of the programme, Trevor thanked the millions of people who had watched the programme over the years, and all those who had worked on it, and ended with the words 'And so finally, it's goodbye *News at Ten*, and from all of us here, goodnight.'

That was it. After thirty-two years, it was all over. Straight commercial pressure, unrestrained by the official regulatory body, the ITC, had killed off Britain's favourite and most successful news programme.

Like the transitions of the British monarchy, however, it was a case of '*News at Ten* is dead. Long live the *Evening News*!' Weeks of preparation had gone into making sure that the launch of the new *ITV Evening News* at 6.30 p.m. the following Monday was flawless. With the Budget due to be unveiled the next day, I was, however, tempted down a path that I might have done better to avoid.

Those responsible for the new programme's launch wanted an 'exclusive' for the first edition, and wondered whether the Budget would provide it. More specifically they hit on the idea of asking Gordon Brown, the Chancellor, for a night-before-the-Budget interview. Even allowing for the fact that the traditional pre-Budget 'purdah' which Chancellors used to observe had largely ceased to exist, it seemed to me that it was unlikely that he would be able to say very much that was genuinely newsworthy. My Editor, Nigel Dacre, acknowledged this, but said that it would be fascinating to hear him talk about the whole process of Budget-making. I imagined that such an interview, with its feature-like feel, would run some way down the bulletin. I was somewhat surprised that the Chancellor agreed to the interview. I was even more surprised when, eventually, it became the lead story on the new bulletin. So, I gather, was the Prime Minister, once he got to hear about it. He immediately put in a call to his Chancellor, I was told later, to ask him 'what you've been telling this fellow Brunson'.

In truth the answer was – not a great deal that we did not know already. There were, however, some very useful hints about what was to come. There had been plenty of speculation about whether the long-promised 10 pence starting rate of tax would at last be introduced. The Chancellor all but confirmed that it would, as he told me, 'People will want to know how we can encourage work, and what the tax rates are for that.' He also talked about 'how we can encourage enterprise, and what the tax rates are for that, and they will also want to know how public investment can contribute towards a more efficient economy and a more successful society'. There was just sufficient in all of that to provide three of the more serious national newspapers the following morning with an extra paragraph or two.

The national television critics, however, went to town over our decision to lead the new programme with what they regarded as a 'soft' interview. They had plenty of fun at my expense, especially as I had dressed the whole thing up with shots of Gordon Brown using not one but two computers in an office in which, under his predecessors, there had not been a single one. The Chancellor, in teasing mood, and with his fingers hovering over the keyboard of the machine that actually contained the Budget, had said, 'Mike, I can show you the Budget now, but I won't!' I had also borrowed his famous red box, and, in an adjoining office, had done my closing 'piece to camera' with my hand casually resting on it.

One critic called the interview, and the fact that it had led the new bulletin, 'a badge of shame'. Allison Pearson in the *Daily Telegraph* wrote a withering, though highly amusing, critique of the programme in general, and my part in it in particular. I had interviewed the Chancellor, she wrote, with 'all the sceptical rigour of a *Blue Peter* presenter invited into the house of Anne Frank'. The same paper, mindful of the famous less-than-heavyweight 'And finally . . .' items which had ended *News at Ten*, actually carried a small separate editorial about the new programme. In it, it referred to what it called the 'saccharine' interview with the Chancellor, headed 'And initially . . .' 'So it's not just a change of time,' the *Telegraph* thundered, 'but a change of function – from news programme to party political broadcast.'

I took consolation from one review in the *Glasgow Herald*. 'A chat like that, the night before the Budget, is unheard of,' the writer trilled. 'It was a great scoop.' No matter that the writer was not exactly unbiased in these matters. The by-line showed it to be the work of the former ITN newscaster Pamela Armstrong.

Perhaps our collective judgement at ITN on the placing of the interview, and the sort of package into which I had incorporated it, were open to question. My other consolation, however, was two-fold: that no one had been able to ignore the lead item at the start of the new programme, and that the BBC, having seen it, made a tremendous fuss about why they had not been given access to the Chancellor as well.

The initial figures for the new *ITV Evening News* were healthy, though it soon encountered mixed fortunes. So did ITV's overall share of the television audience, which the shifting of *News at Ten* was supposed to revive. Figures released after the first hundred days showed that the overall audience in the 10–11 p.m. slot on ITV had gone up by just 200,000, from 5.9 to 6.1 million, which was not exactly the surge that the ITV bosses had hoped for. In fact, the BBC's figures for the same time slot had actually increased by slightly more.

By the end of 1999, the share of the audience watching ITV weekday programmes between 9 and 11 p.m. had increased by just 0.6 per cent. ITV's overall share during the whole of peak-time viewing had gone up by 0.5 per cent. Lift-off had plainly not occurred, which may have been one reason behind the shock resignation of ITV's Chief Executive, Richard Eyre. The Network Centre, however, continued to insist that the changes to the schedule needed time to bed in, and that it was delighted with the way ITN's new programmes had established themselves.

There was, however, no evidence of the gap being filled on any regular basis by the splendid new programming that had been promised. One or two individual programmes were of high quality. I saw, for example, a first-class documentary on Alzheimer's disease – which fitted extremely well into the slot between 9 and 11 p.m., and which a break for *News at Ten* would clearly have wrecked.

For the rest, the newly vacated slot was occupied by a number of programmes that simply failed to take off. Among them was the new current affairs programme *Tonight with Trevor McDonald*, in which ITN was actively involved, though the programme as a whole was produced by Granada. Despite the protestations of the ITV Network Centre that the viewing figures for the programme were respectable, and that the ITV audience liked it, the critics panned it. Soon after the changes to the schedule, the overall late-night figures were boosted by a complete re-run of all the old Bond movies, but that in itself hardly suggested that there was a wealth of high-quality, challenging new material fighting to make it on to ITV.

The audience for the *ITV Evening News* at 6.30 p.m. settled at around the six million mark, and that for the *Nightly News* at 11 p.m. at around three million. Those figures seemed respectable enough, but they represented an overall loss to ITN of around one million viewers when compared with the old schedule that included *News at Ten*. Besides, the viewing figures alone failed to tell the real story.

In the months following the change, countless people told me how they no longer watched any ITN bulletins, and had therefore not seen any of my reports, following the ending of *News at Ten*. Almost without exception, they explained that they were not home in time for the 6.30 p.m. news, and that, as busy people who had to get up early in the mornings, they went to bed before the new *Nightly News* at 11 p.m. It is true that many of the people who spoke to me would not be regarded as regular ITV viewers. Their reaction, however, underlined a further point – that ITN had, by losing its 10 p.m. slot, also lost touch with many of those who could be categorised as 'opinion-formers' – MPs, doctors, lawyers, and other such professional people – and who often watched ITV only to catch *News at Ten*.

But there was also a great deal of anecdotal evidence that people from all walks of life, including, for example, manual workers, felt the same way. Several months after the change, the *Daily Mirror* claimed that just over 5,000 of its readers had called a special hotline on the subject, and that 94 per cent of them wanted *News at Ten* brought back.

Such a finding is one reason why Ministers began to express their unhappiness at the way things had worked out. Speaking seven months after the changes at a Parliamentary Press Gallery lunch, which I was chairing, the Education and Employment Secretary, David Blunkett, said, 'The lack of *News at Ten* on ITV actually disengages another section of the community from a regular understanding of what is going on around us. There's a danger to society when a very large chunk disengages not just from politics but from civic society as a whole.'

While those in charge of ITV continued to insist that nothing but good had resulted from the change, the BBC immediately formed an entirely different view of what had happened. The Corporation's Annual Report for 1998–99, published four months after the ending of *News at Ten*, made a great deal of the BBC's dedication to public service broadcasting. 'We remain committed to comprehensive news coverage in prime time,' the Governors declared. 'There is now a stark contrast between the BBC's commitment to news, and ITV's decision to cease to provide a news bulletin in prime time.'

It was clear that the BBC Governors, like the rest of the nation, regarded 'prime time' as being between 7 and 10.30 p.m. Not for them the legalistic definition of what the 1990 Broadcasting Act called 'peak viewing time' (6–10.30 p.m.), during which ITV was required to transmit a full-length news bulletin. The BBC Governors were stating what I believe the rest of the country had already worked out for itself – that ITV was no longer transmitting its main news at a time when most people expected to see it. In his last major speech before his retirement as the BBC's Director-General, Sir John Birt singled out for particular praise the BBC's coverage of the war in Kosovo. In that context, he referred to 'ITV's abandonment of news in peak time – chillingly one week before Europe's first war for over fifty years'.

However, just as the BBC was repeating its commitment to peak-time news, ITV chiefs were giving indications of their irritation at the placing of news within the ITV schedule. They seemed to have particular problems with the new *Nightly News*, which was supposed to be transmitted each weekday evening at 11 p.m. There was certainly no recognition that any viewers might be switching on simply to watch a late-news bulletin and nothing else, though there was soon evidence that a significant number of people were doing just that. One ITV chief, indeed, defined the late bulletin as something people would 'stick around for', provided that the programming which preceded it was sufficiently interesting. As a result, the starting time of the new bulletin was constantly changed from anywhere between ten minutes to and five minutes past eleven, depending on whatever programme happened to be on before it. ITN received a steady stream of complaints about the shifting start time, including one from the Prime Minister, Tony Blair, through his Press Secretary Alastair Campbell. Only then did the ITV Network Centre respond – by promising that the eleven o'clock news would not, in future, start before eleven o'clock.

At 6.30 p.m. on 8 March 1999, just over 7 million people watched the first edition of ITN's new flagship programme, the *ITV Evening News*. They included Lady Thatcher, who saw it on a large screen at the party that was held to celebrate its launching. Her attention to it, however, was brief. Seeing the bulletin start with my eve-of-Budget interview with Gordon Brown, she immediately realised that even he was unlikely to disclose what he was due to announce the next day, and exclaimed, 'No news there, then.' She returned to the business of haranguing the guests, including the ITN Chairman, Mark Wood, and myself, when I arrived a little later, about the wickedness of getting rid of *News at Ten*. 'I'm going to make a fuss,' she told me. Then, raising her fingers to within a few inches of my face, she declared, 'I still have my sharp nails, you know.'

Why did I not tell her that it was all far too late, and that her Broadcasting Act, nine years previously, had done so much to accelerate the very change she was now criticising? It occurred to me to do so, but it also occurred to me that she would not have listened to a word I said.

CHAPTER SIXTEEN

'And Finally . . .'

There are two pieces of writing that every journalist, indeed every person who is interested in journalism, should read. I have already indicated my admiration for, Evelyn Waugh's novel *Scoop*, which is still, half a century after publication, the funniest, sharpest and best sideswipe at the excesses of the journalistic trade. The other piece is very different, much more serious, and is hardly known at all. It is usually referred to as the Delane editorial, published in *The Times* in February 1852. I was first introduced to it when Sir David English, the former Editor of the *Daily Mail*, read part of it as a tribute at the funeral of Gordon Grieg, who for many years was the *Mail*'s Political Editor.

An official historian of *The Times*, writing almost a hundred years after the Delane editorial was published, called it 'the best and most explicit justification of the duty of the Press to criticise public figures which *The Times* ever printed'. It is even better than that. It is one of the classic definitions of journalism, and especially of political journalism. 'The first duty of the Press', it says, 'is to obtain the earliest and most correct intelligence of events, and instantly, by disclosing them, to make them the common property of the nation.' What clearer definition of the craft could there be?

Dealing in particular with relations between the press and politicians, the Delane editorial goes on,

> The statesman collects his information secretly and by secret means; he keeps back even the current intelligence of the day with ludicrous precautions, until diplomacy is beaten in the race with publicity. The Press lives by disclosures; whatever passes into its keeping becomes a part of the knowledge and the history of our times. It is daily and for ever appealing to the enlightened force of public opinion – anticipating, if possible, the march of events – standing upon the breach between the present and the future, and extending its survey to the horizon of the world.

The circumstances which drove John Thadeus Delane, Editor of *The Times* from 1841 to 1876, to write his famous piece, are both fascinating and as relevant to our own day as they were to his. In the mid-nineteenth century, the influence of *The Times*, printed and published, of course, in London, was almost as strong in continental Europe as in the United Kingdom. The paper had been sharply critical of Louis Napoleon, the nephew of Napoleon Bonaparte, who had staged a *coup d'état* in France in late 1841, and who was later to become the Emperor Napoleon III.

Louis Napoleon, already established, as a result of the coup, as the President of France, was sufficiently outraged at the criticism of himself in *The Times* to communicate directly with its Editor, Delane, by personal letter, in which he made his displeasure plain. As if direct criticism by the leader of another country was not pressure enough, *The Times* was to endure a good deal more of it here at home. So great was the onslaught against the newspaper that our modern complaints about the supposed power and influence of government spin-doctors seem positively petty by comparison.

During debates in Parliament in early 1852, *The Times* was directly attacked and denounced in the Commons by the Prime Minister Lord John Russell himself, and in the Lords by the Leader of the Opposition, the Earl of Derby. Lord Derby set out his view of how journalists should behave. 'It is incumbent upon them,' he declared, 'as a sacred trust, to maintain that tone of moderation and respect . . . which would be required of every man who pretends to guide public opinion.' Even now, as Britain enters a new millennium, there are those politicians and others in public life who still, I suspect, have a sneaking regard for Lord Derby's demands. They would be more than happy if the press showed greater signs of knowing its place, and if it were to show greater signs of adopting a tone of 'moderation and respect'.

Journalists in the British media have, in recent years, established a good track record in defending press freedom, particularly with regard to relations with politicians. Political journalists are certainly not perfect, and there are times when relations between governments and individual journalists can grow too close for comfort, though seldom to the point which prompted Delane to issue this additional, stern warning on the matter 150 years ago. 'To perform its duties with entire independence,' he wrote, 'the Press can enter into no close or binding alliances with the statesmen of the day, nor can it surrender its permanent interests to the convenience of the ephemeral power of any government.' Modern-day transgressions may be relatively few, but it is not a bad quotation for every political journalist to have hanging on his wall.

The challenges facing Britain's politicians and the British press in the new century are, however, of a different order. Journalists will continue to hold governments to account for what they have done and intend to do, but increasingly we shall need to ask whether either, or both, have their priorities in the right order.

One of the most important and immediate issues has been with us throughout the last millennium – that of national sovereignty, of what it is that defines nationhood, not just in this country, but in every part of the globe. As Tony Blair has rightly pointed out, it is a sobering thought that, in Europe, we ended the twentieth century as we began it – with war in the Balkans. Misplaced nationalism has been the cause of countless wars in the past thousand years. Yet that is no reason for failing to realise that national or regional or local identity – the proper sense of belonging to a country or a state or a region – is a very powerful human emotion, which politicians cannot, and indeed must not, ignore.

England has ended the millennium as it began it: 1066 and the Battle of Hastings was about the threat to English sovereignty posed by the invasion of England by a French warlord. Now, along with the rest of the United Kingdom, we are to decide how much more of our national sovereignty is to be given up, through forming a closer union with the rest of Europe, and especially continental Europe, in the European single currency.

Whatever the decision, it is about much more than Britain's economic interests. Membership of a single currency, with interest rates decided, not by the Bank of England, but by the European Central Bank, will tie us to the rest of Europe in a far greater way than ever before. The bond will be of an entirely different nature to that which the existing European single market subjects us. Doing 60 per cent of our trade with Europe is one thing. Having to conduct a major part of our economy with the interests of not just one but around a dozen other countries at heart is quite another.

Britain's relations with Europe are, therefore, redefining the concept of the sovereignty of the United Kingdom at the start of the new millennium. In or out of the single currency, Britain is being forced to reach a decision about what Tony Blair has called 'its ambivalence about Europe', in the certain knowledge that Europe itself is being reshaped. Many of Europe's statesmen and women, whose countries are already full members of the single currency, are unashamedly committed, not just to monetary union, but to full political union too. The degree to which that happens, if it happens at all, will force Britain into yet more difficult decisions about what national sovereignty really means.

Those decisions will, in any case, continue to be shaped by something else. The full effects of constitutional change in the United Kingdom will make themselves increasingly felt. The reform of the House of Lords is already being tackled, though the true impact of the new second chamber as it seeks to redefine its own role, as well as its relationship with the House of Commons, will take time to emerge. It is certain, however, that full-scale reform of the House of Commons will be required. The devolved Parliament in Scotland and, to a lesser extent, the establishment of the Welsh Assembly, coupled eventually with developed government in Northern Ireland, will make reform of the Westminster Parliament inevitable.

It was the Scottish Labour MP Tam Dalyell who first defined what has become known as the West Lothian question. Why should Scottish MPs continue to vote on such matters as health and education in England when English MPs can no longer vote on such matters in Scotland, now that such questions have been devolved to a Scottish Parliament? In response to that question, the demands will grow for an English Parliament. They will be resisted by the majority of MPs at Westminster, who believe that the role of the House of Commons will be fatally diminished by the establishment of such a body, and that the break-up of the United Kingdom will be accelerated by such a move. However, a number of variations on the same theme will also be proposed. The Conservative Leader, William Hague, has already floated the idea of restricting voting in the House of Commons to English members when specifically English matters are before it. Though he does not say so, Hague is, in truth, proposing that the Westminster Parliament should sit, when necessary, as an English Parliament.

To some the idea of English sittings at Westminster, with the full Westminster Parliament, including its Scottish, Welsh and Northern Irish members, only discussing such matters as foreign affairs and defence, over which the devolved bodies in the regions do not have jurisdiction, is total anathema. Again, it is suggested that to have the Westminster Parliament sitting as anything other than the full Parliament of the United Kingdom at all times will demean and diminish it, and will break up the United Kingdom. They point out that in pre-devolution days Scotland and Wales had to put up with English members voting on purely Scottish and Welsh matters. Now, they say, the boot is on the other foot, and England will have to get used to Scottish and Welsh MPs voting on its affairs.

That, however, is a head-in-the-sand argument, a typical 'let's just muddle on as we are' position. It cannot and will not, in my view, simply rest there, though there is little question that a Labour government will try to let it. At present, Labour's hold on power has lulled us into a false sense of security about the workings of devolution. Things will be much more difficult, for example, if a future government, of whatever political persuasion, comes to power with only a tiny majority at a general election.

Imagine, for example, a narrow overall win for Labour, but with the Conservatives commanding a majority of the seats in England. Such a Labour Government would almost certainly depend for its majority on the votes of Scottish and Welsh

Labour MPs, and would never allow any scheme like Hague's 'English votes on English matters' plan to operate, since it would pose the risk of constant defeats for Labour policies in the largest part of the United Kingdom, England. Even that scenario does not allow for the complication of an increasingly powerful Liberal Democrat Party. Devolution, in short, is likely to produce far more questions than answers in the years ahead. We can expect a roller-coaster ride over devolution and constitutional reform.

Whether or not the Westminster Parliament is forced to change as a result of devolution, it is, in any case, in urgent need of change. Some modernisation is taking place, but it is coming far too slowly. There is for example, now, a second debating chamber, running in parallel with the main House of Commons, which has been constructed, at considerable expense, in the large and underused Grand Committee room, just off Westminster Hall. This second chamber is the MPs' talking shop, handling those items like Ten Minute Rule Bills, and Adjournment debates, which MPs use to raise constituency matters, and which, some say, clog up the business of the House. This development, however, does not address the question of whether too much time is spent at Westminster on the concerns of individual MPs. It is an article of faith in the House of Commons that the rights and needs of individual MPs are paramount. They are forever appealing to Madam Speaker to protect those rights, but I believe that the balance has swung too far in their favour.

Parliament, and particularly the Commons, does not do a very good job, in my view, at holding the Government to account. It has difficulty enough in handling and scrutinising the mass of new legislation that all Governments bring forward nowadays. There is precious little time left over for dealing with matters of immediate concern or interest, largely because the Commons is already doing so many other things.

347

Under New Labour, Government, and particularly Number Ten, has the whip hand, considerably helped by its formidable news-management machine. Prime Minister's Questions, particularly since it has been cut back to a single half-hourly session once a week, is an insufficient check on the day-to-day running of the country's affairs. There is a case, in my view, for taking a look at the procedures for emergency debates in the Commons, which at present are in the hands of the Speaker, to allow them to be held more frequently. There is certainly a case for strengthening the Select Committees, which scrutinise the work of individual government departments. They already do valuable work and often deliver tough criticism of the way those departments are run. With better resources, however, and with more permanent staff at their disposal, they could, and should, do much more.

The conduct of business in the House of Commons needs reforming too. There is ample evidence that the public is fed up with the confrontational nature of so much of what they see, hear and read in relation to the Commons. The young daughter of one of my news editors probably got it right when she decided to christen the Commons the 'Shouty-House'. Urgent consideration needs to be given to any and every means of cutting down on 'yah-boo' politicking, particularly when important legislation is being considered. It would help if the far more businesslike approach adopted when Bills are considered 'upstairs' in small committees could be transferred more frequently to the floor of the Commons. It would also help if MPs did not simply face each other across the chamber – a tradition that survives only because the Commons originated, 700 years ago, in a monastic chapel. Most of the world's other legislatures meet in semi-circular chambers. So, now, do the new Scottish Parliament and Welsh Assembly, as do most local councils. Even the new talking-shop chamber at Westminster has been built as a semi-circle.

Perhaps, in the new millennium, the main Commons chamber will be altered to reflect the fact that modern politics in Britain is becoming less and less of a two-party system.

Indeed, one of the greatest changes we may see as the new millennium gets under way is in the make-up of Britain's political parties, a process that the decision on the European single currency will only serve to exacerbate. Will the Conservative Party, for example, have a future as a party of the right if it fails to win forthcoming general elections and if Britain decides that it will join the single currency? For now, the Conservatives are convinced that opposition to the single currency for the foreseeable future is the majority view in Britain. The Conservative Party, however, will be in a very exposed position if Labour continues to govern and wins a single-currency referendum. Will the Conservatives not then face the ever present risk, either of the formation of a breakaway pro-European Conservative Party, or of steady defections of its members to other parties? Or can the Conservative Party so broaden its appeal and recapture the middle ground, thus attracting new recruits to what has become an increasingly old-aged membership, by hammering out a better or more attractive version of Tony Blair's Third Way?

There are plenty of questions for the other parties too. Labour gained power as the last British Government of the old millennium by promising to fulfil the aspirations of the many, not the few. But at what stage do the many decide that their demands for a better quality of life and, above all, better public services, especially in the inner cities and in many pockets of rural Britain, are simply not being met? And do some of the few who have a powerful voice, those who support fox-hunting for example, or who are leading the campaign against genetically modified crops, create such a destabilising effect that Labour's present grip on national politics is fatally weakened? To whom, then, do the disaf-

fected voters turn? Back to a more broadly based Conservative Party? Or will the Liberal Democrats become the ever
more natural home of such voters? Will the Liberal Democrats increasingly take up modernised versions of those positions, on the redistribution of wealth and public spending, for
example, which the Labour Party used to hold so dear?

Questions, rather than suggestions or answers, have begun
to take over this look into the future. I can only plead the old
nostrum that a week is a long time in politics, which makes
the prediction business in politics particularly hazardous,
especially at a time of so many challenges and changes. In
any case, the dilemma, and the fascination, of modern British
politics is that so many ideas are now the common currency of
all responsible political parties that the freedom for man-
oeuvre among them is far more restricted than it used to be.
No latterday British politician seriously advocates, for example, anything but tight control of public spending and inflation. Only the degree of the severity of that control is an issue.
The one certain political prediction is this: that the mixed
economy of private-sector wealth generation with state provision of core public services like health, education and welfare
is here to stay for the foreseeable future. That is not to say,
however, that argument about how broad, or narrow, that
state provision should be will not continue to dominate
political debate.

One other highly complicated issue is likely to demand far
more attention than it does at present. Scientific advances
such as the creation of genetically modified food have, as we
have seen, already begun to produce fierce public debate, and
have raised all kinds of questions over the extent, and the
effectiveness, of political control over such scientific developments.

We are plainly close to the point, for example, where
human beings can be cloned, and where the sex and other

characteristics of children yet to be born can be determined, and decided on, in advance. 'Babies to order' is no longer simply a racy tabloid headline, but an issue that will have to be faced in the very near future. At present, public opinion is firmly against such practices, and the law guards against them. Yet for how long can we rely on such easy certainty? Instances in the past, ranging from *in vitro* fertilisation of human embryos to the crisis over BSE, suggest that governments are very bad at handling such issues. Politicians seem to stagger along on a day-to-day, ad-hoc basis when tackling them, giving the impression of forever being one step behind in their understanding of what is going on, and in constant thrall to what is often conflicting advice from the scientists.

There is now a growing appetite among politicians for draft legislation setting out how they intend to frame new laws, and inviting public debate upon them. That process is still, however, largely reactive – seeing that a problem has arisen, but taking a little more time than usual in finding the way to tackle it. Perhaps, now, there needs to be an extension of the process that provides politicians with an early-warning system of such things as major scientific advances. Perhaps, also, some kind of cross-party national forum is needed at which politicians and others can, without any firm commitment to legislation, begin to toss ideas around as to whether legislation is either possible or desirable.

It is a function that the so-called think-tanks, which proliferate in and around Westminster, try to perform at present, as do some of the excellent and almost completely unknown committees of the House of Lords. The process, however, is haphazard. Whether it can be made less so, possibly in some kind of permanent, national think-tank, and whether those in public life should spend more time considering what lies ahead, as well as managing the present, needs itself to become a matter of debate. Early attention to issues that may well become the problems of the future is, for example, a role that the new, reformed House of Lords might well wish to expand, alongside its continuing function as a revising chamber.

If the politicians have much to reflect on as the new millennium begins, so do journalists, and, in particular, those who work in television news. Within the space of the last thousand years, of course, journalism is a relative newcomer, though the concept of the messenger, the person who brings us news, has been with us from the earliest times – witness the honoured place which the 'messenger' holds in the classical Greek tragedies. It is clear that the latterday messengers – journalists of all kinds – will be no less busy during the new millennium, though the way in which the message is delivered is changing and developing with astonishing speed.

There are already, however, worrying trends within television news. As I have already made clear, I remain utterly dismayed at the way the removal of *News at Ten* has pushed television news to the outer edges of peak-time viewing on ITV, though the BBC has made clear its continuing commitment to news on BBC1 during the main viewing hours. That aside, the question still remains: Are television news bulletins using precious viewing time in the right way?

There is much talk of the dumbing down of television news. Those who deny it point to what they call a broadening up, suggesting, for example, that the range of information that news on television can now provide has been greatly enhanced, as technology has advanced. Live reports from war zones, for example, are only limited by the danger to which correspondents and technicians may be subjected as they deliver them, or the control that the military authorities choose to exercise to keep such reporting at bay. Decisions from Parliaments or courts or sporting arenas around the world can be shown as they happen, as can the immediate reactions to them. In addition, the argument runs, news is such a competitive business, with information increasingly available on alternative sources like the Internet, that television news has been forced to become much more user-friendly.

It is in fulfilling the 'user-friendly' requirement, however, that I see the greatest dangers. There is an increasing reliance by those in charge of television news on their perception of what viewers want to see or hear, rather than the simple provision of information about what has happened, or is about to happen. In May 1999, for example, I was reporting the day's events in the Commons, and the massive revolt by Labour backbenchers, as the Government sought to introduce new laws which would change future welfare provision for tens of thousands of disabled people in Britain. My report for the *ITV Evening News* at 6.30 p.m. was one minute and forty-five seconds long. It ran, not at the start of the bulletin, but after stories about the conviction of a rapist, three reports about the seven-week-old war in Kosovo, staff cuts at Barclays Bank, and the ongoing row about genetically modified food. The reports from the war zone in Kosovo were rich in picture and human emotion. One concerned the joyful reunion of a family in one of the refugee camps. The other reports fell easily into that currently modish category of 'lifestyle' stories. Against such reporting, a story that could, in fact, have affected thousands of lifestyles in Britain, was considered to be much less important.

There is a growing reluctance throughout much of television news – some, indeed, might add throughout television generally – to confront viewers with items or issues which are intellectually demanding. There are many honourable exceptions to that observation, but what is not in doubt is the preoccupation in present-day television news with form over content. Large sums are spent on the designing and construction of the elaborate sets from which the news is presented.

Long gone are the days of a plain blue background, and a little panel hanging behind the newscaster on to which the odd image could be projected. That, however, is precisely the set-up which was good enough for *News at Ten* during the many years in which it was the clear leader among television news bulletins in Britain.

There is endless discussion over how those who present the news should look and sound. More insidiously, there is evidence that the content of news bulletins is being increasingly tailored to the supposed tastes of the audience watching it. At one point during the war in Kosovo, for example, the ITV Network Centre ordered ITN to cut down on the number of reports from the refugee camps, on the ground that the British audience was suffering from 'refugee fatigue'. It meant that, on one particular day, a moving report about a young victim of shell-shock, which truly brought home, to me at least, the terrible suffering of those refugees, was shown only at lunchtime. In later bulletins, it was replaced by a story that demanded less of the audience, involving a young child who had been discovered alive, many hours after a devastating tornado had hit parts of America.

In addition, ITN bulletins are increasingly carrying promotional plugs for other programmes on ITV – one clear result of those bulletins being deliberately rebranded as ITV programmes. After the revamping of the schedules in March 1999, the *ITV Evening News* began the practice of regularly carrying details of the current affairs programme *Tonight with Trevor McDonald* later in the evening, regardless of whether or not that programme had anything newsworthy to report. The dangerous erosion of ITN's editorial independence also resulted, for example, in a shameful news report about the routine return of the ITV game show *So You Want To Be A Millionaire*. ITN's bulletins should carry genuine news, not puffs for other programmes.

For the moment, political reporting in newspapers and on radio and television is holding its own. Indeed, it is doing better than that. In many cases, the press is doing a more thorough job of holding the Government to account than Parliament. Television and newspaper reports are constantly being quoted in Parliament as evidence that Ministers and the departments are at fault. That is why recent academic studies about the nature and extent of political news coverage, which are based on the simple statistics of how much time and space has been devoted to it, are misleading. Such enquiries mistake quantity, or the lack of it, for quality. They also make no allowance for the fact that politics, like everything else, has its busy and its not so-busy periods. There are competing claims on our attention like the recent war in the Balkans. In any case, political reporting is undergoing something of a renaissance, with a return to straightforward reporting of proceedings in the Commons and the Lords. The BBC's venerable *Yesterday in Parliament* is making a return to Radio Four's main morning schedule, and the *Daily Telegraph* and *The Times* have brought back sections devoted to straight Parliamentary coverage. Live coverage of Parliament is now available to an increasing number of television viewers on cable and satellite. I welcome such moves, and hope that they are the start of a wider trend. Democracy is ill served if journalism, and particularly political journalism, cops out or dumbs down too far.

I am the first to admit that news judgement, the definition of what it is that makes a story important to an audience, is the hardest thing in journalism to get right. At one stage, ITN used to include a lot of reports about older people and their health problems in its lunchtime news bulletins, because it was known that a lot of older people watched the news at that time. Some research, however, revealed that the very last thing old people wanted to see on the news is stories about the sort of aches and pains they endure, and they wanted to be told a lot more about what young people like Princess Diana had been doing. As a result, a lot more 'Diana' stories began to be shown.

My test of what makes a story is this. Could I walk into a pub with the information I have, saying to those around the bar, 'Listen, you'll never believe what's happened,' or 'Something really interesting went on today,' and still hope to retain their interest as I gave them the details? Could I also hold their attention by declaring, 'I've discovered that something very important or disgraceful or strange is going on out there,' and successfully make the case for claiming their attention while I set out what that 'something' is? Diamond-hard news, clearly and popularly presented, is what should fill news bulletins, and the programmes on which I have worked over the years have always been most successful when they have followed that rule.

Perhaps journalists should rework and adapt, as a motto, the legal phrase *in loco parentis*, used to describe someone who stands in for a mother or father. Journalists stand *in loco populi*, being present for ordinary people in those places and at those times where they cannot be present themselves. We are entrusted with the job of showing and telling them what has happened, or what is likely to happen, when they are not in a position to do so for themselves. We are entrusted with the job of asking the questions that they cannot ask, and of helping them to understand or assess matters that may be important but are obscure and complex, or about which the whole truth may not have been told. Trying to do so, during my professional life, has been extremely demanding, but it has often been hugely enjoyable too. Very seldom has it been boring.

There are, after all, very few occupations that offer a completely new challenge every single day, but television journalism is one of them. It's one of the reasons why it has been such a stimulating and satisfying career. Sometimes, of course, a wholly unexpected event may occur – an accident or a natural disaster, a ministerial resignation or a sudden death – and the race is then on to get everything together in time to tell the viewer what has happened and why. Adrenalin and experience take over and carry you through – often helping you to overcome what appear to be impossible practical obstacles and to meet seemingly impossible deadlines.

At the end of those crazy, busy days, there are sometimes congratulatory messages from the powers-that-be for your efforts, which are known in the trade as 'hero-grams'. I always tell people, though, that the real 'hero-grams' should be handed out on those apparently unpromising days when little has happened and when the agenda looks all too familiar. I think that producing reports, and constructing a television news bulletin that people will still watch, on what we call the slow days is an even greater challenge than coping with the sudden crises. If you can't handle the fast-breaking story, you shouldn't be in journalism at all. On the quieter days, when it's all down to you, you still need all your professionalism to keep up your enthusiasm, and even if you can't manage that, not to let the lack of it show too much.

Something, however, usually helps you through. However familiar the story may look at nine o'clock in the morning, it will have some new twist to it by ten or eleven o'clock at night. Familiar early headlines like 'Another Tory split on Europe' or 'Chancellor urges prudence and caution over public spending' will often provide the starting point for more exploration of an existing story, or for another angle to be pursued, or a new development in an ongoing tale to be followed through.

Then there is the daily challenge of turning it all into a report for television. Words must be matched to pictures, and, if there aren't any pictures, they must be found. Interviews must be sought and conducted, and if interviewees are not available, the viewer must sometimes be told why. You must take in your stride the day's many other practical problems. There may, for example, be camera crews or picture editors whose equipment has failed – though it's a tribute to their professionalism that it usually does not. Bookings for satellites or other links, or for studios, may not be available when you most want them. There are many links in the chain of television broadcasting, and any one of them has the potential to fail.

In my worst moments, and faced with such difficulties, I have often shouted at colleagues that I wished I worked in radio or newspapers. In my heart of hearts, though, I have never really meant it. Done well, television news is where it's at. It gives people the whole picture, both literally and figuratively. That is why from the very first day that high-quality news bulletins on television became a practical reality, it has been the medium through which the majority of the population get most of their information. I know, because people tell me so, that the public appreciate the effort that I, and many others like me, have made to get that full news picture to them and to put it all in some kind of context for them.

Now, though, it is time to step back, and to let others carry on the round of daily television journalism. Once a journalist, always a journalist, I suspect, and I am not yet ready for a full retreat to the rose garden or the vegetable patch. However, as one of my old BBC bosses put it, it probably *is* the moment for a little less reporting – and a little more thinking.

Index